WEBER, THE IDEAL TYPE, AND
CONTEMPORARY SOCIAL THEORY

Weber, the Ideal Type, and Contemporary Social Theory

SUSAN J. HEKMAN

UNIVERSITY OF NOTRE DAME PRESS
NOTRE DAME, INDIANA

Library of Congress Cataloging in Publication Data

Hekman, Susan J.
  Weber, the ideal type, and contemporary social theory.

  Bibliography: p.
  1. Sociology—Methodology. 2. Social sciences—
Methodology. 3. Positivism. 4. Phenomenological
sociology. 5. Structuralism. 6. Weber, Max, 1864-
1920. I. Title.
HM24.H456   1983   301'.01   82-40381
ISBN 0-268-01931-2

For My Father

Contents

Acknowledgments   ix

1. Introduction   1

2. Weber's Theory of the Ideal Type   18

   1. The Epistemic Problem   18
   2. The Ideal Type in Weber's Methodology   26
   3. Varieties of Ideal Types   38
     A. Historical and General Sociological Types   39
     B. Epistemology of Action Types   43
     C. Development of Structural Types   49
   4. Conclusion   59

3. The Subjective Critique   61

   1. Introduction to the Critiques   61
   2. Nature of the Subjective Critique   64
   3. Phenomenology   66
   4. Ordinary-Language Analysis   77
   5. Conclusion   95

4. The Objective Critique   101

   1. Nature of the Objective Critique   101
   2. Structuralism   104
   3. Critical Theory   123
   4. Conclusion   145

5. Logical Status of Social-Scientific Analysis   149

   1. Introduction   149
   2. Weber's Concept of Objectivity   153
   3. The Social Scientist and the Social Actor   161

4. The Relationship among Social-Scientific Theories   165
5. Social-Scientific Analysis of Other Cultures   176
6. Conclusion   191

Notes   194

Bibliography   201

Index   211

Acknowledgments

Over the years many colleagues and friends have helped me to clarify the arguments presented in this book, but I would especially like to thank Richard Flathman and Guenther Roth for their invaluable assistance. Without their continuing criticism and encouragement this manuscript would not have reached its present form. I would also like to thank Guy Oakes for his comments on the manuscript and David Easton for his advice and support. Finally, I thank Fred Dallmayr, not only for his support of the manuscript but also for his insightful critique of my arguments. Incorporating the suggestions of these critics and friends has, I hope, made this a better book.

1. Introduction

Over half a century ago Max Weber attempted to sort through the complex problems involved in defining a methodology for the social sciences. He did so in a series of articles that critiqued the theories of his contemporaries rather than in a single, comprehensive treatment of the subject. Weber's methodological views have enjoyed a mixed fate, both in discussions in his day and in contemporary discussions of the philosophy and methodology of the social sciences. While certainly not ignored, Weber's methodological views have not been taken as seriously as those of theorists who stated their views in a more comprehensive fashion. By and large, although acknowledged to be of historical interest, Weber's views have been dismissed from serious consideration on the grounds that they are fragmented and lacking in philosophical sophistication. It is the intention of this study to reassess this judgment.

Although Weber's presentation of his methodological views is indeed fragmented and, at certain points, philosophically naive, one aspect of his views, the theory of the ideal type, ought to be taken seriously as a significant contribution to the methodology of the social sciences, and of much more than historical interest. Weber's theory of the ideal type is directly relevant to the current unresolved problems in the philosophy and methodology of the social sciences, for it synthesizes aspects of social-scientific analysis that are central to the critiques of positivism which dominate today's discussions. The purpose of this book, then, is to examine Weber's ideal type in the context of contemporary issues and to present an argument for its relevance to the modern attempt to construct a coherent methodology for the social sciences.

To be successful that argument must begin with an assess-

1

ment of the current status of discussions in the philosophy and methodology of the social sciences. And this is not easy, for if anything can be said to characterize these contemporary discussions, it is lack of unanimity. A staggering number of books and articles concerning the methodology of the social sciences have appeared in recent decades, but this extensive discussion has not resulted in consensus on the issues under consideration. Rather, the discussion has spawned new approaches to these issues, and their resolution seems more distant than ever. The reason for this lack of consensus, we are told by an increasing number of participants, is that the social sciences are undergoing a "revolution." Thus defining what this "revolution" is about seems a good place to start in assessing the debate.

If there is one point of agreement among the disputants in the debate over the methodology of the social sciences, it is that the cause of the revolution is dissatisfaction with positivism as a basis for that methodology. Although the disputants differ on the precise definition, they generally agree that positivism has been the dominant paradigm in the social sciences for most of the twentieth century. There is also general agreement on why positivism was initially so attractive to the social sciences. As Anthony Giddens puts it, the social sciences were "born in the shadow of the triumphs of the natural sciences" (1976:12).

In the nineteenth century it was natural that the infant social sciences should want to duplicate the triumphs of the natural sciences by mimicking their methods. Thus, at the outset, the appeal of what social scientists took to be the positivist methodology of the natural sciences was overwhelming. It was assumed that if the social sciences applied this methodology to the study of social life, the result would be the discovery of "objective truths" about society that would lead to scientific breakthroughs on the order of those achieved in the natural sciences. All that was required, it seemed, was for the social sciences to produce their Newton. In short, the positivist methodology which the social sciences ascribed to the natural sciences, and which they credited with the triumphs of the latter, created an ideal for all scientific activity: the goal of science is the production of "objective truth" as defined by positivism.

An understanding of the current revolution in the social sciences must thus begin with the positivist definition of scientific activity. Briefly, positivism is based on a conception of science that defines scientific activity largely in terms of induction from occurrences in a visible, tangible, world. Initially, positivists maintained that the scientist examines such occurrences, utilizing a theory-free observation language to discover the "how" (rather than the "why") of events in the visible world. Positivist science, furthermore, rejects out of hand the exploration of "unobservable entities." Analysis of such entities, the positivist asserts, is simply not the business of science (Horton, 1973:297). The "objective truth" which the positivist pursues, then, is a result of the theory-free observation of events in the visible, or "real," world. The concern of the following discussion will not be to elaborate on this definition of positivism but to comment on the current status of the revolution against the positivist conception of scientific activity.

The revolution has been pursued along two related lines. Social scientists have questioned the appropriateness of this positivist ideal of science for the analysis of social life because its definition of scientific activity restricts the social sciences to examination of how events occur in the visible world. Many social scientists have argued that these restrictions make it impossible for the social sciences to assess the subject matter of their science adequately. Specifically, it has been argued that the business of social science is to explain *why*, not *how*, events occur in the social world, and furthermore, that these events can be explained only by reference to what positivists label "unobservable entities." Two major categories of social-scientific analysis fall under this definition of "unobservable entities": exploration of social actors' "subjective meanings" and exploration of the structural, or institutional, forms of social life. The first major aspect of the revolution against positivist methodology for the social sciences, then, has been to point out that a positivist social science simply cannot supply the social sciences with the kind of analytic tools that analysis of social life demands.

The second argument in the revolution against a positivist social science involves a more comprehensive approach that has its origins in the philosophy of natural science. In recent decades, philosophers of science have argued that positivists' understanding of scientific activity is itself inadequate; that is, the ideal of scientific activity established by positivism is an inaccurate description of scientific practice. The positivists' emphasis on induction, their rejection of "unobservable entities," and their positing of a theory-free observation language have been called into question by the philosophy of science.[1]

At this point in these discussions, it can be asserted that the positivist ideal of science that initially attracted the social sciences is no longer espoused by modern philosophers of science, and furthermore, that it has been shown that positivism provides an inadequate understanding of the activity of the natural scientist. The implications of this line of argument for the social sciences are beginning to be pursued in contemporary discussions in the philosophy of social science,[2] and these discussions have revealed that if the positivist ideal of science is discarded altogether, the social sciences can cease apologizing for their "unscientific" status. They can, in other words, cease waiting for their Newton.

Both of these lines of criticism will be pursued in the course of this study, but the thesis that will be advanced with regard to Weber is concerned not with the historical development of these lines of criticism but with the current status of the revolution against a positivist methodology of the social sciences. The first notable aspect of recent discussions of this subject is that many commentators now claim that the revolution against the positivist methodology has already been won. Giddens states confidently that "those who still wait for a Newton are not only waiting for a train that won't arrive, they're in the wrong station altogether" (1976:13). What he means by this is that modern philosophers of social science have, at long last, abandoned the positivist ideal of science as a realizable or even desirable goal of social-scientific activity. The seemingly endless critiques of positivism that have appeared in the past half-century, Giddens claims, have finally laid to rest the notion that we are waiting for our Newton.

Although the social-scientific community would not unanimously accept Giddens' assessment of the situation, the existence and nature of the revolution against positivism has been widely discussed. Gouldner (1970) claims that the social sciences are in a state of "crisis," Bernstein (1976) declares that social and political theory are being "restructured," and Harre' and Secord (1972) join Giddens in the proclamation that the revolution has succeeded. Although there is considerable difference of opnion as to the status of the revolution, it can be confidently asserted that one can search in vain for a contemporary defender of the positivist ideal in its pure form—that is, a defender of the goal of scientific, "objective" truth for the social sciences. Indeed, this naive positivist position has become a strawman in the debate over the proper philosophy of the social sciences. It is easily refuted, and even those whom their opponents label "positivists" do not defend it.

The second and, for the purposes of this study, more important point that can be made about the status of the debate is that although naive positivism can no longer be defended as an adequate philosophy for the social sciences, it cannot be maintained that positivism has been replaced as the dominant paradigm. Why this is the case can be attributed primarily to two factors. First, as Radnitzky points out, the legacy of positivism in the social sciences has been to create an ideal of science which is firmly entrenched in the minds of social scientists. This ideal, although it has been repeatedly refuted, will not simply disappear because it has been proved logically indefensible. Rather, it may take generations for this ideal to be replaced by another (Radnitzky, 1970:69). This means in a practical sense that, for practicing social scientists, positivism is still the "dominant standpoint" (Giddens, 1976:13). Although philosophers of social science may regard positivism as a dead issue, it continues to guide most research activities undertaken by social scientists.

The second factor in the failure to replace the positivist paradigm is closely related to the first. To continue the revolution analogy, it can be asserted that the assault on positivism has been a series of isolated attacks rather than a unified offensive. Many critiques of positivism have been developed, and many contenders for positivism's position as the dominant paradigm of the social sciences have emerged, but none, as yet, has been able to capture positivism's mantle. Instead, the various critics of positivism have coalesced into camps which expend as much effort disputing among themselves as in attacking their common enemy. Thus positivist research methodology and the positivist ideal of science have not been replaced by a single, coherent alternative. Positivism remains the dominant standpoint because none of the alternative standpoints has managed to assume the prominence enjoyed by positivism.

It is the existence of competing antipositivist camps that creates the impression of lack of unanimity, or even confusion, in contemporary discussions in the philosophy and methodology of the social sciences. It might be supposed that, because all these approaches object to a positivist philosophy for the social sciences, they share a basic orientation to the methodology of the social sciences, but this does not appear to be the case. The antipositivist camps include many diverse groups: phenomenology, ordinary-language analysis, ethnomethodology, hermeneutics, critical theory, and structuralism. Each of these approaches has a distinctive viewpoint, has developed a vocabulary that frequently is incomprehensible to the uninitiated, and has generated a loyal following committed to its particular perspective. Each sees positivism to be in error, but each has defined a different aspect of the positivist approach as the source of that error. The alternative methodology that each advocates is based on this definition of the principal deficiency of positivism; hence each defines its approach as the only correct antidote to the deficiencies of the positivist methodology for the social sciences.

Without ignoring the range and complexity of positivism's errors which have been uncovered by these various approaches, it is nevertheless possible to discern two distinct themes in these critiques which correspond to the two principal deficiencies of positivism as a philosophy of social science. The first of these deficiencies is the inability of positivism to account for what has come to be labeled the "subjective meaning" of the social actor. Several contemporary antipositivist critiques have focused on this deficiency, making it the central element in their rejection of the positivist methodology. It follows quite naturally that these approaches should make the interpretation and understanding of the social actors' subjective meaning the basis of the alternative methodology which they advance. Phenomenology, ethnomethodology, hermeneutics, and ordinary-language analysis are the approaches which have received the most attention in recent years.

Although there are important differences between the antipositivist approaches which center around the social actors' meaning, there are important similarities as well. These similarities, furthermore, are coming to be well documented in the literature. Bernstein (1976), Giddens (1976), Roche (1973), and Apel (1967) are recent examples of this trend, and all discuss the similarities between the various "interpretive" approaches to the methodology of the social sciences. The shared emphasis of these schools on interpreting the meaning of the social actors is seen by most commentators to be a positive and necessary corrective to the positivist approach, but discussions of the similarities among the interpretive approaches have also pointed to a deficiency in their alternative methodological stance. An approach which focuses exclusively on the social actors' meaning cannot account for the institutional and structural aspects of social organization (Giddens, 1976:92). It has been argued that, in a sense, these approaches have thrown out the baby with the bath. In their desire to correct the positivists' dismissal of subjective meaning, they have refused to consider any aspect of social life other than the social actors' concepts. Their opponents argue, however, that social-scientific analysis must do more than merely interpret actors' concepts. It must be able to examine the broader, structural elements of social life as well.

It is precisely the demand that social scientists analyze and critically assess the structural elements of social life that defines the second theme of contemporary antipositivist critiques. Positivist methodology in the social sciences is deficient, it is argued, because employing a positivist methodology prevents social scientists from critically examining structural arrangements, from assessing the impact of social institutions, and from passing judgment on the appropriateness and effectiveness of one institutional structure as opposed to another. Arguing that positivist social science can do no more than examine the operation of social life inside a given institutional structure, several contemporary antipositivist critiques have focused on establishing an alternative methodology which allows the social scientist to assess the structural elements of society, to trace the development of different structural arrangements in human societies, and to provide means of comparing one structural arrangement with another. The antipositivist schools that are most representative of this category are critical theory and structuralism.

What is being argued, then, is that two distinct deficiencies of positivism—its inability to account for social actors' subjective meaning and to critically assess structural arrangements—have generated two distinct themes of antipositivist criticism in the social sciences. It must be kept in mind that within each of these two categories important differences between the approaches remain. It is not my intention to suggest, for instance, that critical theory and structuralism approach the social sciences from the same perspective. Collapsing phenomenology and ordinary language into a single approach would likewise do violence to important aspects of both theories. But despite these differences, agreement within the two categories can be discerned on two key issues: the central deficiency of positivism and the goal of social-scientific analysis. The first category, which in the following discussion will be labeled the "subjective critique," faults positivism for its rejection of the actors' meanings and claims that the goal of social-scientific analysis is the interpretation and understanding of the subjective meaning of the social actors. The second category, which will be labeled the "objective critique," faults positivism for its inability to assess structural arrangements and argues that such critical assessment is the goal of social-scientific analysis.

But it cannot be assumed that identification of these two themes within the antipositivist camps brings the social sciences any closer to a single methodological stance, for the differences between the "subjective" and "objective" critiques are formidable. Commenting on this bifurcation in the antipositivist critiques, Touraine remarks that the division forms an "unbridgeable gulf" in contemporary social theory (1974:91). In other words, even though the "subjective critique" and the "objective critique" both reject positivism, the gap between them appears to be just as wide as the gap between each critique and positivism itself.

Faced with this lack of consensus on the proper methodology for the social sciences, the reaction of some social theorists has been simply to accept this "polyparadigmatic" state. Thus Martins, in his preface to a discussion of contemporary social-scientific methodology, comments: "There is no New Paradigm in sociology or social/cultural anthropology or political science, although plenty of paradigm claimants" (1974:249). Other social theorists, however, are less content to accept this lack of unanimity on so fundamental an issue. Their reaction to the current state of social theory is to attempt to create the "New Paradigm" through a synthesis of existing approaches.

Two types of syntheses have been suggested in the contemporary literature. The first one attempts to join the insights of the humanist or *Verstehen* approach with the analytic rigor that characterizes positivist/behaviorist social science. The nature of this synthesis is most clearly articulated by Fay and Moon in an article entitled (appropriately) "What Would an Adequate Philosophy of Social Science Look Like?" (1977). They argue that a contemporary philosophy of social science requires a synthesis that transcends the dichotomy between what they refer to as the "humanist" and the "naturalist" (positivist) traditions that have dominated discussions in the social sciences in the last twenty years (1977:209). Their outline of such a synthesis is, by their own admission, only a sketch, but it reveals the considerable gulf between the two traditions and the deficiencies of both approaches. They point out that the naturalists very competently assess the empirical, causal, or "actual" situation in their analysis of social life while the humanists reveal the constitution of the situation through the actors' self-understanding. But each tradition is severely limited by its approach: naturalists fail to see the significance of the difference between the actors' self-understanding and the actual situation, and humanists are limited by their refusal to go beyond the actors' self-understanding. But both of these deficiencies could be remedied, they argue, by synthesizing the two approaches (1977:226). Much the same sort of synthesis is suggested by Radnitzky's analysis of contemporary schools of social science (1970). He argues that a humanist analysis must "tack" to causal, empirical analysis when events do not match the stated intentions of the actors—or, as he puts it, when "the agents are not transparent to themselves to a relevant degree" (1970:96).

The synthesis proposed by Fay and Moon, as well as Radnitzky, would thus allow the social sciences, in a sense, to have their cake and eat it too. They propose a social-scientific methodology that combines the "good" elements of positivism—that is, its analytic rigor and empirical techniques—with the interpretive techniques of the humanist approaches.

However, another kind of synthesis is proposed in contemporary discussions of social theory: between the two major categories of the antipositivist critique, the categories labeled above as the "subjective" and "objective" critiques. But the call for synthesis between these two theoretical groups is quite different from that discussed above. This second kind of synthesis is based on the conviction that any aspect of the positivist tradition must be excluded. Advocates argue that because positivism has been shown to be an inadequate basis for the methodology of the social sciences, it should be discarded altogether. What is needed, they argue, is a synthesis of the major strands of the contemporary antipositivist critiques, a synthesis that might be labeled "postpositivist." Keat and Urry state the call for this synthesis very clearly. The key problem for contemporary social theory, they assert, is to develop a theory that satisfactorily synthesizes the structural analysis of social formations and the explanation of human action in terms of subjective states and meanings (1975:229; cf. Collins, 1975).

To date, the most ambitious attempt to effect such a synthesis can be found in the work of Jürgen Habermas, who attempts to incorporate the insights of interpretive social science— specifically, ordinary-language analysis, phenomenology, and hermeneutics—with what he calls the "objective framework" of social action that transcends the actors' concepts. He argues that employing interpretive techniques in the social sciences does not preclude, as many interpretive social scientists maintain, the critical assessment of social arrangments. Because of Habermas' emphasis on the objective framework of social action and the critical assessment of social forms, his position, as well as his attempted synthesis, will be placed under the rubric of the "objective critique" and discussed at length in chapter 4.

Various attempts at synthesis along these lines have been made by other social theorists. Berger and Luckmann, in *The Social Construction of Reality* (1966), attempt to synthesize two perspectives normally taken to be incompatible: viewing human society as constituted by the social actors' bestowal of meaning on their actions, and viewing social actors as products of the social structure in which they live. To accomplish this synthesis, they divide their book into two parts. In the first part, social actors are described as producers, and the authors examine how social actors create their society through the bestowal of meaning on everyday actions. In the second part of the book, however, the social actors are described as products, rather than producers, and the authors explicate how social actors are created and shaped by the social structure in which they find themselves. In an article published the same year as the book, Berger and Pullberg succinctly state the nature of the synthesis attempted in the book: "Man produces himself as a social being through social structure" (1966:63).

Although it is generally acknowledged that the synthesis attempted by Berger and Luckmann is noteworthy, its success is generally denied. Keat and Urry specifically reject it (1975:184ff.), most other theorists simply dismiss it—and it is not difficult to understand why it has not had the desired impact on social theory. Although the authors make a persuasive case for social actors as both producers and produced, they do not provide a single, conceptual, theoretical approach that can bridge the gap between these two perspectives. In short, they do not *synthesize* these two aspects of social theory; they fail to develop a theoretical perspective by which both aspects of human social life can be conceptualized. Serial descriptions of these two perspectives on social life, between the covers of one book, do not, unfortunately, constitute a synthesis.

The clearest description of what is required if such a synthesis is to be successful has been supplied by Anthony Giddens. Beginning with the assertion that connecting the subjective orientation of action with institutional structures is "enormously difficult," he goes on to specify the nature of this difficulty (1977:86). The problem stems from the fact that "structuralists" interpret social structure as a restraint on human action while humanists interpret it as a human creation, that is, the product of meaning bestowal. These two perspectives can be reconciled, Giddens argues, through what he refers to as the "duality of structure":

> Structure enters into the explanation of action in a dual way: as the medium of production and at the same time as its outcome in the production of social forms. [1977:130]

Social structure, then, must be seen as produced and *re*produced by human action. It is both a restraint on human action and, at the same time, an enabling medium through which human action becomes possible:

> The reflexive rationalization of action must be seen as operating through the mobilization of structural properties, and at the same time thereby contributing to their reproduction. [1977:86]

The virtue of Giddens' approach, however, lies not only in the fact that he clearly defines the nature of the needed synthesis, but also in the fact that he defines precisely what is missing in the Berger and Luckmann approach: the conceptual and theoretical problem which the social scientist must face if social actors are to be interpreted as both producers and products of social structure. If, in Giddens' terminology, social structure is interpreted as a "duality," what is needed on the conceptual level is recognition that the social scientist is engaged in a "dual hermeneutic" (1976:12). The social scientist's concepts, he asserts, must be determined by both the actors' concepts and the concepts of the scientific community.

The problem that Giddens addresses with his conception of the social scientist's dual hermeneutic is complex. Since it is also the problem that will be the principal focus of the following, it is important to define it clearly at the outset. Giddens realizes that his call for a synthesis of the humanist and structural approaches to social theory faces a nearly insurmountable conceptual problem because the two perspectives are based on radically different understandings of the origin of the social scientist's concepts. Humanists, or those engaged in the subjective critique, base their approach to social theory on the assumption that the concepts they utilize must be those of the social actors themselves, and this assumption is the central issue in the subjective critique of positivism. But the second approach, the objective critique that seeks to analyze and assess structural arrangements, is entirely different conceptually. Advocates of this approach assume that if social scientists are to engage in structural analysis, their concepts must, in some sense, transcend the actors' concepts. The social scientist must be able to replace the actors' concepts with scientific concepts that uncover the structural arrangements of society, which are opaque to the actors themselves.

It is this problem that Giddens addresses when he asserts that the social scientist's concepts must subscribe to a "double hermeneutic." He sees what Berger, Luckmann, and Pullberg failed to see: If the subjective and structural perspectives are to be synthesized into a single social theory, the conceptual dichotomy between these two approaches must be resolved. If one approach insists that the social scientist's concepts are determined by the social actors' concepts and the other that the social scientist's concepts are determined by the scientific analysis of structural forms, then—before these two approaches can be synthesized—the social scientist must be supplied with concepts which are determined by the frame of reference of both the actor and the social scientist. And since the actors' frame of reference is everyday social life and the social scientist's is the "technical conceptual schemes" of scientific analysis, this problem is substantial (1976:79). Giddens does not pretend to have solved the problem, although he has clearly outlined the direction in which theoretical efforts must move.

The foregoing outline of the current status of discussions in the philosophy and methodology of the social sciences provides a necessary background for the statement of the thesis of this book. Also, the argument for the relevance of Weber for contemporary social theory is predicated on several conclusions drawn from this discussion. The first conclusion is that, at this point in the discussion, more critiques of positivism are not necessary, and may even hinder the progress of the discussion. Since Weber's day, a great number and variety of critiques of positivism have been produced by social theorists and philosophers. Some of these have been discussed above and more will be discussed in detail in the course of the book, but the formulation of one more critique of positivism is decidedly *not* the purpose of the following. Rather, it will be assumed that the critiques of positivism which have appeared since Weber's time have succeeded in their task. Although elements of the positivist philosophy are defended by contemporary social theorists, no contemporary social theorist can be said to defend the naive positivist position that is the object of many contemporary antipositivist critiques. Attacking this naive positivist position, as one author has recently noted, is like flogging a dead horse (Briskman, 1978:81). Ralf Dahrendorf makes much the same point when he refers to the orthodox positivist position as the "third man" in the contemporary debate (1976:125). Therefore, it will be assumed that positivism has been shown, quite decisively, to be an inadequate basis for the methodology of the social sciences.

The second conclusion that will be drawn from this discussion is more in the nature of an argument than a conclusion. Current discussions in the philosophy and methodology of the social sciences seem to indicate that what is needed, if the social sciences are to construct a new paradigm to replace the discredited positivist paradigm, is a synthesis of relevant aspects of the antipositivist schools that have developed in recent years. Specifically, what is needed is a synthesis of the type so clearly stated by Giddens, which unites the two major categories of the contemporary antipositivist critique: the subjective critique, which focuses on the actors' meaning, and the objective critique, which focuses on the structural arrangements of social life.

Throughout the book, arguments will be advanced to support this particular version of contemporary social theory, but the principal argument rests on the validity of this interpretation, for it will be the task of the book to show that Max Weber's philosophy of social science points precisely to the kind of synthesis that Giddens discusses.[3] It will be argued that Weber's approach to the methodology of the social sciences, an approach that was formulated as a corrective to the positivism of his day, is directly relevant to the attempt by social theorists to formulate a new paradigm for the social sciences. It is relevant because, in his theory of the ideal type, Weber effected a synthesis between the analysis of subjective meaning and the assessment of structural forms.

The contemporary relevance of Weber's philosophy of social science, however, is not readily acceptable to contemporary social theorists. His methodology of the social sciences occupies a curious position in contemporary discussions of the philosophy and methodology of the social sciences. On one hand, it can be observed that Weber's methodology of the social sciences has enjoyed a certain popularity in recent years. Numerous articles and books have examined Weber's views on methodological questions, views which, in many cases, have gone unexamined for decades. In some cases, this has led to outright advocacy of Weber's position. Fay and Moon, for instance, note that "a return to Weber would be a progressive step in the philosophy of social science" (1977:216). Likewise, Keat and Urry state that "an understanding of [Weber's] complex views is an essential starting-point for most of the discussion which follows" (1975:144).

But this praise of Weber's methodological views is far from unanimous. Many theorists who have "rediscovered" Weber in recent years have done so either to discard or criticize his methodological approach. Even those theorists who discuss Weber's position at great length often come to the conclusion that his views are outdated. For example, in the preface to his book on Weber's theory of concept formation Thomas Burger states that Weber is of great historical interest but little contemporary relevance (1976:x). Anthony Giddens, who also makes extensive reference to Weber's work, writes off Weber's theory as "obsolete" in the light of recent discussions (1976:23). Those who criticize specific elements of Weber's views, furthermore, usually do so from the standpoint of a particular methodological perspective. All of the contemporary antipositivist approaches mentioned above have expressed serious objections to aspects of Weber's theory. Each of these schools has found particular elements of Weber's theory to be incompatible with their theoretical position, and it is these objections that constitute much of the contemporary literature on Weber.

The nature of contemporary criticisms of Weber, however,

is instructive in itself. Whereas earlier critics of Weber's methodology were likely to take him to task for his alleged positivism (notably L. Strauss), contemporary critics have taken a different approach, and their criticisms fall into two distinct categories. On one hand, Weber has come under attack by each of the antipositivist schools for not clearly specifying the particular element of social theory which that school defines as the focal point of social-scientific methodology. For example, Schutz faults Weber for not supplying a clear understanding of subjective meaning, and Habermas faults him for not providing a means by which the rationality of social structures can be assessed. But another line of criticism of Weber is equally significant. Weber has been frequently attacked in recent discussions for his eclecticism, that is, for his attempt to wed theoretical elements that his critics see as incompatible. Winch, for instance, while praising Weber for focusing on the social actors' subjective meaning, criticizes him for including causal analysis in his list of legitimate tools of social-scientific analysis. Other critics have attacked Weber for failing to synthesize the disparate elements of his theoretical approach. Brittan, for example, argues that Weber merely accepts, but does not resolve, the "duality" between, on one hand, an analysis of subjective meaning and, on the other, an "avowedly empirical" approach (1973:11).

This charge of eclecticism is particularly relevant to the present discussion of Weber, for it will be shown that Weber has succeeded in synthesizing the apparently disparate elements of his methodological approach. It will also be shown that the key to this synthesis is the ideal type, and that this synthesis is directly relevant to the issues raised in contemporary discussions. The relevance of the synthesis that Weber effects in the ideal type lies in the fact that, on one hand, it is firmly rooted in the social actors' subjective meaning and, on the other hand, without losing this subjective grounding, it provides a tool for the structural analysis of social institutions.[4]

It should be noted at the outset, however, that Weber's ideal type is not presented as the single answer to all the problems raised by contemporary philosophy and methodology of the social sciences. Weber's theory, at certain points, is vague and even confused, and lacks the polish and precision of a sophisticated philosophical account. Discussion of these flawed aspects of Weber's theory will frequently draw on relevant aspects of contemporary antipositivist critiques which have clarified points that Weber glosses over. But although Weber's theory lacks the philosophical sophistication of some of the contemporary accounts, it is relevant to the contemporary controversy because, in his theory of the ideal type, Weber bridges the gap between interpretation of social action in the actors' terms and assessment of structural forms. This parallels the attempt of contemporary theorists to bridge the gap between the subjective and objective critiques of positivism.

Interest in Weber's methodology of the social sciences has revived in recent years precisely because it was formulated as a foil to the positivism of his day. It is frequently rejected in current discussions because Weber, so to speak, has a foot in both camps; that is, his theory contains elements of both the subjective and the objective critiques of positivism. But Weber's theory has been too quickly dismissed by these critics. It will be argued—against them—that Weber can be absolved of the charge of inconsistency and, more importantly, that the synthesis he effects in the ideal type can serve as a useful point of departure for the attempt of contemporary social theorists to synthesize the analysis of subjective meaning and the critical assessment of structural forms.[5]

To substantiate this thesis with regard to Weber's theory, the argument will move in carefully circumscribed steps. Rather than attempt an overview of Weber's methodological corpus, the examination will focus on the ideal type, bringing in other elements of his theory as they are relevant to the discussion. First, the epistemic problem Weber faced when he attempted to formulate the ideal type will be examined. His answers to this problem—that is, the epistemological status of his concept of the ideal type—will then be carefully detailed. This examination will lay the groundwork for thorough analysis of the different kinds of ideal types employed in Weber's extensive works. Generally, the aim of this analysis will be to show that Weber's ideal types have the same epistemic base, and specifically, to uncover the connection between the ideal types of action and the ideal types of structural forms. The latter point, as the subject of contemporary critiques of Weber, is particularly crucial to the argument.

The examination of Weber's concept will be followed by a more detailed analysis of four of the modern antipositivist schools mentioned in the foregoing. Using Weber's theory as the point of departure, the analysis will seek to uncover elements of those theories which can be used to construct a contemporary postpositivist synthesis. As a means to that end, each of these school's criticisms of Weber's theory will be used to isolate the elements of that approach which can be utilized in the construction of such a synthesis. The schools that will be considered under the heading "subjective critique" are ordinary-language analysis and phenomenology, and those under the heading "objective critique" are Althusser's structuralism and the critical theory of Jürgen Habermas.

In the examination of these modern schools, no attempt will be made to present a comprehensive analysis of their positions. Rather, the intent will be to isolate the elements of these approaches which offer the most significant contributions to the attempt to construct a postpositivist paradigm for the social sciences. Also, an attempt will be made to identify some of the major issues which, to this point, have prevented a synthesis of the positions of the various schools, within each category and between the two. Thus with regard to the "subjective critique," the issue of "inner events" will be considered in detail. With regard to the "objective critique," the issue of the status of the social scientist's critical assessment of structural forms and social arrangements will be examined.

In the final chapter, the discussion will return to analysis of Weber's position in a general examination of the logical status of social-scientific analysis. After examining Weber's theory of "objectivity," an attempt will be made to sketch what might plausibly be defined as a postpositivist conception of the "objectivity of the social sciences."

2. Weber's Theory of the Ideal Type

1. The Epistemic Problem

Weber formulated his conception of the ideal type in the course of his attempt to define the epistemological status of social-scientific investigation. It should be noted, however, that this exploration of epistemological issues arose directly from his involvement in concrete scientific research. Weber had no interest in epistemological or methodological questions per se, but addressed himself to these issues only because their resolution was necessary to explain the method he employed in his investigations. Thus Weber did not consider the ideal type to be a new conceptual method but, rather, an explication of existing practice (Giddens, 1971:141). Although Weber's definition of the ideal type arose from the context of his own investigations, his exploration of the epistemological questions involved in defining the nature of social-scientific knowledge was cast in terms of the theories advanced by his contemporaries. An accurate understanding of Weber's definition of the ideal type, then, must begin with examination of his epistemological problematic as it was defined by the theorists of his day.

In recent years, tracing the philosophical origins of Weber's methodology has become a popular topic among social theorists. In Germany, discussions of this issue have grown into heated debate over the proper designation of his philosophical roots (Janoska-Bendl, 1965). A full exploration of this issue would necessarily involve examination of the positions of Windelband, Dilthey, Rickert, and Simmel, as well as assessment of the major issues of the *Methodenstreit* of the 1880s and 1890s. In the

18

following, no attempt will be made to undertake such an exploration, for two reasons. First, such an exploration would be redundant. Perfectly competent accounts of Weber's relationship to his contemporaries already exist in English as well as German (Burger, 1976; Hughes, 1958; Iggers, 1968). Second, and more importantly, such an examination would divert the essay from its major purpose: relating Weber's position to contemporary issues in the philosophy of the social sciences. The aim of this examination is to place Weber's conception of the ideal type in the context of theories of *our* contemporaries, not his. In the following examination, therefore, although it will be necessary to define Weber's epistemological problematic in general terms, no detailed consideration of the origins of that problematic will be attempted.

Weber developed his theory of the ideal type as a consequence of his participation in heated discussions over the nature of social-scientific knowledge which characterized the *Methodenstreit* of his day. The two poles of the *Methodenstreit* were represented by subjectivists and positivists, and their dispute, in its simplest terms, can be reduced to an argument over the nature of social-scientific knowledge. The subjectivists maintained that social-scientific knowledge is inherently subjective—that is, concerned exclusively with human meaning and values—and thus is radically different from the knowledge of the natural sciences. The positivists maintained just the opposite: social-scientific knowledge could be obtained through the same methods as those employed in the natural sciences and thus social-scientific knowledge is just as "scientific" as that of the natural sciences.
In the broadest terms, Weber's position can be interpreted as an attempt to synthesize the best aspects of both these positions. His intent was to retain the subjective grounding of the social sciences while, at the same time, providing a "scientific" basis for social-scientific research. But Weber's position was profoundly influenced by other attempts at synthesis advanced by participants in the *Methodenstreit*, particularly Rickert and Windelband, as well as by the theories of Emil Lask. The basic assumptions which Weber brought to the dispute can be organized under two headings: his assumptions concerning the nature of knowledge and reality; and his assumption that the major issue to be addressed is the distinction between the nature of knowledge in the natural and the social sciences. Weber's

assumptions concerning the nature of knowledge and reality have generally been placed under the "neo-Kantianism" label. Along with the neo-Kantians, Weber defines reality as an "infinite flux" which cannot be apprehended in its totality. He assumes, further, that all knowledge is abstraction from the concreteness of reality; in other words, that "knowing" anything about this infinite flux means removing (abstracting) particular elements from the concretely real. A corollary of this neo-Kantian position, to which Weber also subscribed, is that no knowledge is possible without conceptualization, because concepts are the means by which abstraction from the concreteness of reality is effected.

The second set of assumptions which informs Weber's participation in the *Methodenstreit* revolves around the distinction between the knowledge sought by the social scientist and that which is the province of the natural sciences. The first set of assumptions concerning the nature of knowledge and reality, however, determines Weber's approach to this question. Because of his assumption that all knowledge is acquired through a process of abstraction from reality itself, and furthermore, that this process of abstraction is accomplished through conceptualization, Weber's exploration of the nature of social-scientific knowledge concerns the process by which the concepts of the social scientist are selected. This question, in turn, he phrases in terms of the nature of the distinction between the concepts of the natural and the social sciences. And in his discussion of this distinction Weber was definitely influenced by his contemporaries' definitions.

Two different conceptions of the distinction between the natural and the social sciences were discussed by the methodologists and philosophers of Weber's day, and Weber incorporated certain elements of both these theories in his conception of the division between the sciences. The first conception of the distinction concerned the difference between the subject matter of the natural and the social sciences, and should be very familiar to contemporary readers because it has figured prominently in recent discussions of the philosophy of social science. The basic difference between the natural and the social sciences, according to this view, is that the subject matter of the latter is radically different from that of the former. In Weber's time, the distinction was defined in terms of "value." Thus it was argued that the subject matter of the social sciences is defined in terms of its reference to values whereas that of the natural sciences is not (Rickert, 1962:13). Today, this distinction is more often defined in terms of the social actor's constitution of meaning; contemporary theorists argue that the subject matter of the social sciences is constituted by the social actors themselves whereas that of the natural sciences is not. But in either formulation the distinction comes to much the same thing: the social sciences differ from the natural sciences in that the subjects of the social sciences (social actors) participate in the creation of the subject matter of those sciences.

This distinction between the social and natural sciences, though recognized and utilized by Weber, was not, in his view, sufficient to capture the full extent of the division between the sciences. Furthermore, this definition of the distinction between the sciences created a set of problems that Weber was at pains to avoid. Specifically, it encouraged social scientists to think of their discipline as "subjectifying"—that is, set apart from the natural sciences because it deals exclusively with values, subjective meaning, and other "imprecise" phenomena. To avoid what he considered the dangers of such an attitude, Weber, following Rickert and Windelband, proposed a second way of conceptualizing the distinction between the natural and the social sciences, based on method rather than subject matter. These theorists saw their conception not as superseding the distinction based on subject matter, but as supplementing it.

Rickert, who articulated the nature of this distinction most clearly, argued that there are two kinds of sciences of empirical reality: individualizing (or idiographic) sciences, which are concerned to describe and explain individual events, and generalizing (or nomothetic) sciences, which are concerned to formulate universal laws.[1] These two kinds of sciences, furthermore, are identified with two distinctive scientific methods: the individualizing or historical method, which relies on the formation of individual concepts, and the generalizing method, which relies on the formation of general concepts (Rickert, 1962:14–15). By definition, both methods of conceptualization rely on abstraction, but the purpose of each method is distinctive, matching the purpose of the science it serves. The purpose of individual concepts is to retain the unique while that of general concepts is to synthesize the common.

Rickert's formulation of the methodological distinction between the two kinds of sciences is of crucial importance to understanding Weber's epistemological problematic.[2] Weber formulated his conception of the ideal type in terms of what he perceived to be the problems created by Rickert's definition of the methodological distinction between the natural and the social sciences, on the basis of which Rickert concluded that the characteristic method of the social sciences involves the formation of individual concepts while the method of the natural sciences involves the formation of general concepts. Rickert conceded certain "twilight zones of investigation" in which the method of one branch of science may be employed in investigation in the other branch; thus the natural sciences will occasionally employ individual concepts and the social sciences may utilize general concepts (1962:15). When the latter occurs, Rickert asserts, the result is a "positive natural science" of human life (Outhwaite, 1975:39), but he saw these cases as exceptions which do not negate the general rule.

Although Weber was in basic agreement with most of Rickert's theory, he was troubled by some of the consequences of the division between the sciences that Rickert proposed. Particularly, he questioned Rickert's assertion of a "positive natural science" of human life. Rickert was asserting, in effect, that when social scientists depart from the individual concepts on which their discipline is based, they must necessarily utilize general concepts which are, epistemologically, of the same structure as those employed by the natural scientist. This was the case because Rickert recognized only two methods of conceptualization, the individualizing method and the generalizing method; and this disturbed Weber, because, as a practicing social scientist, he regularly employed concepts that are neither individual nor general in the sense defined by Rickert. Weber knew that some of the concepts in social-scientific research cannot be labeled "individual" because they were designed to synthesize characteristic and significant aspects of a broad range of phenomena, not to retain a phenomenon's uniqueness. Nor can these concepts properly be labeled "general." The synthesized aspects are not the common but the significant elements of the phenomena under examination. Thus Weber saw his problem as an attempt to describe and define these nonindividual, nongeneral, synthetic concepts which are commonly employed by social scientists. His answer to the problem was the ideal type. To arrive at his definition of this concept, Weber was forced to depart from Rickert's neat division between individual and general concepts.

Weber's definition of the ideal type can best be described by interpreting his efforts as an attempt to carefully reconstruct the process by which the concepts of the social scientist are created. His reconstruction relies both on conceptions of the distinction between the social and natural sciences utilized by his contemporaries, and on distinctions based on subject matter and on method. Weber's understanding of how these differences combine to distinguish the nature of investigations in the social sciences from those in the natural sciences, however, moves beyond these theorists, and his examination can be divided into two stages. In the first stage, he concentrated on subject matter. How, he asked, does each kind of science define the "basic facts" it studies? In the second stage of the examination, he turned to method, exploring the principles that guide construction of the synthetic concepts in the natural and social sciences. The conclusions that arose from this two-stage investigation—that is, his conclusions regarding the logic of concept formation in the two branches of science—constitute the basis for his theory of the ideal type.

In the first stage of his problem, Weber asks how the basic facts of the natural sciences differ from those of the social sciences. That the subject matter of the natural and the social sciences is composed of a distinct category of "facts" which must first be conceptualized *as* the proper subject matter of each kind of science seems to be self-evident from the perspective of contemporary philosophy of science, but it was not self-evident to Weber. At certain points Weber seems to imply that the elements which are used to construct the concepts of both the natural and the social sciences are lifted directly from the "infinite flux" of reality without prior conceptualization (1949:72). This is one of the most serious philosophical errors in Weber's theory, but it is limited almost entirely to his understanding of the natural sciences and, therefore, can to a large extent be ignored in the present context. Although Weber occasionally lapses into this error in his discussion of the social sciences, in the most comprehensive statement of his position he clearly argues that prior conceptualization is involved in the constitution of the "facts" of the social sciences. He declares that something becomes a "fact" of the social sciences if, and only if, it is endowed with meaning by social actors, that is, if it has "cultural significance." Thus the facts of the natural sciences differ from those of the social sciences because the latter cannot become "facts" unless they are endowed with meaning by the participating social actors. To put it most simply, social facts depend for their existence on culturally endowed meaning; natural facts do not. In terms of the division between natural and social science, this means that the subject matter of these two branches of science is radically different.

Although Weber is much clearer than Rickert in his assertion of the prior conceptualization involved in defining the subject matter of the social sciences, his definition of the distinctive subject matter of the social sciences does not, in itself, depart from Rickert's approach. But as he goes to the second stage of his examination, Weber begins to strike out on his own. The second stage involves a description of the process by which the constructed or synthetic concepts of the natural and social sciences are formed. It is obvious to Weber that both natural and social scientists alike employ concepts which are syntheses of aspects of the category of facts that comprise the subject matter of that branch of science. Rickert had defined only two principles of synthesis by which the characteristic concepts of the two branches of science could be constructed: the selection of unique elements and the selection of common elements; and Weber broke from Rickert at this point by asserting a different principle of synthesis for the social sciences, a principle which subsumes Rickert's understanding of "individual concept" under a broader principle. Weber begins his definition of this principle by comparing the process by which the natural and the social scientist construct their synthetic concepts. Both must begin by selecting a group of concepts from the category of facts available to that science. Keeping in mind that these categories are significantly different for the natural and the social sciences, Weber maintains that in both cases this initial selection is made on the basis of the theoretic interest of the investigator. In other words, the first step in construction of a synthetic concept in both sciences is selection of a group of facts determined by the investigator's interest.

In the second step of constructing a synthetic concept, however, natural and social scientists take different paths. In the first step, both selected a group of facts on the basis of their theoretic interests; so Weber's next problem is to define for each scientist the principle by which certain aspects of these facts are synthesized into a new, constructed concept that can be employed as a tool in the investigation at hand. Rickert had already defined this principle for the natural scientist: guided by the theoretic interest of the investigation, the natural scientist selects the common traits of the facts under consideration and synthesizes them into a general concept. But Weber defines a distinctly different principle of synthesis for the social scientist, and this definition is his unique theoretic discovery. Unlike the natural scientist, the social scientist is not interested in the common or average aspects of the facts under consideration; rather, the social scientist is interested in their characteristic traits, their cultural significance, and their meaningful interrelationships as defined by the problem at hand. The selection of aspects of these concepts, therefore, is based not on commonality but on the interrelationship of the meaningful aspects of the facts that can be utilized to answer the question under investigation. The result is not an average but a "one-sided accentuation" of aspects of those concepts related to each other on the basis of the "logic" inherent in the meaning of the concepts. These aspects are synthesized into a concept that is the primary and necessary tool of social-scientific analysis: the ideal type.

This outline of the nature of concept formation in the natural and the social sciences is the epistemic basis for Weber's discussion of the ideal type and it will be expanded and substantiated in the subsequent discussion. Weber's actual discussion of the ideal type was not, of course, as neat as this outline suggests, but sketching Weber's theory in this highly schematic form has two advantages: it provides guidelines for the detailed examination to follow and it reveals why the ideal type is so central to Weber's methodology.

Weber articulated his theory of the ideal type because, for his purposes, Rickert's theory of concept formation could not adequately describe the functioning of the social scientist's concepts.[3] Restricting the conceptualization of social science to the examination of "historical individuals," as Rickert proposed, was unacceptable for Weber. It was likewise unacceptable to assume that when social scientists depart from such individual concepts, their only recourse is to the general concepts of the natural scientist. Thus Weber was forced to create a concept that was neither individual nor general in order to legitimize the conceptual activity of the social scientist. He did so by creating a concept that subsumes Rickert's understanding of the "individual concept" under a principle of synthesis that allows the social scientist a broader range of investigation.

Weber's theory of concept formation does not provide as neat a division between the natural and the social sciences as Rickert's theory of individual and general concepts, but his understanding of the ideal type identifies similarities and differences between concept formation in the natural and the social sciences that Rickert overlooked. The most significant similarity is the role of the investigator's theoretic interest in both cases of concept formation. Weber asserts that the group of facts which is selected from the separate categories of facts available to each branch of science is *always* determined by the nature of the investigator's interest; this is not a peculiarity of social science.[4] The uniqueness of concept formation in the social sciences that Weber finds to be decisive rests on two key differences: the category of facts available to the social sciences is unique because it is preselected by the social actors' bestowal of meaning; and the principle which guides construction of the synthetic concepts of the social sciences is distinct from that which is used to construct the general concepts of the natural sciences because the former is based on meaningful interrelationships rather than commonality.

2. The Ideal Type in Weber's Methodology

The first step in filling in the bare bones of the preceding outline of Weber's theory is to examine the description of the ideal type in his methodological works, but the attempt to derive a coherent and consistent theory of the ideal type from Weber's strictly methodological works is difficult for at least two reasons. First, Weber is clearly not an epistemologist, and even refused to describe himself as a methodologist. Several points in his theory that are, from an epistemological point of view, very crucial, are not clearly defined. These oversights cannot be excused, but they can be explained by Weber's somewhat disdainful attitude toward methodological issues. He insists repeatedly that methodological work is not a precondition for fruitful research, and he puts this point rather strongly: methodological work is no more a precondition for proper scientific research than knowledge of anatomy is a precondition for walking (1949:115). For Weber, methodological work is appropriate only if it arises from the context of substantive problems.

Second, Weber's entire methodological corpus represents his effort to steer a path between the erroneous elements of the two poles of the *Methodenstreit*, positivism and subjectivism, and this creates several problems of interpretation. It forces the modern reader to endure Weber's lengthy critiques of unknown authors and obsolete positions. Moreover, Weber's concern with revealing the errors of others frequently obscures the elements of his own position. Weber appears to be much more comfortable attacking the positions of others than formulating one of his own. Thus defining his position in the context of these polemics must begin with an account of his objections to these two doctrines.

The occasion for Weber's most specific discussion of the ideal type is an article he wrote as a statement of the editorial policy of *Archiv für Sozialwissenschaft und Sozialpolitik*, the article now known as "Objectivity in Social Science and Social Policy." This task provided him a perfect opportunity to expose the errors of both positivism and subjectivism with regard to the methods of social-scientific research, and to counter these positions with his own. Each school advocated a distinctive methodology for the social sciences, based on an equally distinctive definition of the goal of social-scientific research. The positivists argued that social scientists should employ the same methods utilized by natural scientists, because the goal of the two branches of science is the same: the formation of universal laws. The subjectivists, on the other hand, argued that the methods of the social sciences are unique because the goal of social-scientific analysis is to minutely reproduce social reality through a process of "intuiting" or "reliving" the actions of social actors. The subjectivists, therefore, eschewed all abstraction from the concreteness of social life, asserting that the formation of laws and concepts is inappropriate to the goal of social-scientific analysis. In the course of his discussion, Weber rejected elements of both positions; yet he began his analysis by revealing one respect in which the theories are identical. Both assume that the facts the social scientist studies are "given" or "immediate," that is, that they can be apprehended by the social scientist without presuppositions. This assertion is the first object of Weber's polemic.

"The type of social science we are interested in," Weber begins, "is an *empirical* science of concrete reality" (1949:72). The central problem in defining such a social science is to explain how concrete reality is apprehended and analyzed. But this is no easy task:

> as soon as we attempt to reflect about the way in which life confronts us in immediate concrete situations, it presents an infinite multiplicity of successively and coexistently emerg-

ing and disappearing events. . . . The absolute infinitude of this multiplicity is seen to remain undiminished even when our attention is fixed on a single "object." [1949:72]

Given this understanding of the nature of reality, however, the position that any aspect of reality can be apprehended without presuppositions—that is, without assuming some "point of view"—is obviously absurd. Thus, at the outset, Weber rejects out of hand one of the central positions of both positivism and subjectivism; the "presuppositionlessness" of the facts of the social sciences. He turns instead to the problem of formulating the nature of the presuppositions that are the necessary conditions of social-scientific research:

> Order is brought into this chaos only on the condition that in every case only a *part* of concrete reality is interesting and *significant* to us, because only it is related to the *cultural values* with which we approach reality. [1949:78]

At the very least, then, the presupposition that is fundamental to all social-scientific investigation can be identified as the relationship to cultural values. In other words, that part of reality which forms the subject matter of social science is defined by its relationship to the cultural values by which reality is apprehended.

These opening passages establish a position fundamental to Weber's approach. Identifying the "necessary presupposition" of social-scientific analysis and, hence, defining the subject matter of the social sciences is an exceedingly crucial point, yet one which Weber, at least in this context, passes over too swiftly. Unfortunately, stating that "cultural significance" is the principle by which the chaos of reality is ordered for the purposes of social-scientific research raises more questions than it answers. Weber is not clear on how "cultural significance" is defined within a given society. Is it defined in terms of what a majority of the members of the society consider to be significant or by what the social scientist who studies the society deems significant? Weber is also unclear on how "cultural significance" is defined in a comparative or historical analysis. Should social scientists, studying a foreign or historical society, define "cultural significance" in their own terms or in the terms employed by the society under investigation? Weber offers no satisfactory answers to these questions.

But Weber's pronouncements on the necessary presupposition of social-scientific research that defines its subject matter are

not limited to the "Objectivity" article. His most explicit statement of the basic problem, the constitution of the category of
mprises the subject matter of the social sciences, can
a brief passage in *Critique of Stammler*. Because it is
w instances in which Weber deals directly with this
orth quoting at length:

> suppose that two men who otherwise engage in no
> relation"—for example, two uncivilized men of dif-
> races, or a European who encounters a native in
> Africa—meet and "exchange" two objects. We are
> d to think that a mere description of what can be
> d during this exchange—muscular movements and,
> words were "spoken," the sounds which, so to say,
> ite the "matter" or "material" of the behavior—
> in no sense comprehend the "essence" of what hap-
> his is quite correct. The "essence" of what happens is
> ited by the "meaning" which the two parties ascribe
> ir observable behavior, a "meaning" which
> "regulates" the course of their future conduct. Without this
> "meaning," we are inclined to say, an "exchange" is neither
> empirically possible nor conceptually imaginable.
> [1977:109][5]

This same thesis is stated more succinctly in the opening
passages of *Economy and Society*, where Weber defines sociology
as "a science concerning itself with the interpretive understanding of social action" and then states that

> we shall speak of "action" insofar as the acting individual
> attaches a subjective meaning to his behavior. [1968:4]

This is considerably more satisfactory than a vague appeal
to "cultural significance." In these passages Weber states unambiguously that the "facts" of the social sciences are constituted by
the meaning bestowal of social actors. Many critics of Weber's
approach have noted that he never accords this issue the attention it deserves, which is undoubtedly true; but although Weber
does not elaborate on this essential point, his intention is quite
clear: the "subjective meaning" of social actors is the foundation
for all social-scientific analysis.

Instead of developing this theme in the "Objectivity" article, Weber's attention is focused on other issues that he appears
to find more noteworthy. Defining the subject matter of the

social sciences as that part of reality on which the social actors bestow meaning is only the first stage in the process by which the social scientist selects objects for analysis. The social actors' bestowal of meaning creates a broad category of facts which are appropriate objects of social-scientific analysis, but Weber must now explain how the social-scientific investigator chooses a particular segment of facts from that broad category. This second stage in the selection process is accomplished by the choice of a particular topic for investigation, a choice that derives from the investigator's individual values:

> . . . without the investigator's evaluative ideas, there would be no principle of selection of subject-matter and no meaningful knowledge of the concrete reality. [1949:82]

Weber is arguing, then, that all social-scientific analysis begins with a two-stage selection process: first, creation of a category of appropriate facts through the social actors' bestowal of meaning, then the choice of a particular segment of those facts, based on the investigator's interest.

It is important to note at this point precisely what Weber accomplished through articulation of this two-stage selection process. First, he has shown that no knowledge of social reality is presuppositionless—the original point he was attempting to establish against both subjectivists and positivists. Against them, he argued that two sets of presuppositions enter into the selection of facts for any social-scientific investigation: the meanings of the social actors and the investigator's individual values which are reflected in the nature of the question which is posed. Second, he has shown that analysis of social reality always involves abstraction. The "infinite multiplicity" or "chaos" of reality, which he mentions at the outset, is ordered by the two-stage selection process, which he outlines, and the result is a collection of facts which represent an abstraction from that reality. Furthermore, Weber makes the point that this abstraction is always effected through the use of concepts, which are constitutive of both stages of the selection process.

It is clear from the passage in the Stammler article that the basic category of facts available to the social scientist is the concepts of the social actors.[6] The social scientist also employs concepts in selecting particular elements from that category of facts, and the social scientist's necessary reliance on conceptualization is an important point in Weber's rejection of the subjectivists' position that it is the aim of social-scientific investigation to reproduce reality in all its concreteness (1949:74). Thus Weber has definitely shown that such a reproduction is impossible.

Despite the attention Weber devoted to outlining this two-stage selection process, he almost ignored one aspect of the process: the role played by the theoretical presuppositions of the scientific community, of which his hypothetical social scientist is a member. In his critique of Weber's methodology, Runciman makes this point very clearly; he remarks that Weber sees the presuppositions of social-scientific investigation as rooted entirely in the social scientists' individual and cultural values (1972:40). But, as Runciman accurately notes, many of the presuppositions which structure social-scientific analysis derive not from the investigator's personal or cultural values but from the "values" or theoretical presuppositions of the scientific community. The reasons for Weber's refusal to acknowledge the significance of such theoretical presuppositions are to be found in his attitude toward the status of scientific method itself, an issue which will be addressed in depth in the concluding chapter. At this point, however, it is important to note that, theoretically, Weber placed the presuppositions of the social-scientific community under the general heading of "investigator's evaluative ideas," a categorization which is, at best, confusing.

Having defined the principles which govern the selection of facts for social-scientific analysis, Weber's next task was to explain how these selected facts are synthesized into a conceptual tool which can be utilized by the social scientist, and it is at this point that Weber introduced his famous definition of the ideal type:

> An ideal type is formed by the one-sided *accentuation* of one or more points of view and by the synthesis of a great many diffuse, discrete, more or less present and occasionally absent *concrete individual* phenomena, which are arranged according to those one-sidedly emphasized viewpoints into a unified *analytical* construct. [1949:90]

This passage is Weber's most concise statement of the status of the ideal type, but in a subsequent definition he elaborates his point:

> Thus in the reality of the historical given we find particular individual characteristics of a variously mediated, refracted sort, more or less logical and complete, more or less mixed

with other heterogeneous characteristics. The most prominent and consequential of these features are selected and
combined according to their compatibility. [1978:1111]

In both of these passages, Weber attempted to describe the
nature of the act of synthesis which creates the conceptual tool of
the social scientist, the tool he has now identified as the ideal
type. He argues that creation of the ideal type involves the synthesis of various features or characteristics of the facts which
have been selected by the social scientist. What is crucial here,
however, is his definition of the principle which guides this synthesis, and in these passages Weber discusses two factors. The
first is the nature of the question posed in the investigation. This
question, which determines the initial selection of facts from the
broad category of meaningful action, is also instrumental in
determining construction of the ideal type itself. The nature of
the investigator's question determines what particular aspects of
the selected facts can logically be combined to formulate an
answer to the question. In another article, Weber reiterates this
point. The unity of the synthetic construct, he states,

is constituted by the selection of those aspects which are
"essential" from the point of view of specific theoretical
goals. [1975:168]

The second factor which Weber mentions is the "logic" inherent in the concepts themselves. When Weber states that the
features which make up the ideal type will be combined "according to their compatibility," his point is that concepts cannot be
thrown together in arbitrary fashion. Ideal types are not the
product of the whim or fancy of a social scientist, but are logically constructed concepts. Because certain factors of the facts
under consideration are logically compatible and others are not,
these relationships determine the structure of the concepts.

Finally, Weber carefully distinguished the logic that
governs construction of ideal types from that which governs construction of "average" types. He states that, in the majority of
cases of action important to history and sociology, "average"
types cannot be formulated and hence are not appropriate tools
of analysis in these disciplines (1968:21–22).

Discussion of Weber's understanding of the "logic of concepts," however, must proceed with a good deal of caution. It is

tempting to observe that Weber here anticipates the modern discussion of the logic of concepts which has arisen from the ordinary-language tradition of Wittgenstein. But although this supposition is not wholly inaccurate, it must be qualified substantially. On one hand, Weber's understanding of the logic of concepts has much in common with the Wittgensteinian understanding. Both emphasize that the "ordinary language" concepts of social actors have a "logic" in the sense that a wrong and a right way to employ these concepts can be determined. Weber would certainly agree with Winch's point that rules of usage can be determined for ordinary-language concepts and that the determination of these rules is essential to an understanding of social action.

But it is also the case that Weber's understanding of the logic of concepts does not derive from the same context as that of the Wittgensteinians. Most importantly, Weber, unlike Wittgensteinians, is not sensitive to the distinction between the "logic" inherent in ordinary-language concepts and the "logic" that informs the scientific method. The context of Wittgensteinians' discussion of the logic of ordinary discourse is defined by their concern to reveal the distinctiveness of this logic in contrast to the rigid, formalized logic of scientific method. The context of Weber's discussion of the logic of ordinary discourse is quite different. He is primarily concerned with specifying the logic of the social scientist's analysis of subjective meanings; his aim is to show the similarity between the logic with which the social scientist analyzes the subjective meanings of social actors and that with which the physical scientist analyzes events in the natural world.

Weber's isolation of the factors which guide the synthesis of ideal types, then, clarifies his understanding of the distinction between the process of constructing ideal types and that involved in formation of the general concepts of the natural sciences. He asserts, in sum, that general concepts are syntheses of average or common features, while ideal types are syntheses of characteristic or significant features constructed on the basis of logical and meaningful compatibility (1949:100–101). Once he has clearly established the nature of ideal types, he can turn, finally, to the function of ideal types in empirical research. Weber supplies a list of these functions in almost staccato style: they are neither hypotheses nor descriptions of reality, but "yardsticks" with which reality can be compared; they are neither historical reality nor "true reality," but purely limiting concepts or utopias; the purpose of ideal types is to provide a means of comparison with concrete reality in order to reveal the significance of that reality (1949:90–93). Or, as he puts it elsewhere, the abstraction of historical reality made possible by the ideal type facilitates the understanding of that reality (1968:110).

Because the critical literature has made much of the "unreality" of Weber's concept of the ideal type, precisely what he means in this context should be clearly stated. Weber's position is that ideal types are "abstract" in the sense that they are selective; that is, they are syntheses of elements selected from the concrete totality of reality. The fact that the ideal type, like all concepts, is "unreal" is thus a function of the fact that no concept can fully reproduce the concreteness of reality. There is, however, one sense in which these criticisms have isolated a weak point in Weber's theory. Weber states that the function of an ideal type is to facilitate a comparison with historical reality: ideal types are never found precisely in this reality, and thus in every case the relationship between the ideal type and reality is different and must be specified (1949:90). But Weber is not always as clear as he should be on the nature of the "reality" from which the ideal type is drawn and to which it is compared. It is not the "infinite flux" he refers to at the beginning of the "Objectivity" article; rather, it is the reality created by the social actors' bestowal of meaning. This reality, the subject matter of the social sciences, is constituted by the subjective meanings of the social actors and is thus preselected. Weber's failure, at certain junctures, to specify the nature of this reality is clearly an oversight and an instance of the kind of mistake he would not have made if he were a careful epistemologist.

One of Weber's concerns in his discussion of the use of ideal types in empirical research is to distinguish the theoretic status of the ideal type from that of the concepts and laws of the natural sciences. But with regard to this question, as with many others, Weber's position is not either/or. Rather, his aim is to identify similarities and differences between the concepts of the natural and the social sciences. His understanding of this issue, however, is closely tied to his concepts of objectivity and the scientific method. Full discussion of these issues will be postponed until the last chapter; at this point, however, several aspects of Weber's understanding of the role of ideal types vis-à-vis the concepts of the natural sciences should be noted. The similarities he identifies between the two types of concepts is informed by his position that the logic of the scientific method is the fundamental basis of the methods and concepts of both the natural and the social sciences. He notes that both employ "constructed" concepts and insists that although the process of their construction differs, the *use* of these constructed concepts is the same in both branches of science—but precisely what this similarity amounts to is never clearly specified. Weber declares that ideal types cannot be employed in the same way as the general concepts, laws, or hypotheses of the natural sciences. Given these exclusions, it is difficult to determine the nature of the similarity Weber has in mind. The only concrete similarity he can point to is the rules of logic, which, he claims, characterize the scientific method.

Weber's discussion of the differences between the theoretic status of ideal-typical analysis and analysis in the natural sciences, however, is much more substantive. His understanding of these differences derives from his specification of the basic division between the two branches of science, a theory he borrows from Rickert. Weber declares that one branch of science is concerned with elucidating the meaning of concrete reality, the other with the formation of universal laws. This division corresponds in most cases to the division between the social and the natural sciences, although exceptions to this rule can be found.[7]

Furthermore, Weber identifies the "concrete reality" that it is the concern of the social scientist to elucidate as concrete *cultural* reality. This distinction between what Weber refers to as the "sciences of concrete reality" and those designed to formulate universal laws allows him to catalogue a number of significant differences between the methods of the two branches of science. The first is rejection of the use of universal laws in the sciences of concrete reality in general and in the social sciences in particular. Weber adduces a very practical reason for this exclusion. Scientists who are concerned to formulate universal laws are interested in specific events only as instances of these laws; they are not, like social scientists, interested in specifying the meaning of the events themselves. In addition, specific events cannot be "deduced" from laws. Thus the discovery of a universal law, however significant in some scientific investigations, is not significant in the social sciences because laws can reveal nothing about the occurrence of concrete events. Hence he concludes that universal laws are simply not relevant to the concerns of the social sciences and must be rejected as the proper methodological tools of the social scientist.[8]

This division between the two branches of science also informs Weber's discussion of a second difference between the methods of the two branches: the range and permanence of ideal-typical concepts. Weber argues that ideal types make no claim to general validity; they are not hypotheses and thus cannot be "refuted" by a case that contradicts the concept. In the natural sciences, discovery of only one contradictory case refutes a hypothesis because the hypotheses of the natural sciences necessarily make claims to general validity. Discovery of contradictory cases in ideal-typical analysis, however, reveals not the error of the concepts but that the selected ideal-typical concept is not relevant to the problem at hand (1975:190). The only test of the "accuracy" of an ideal type is whether it *explains* the phenomena under investigation.

A third and particularly problematic difference between ideal types and concepts in the natural sciences revolves around conceptual change. If the selection and synthesis of ideal types is determined by both the meaning bestowal of the social actors and the interest of the investigator, it follows that these concepts must be subject to continuous change. Weber readily admits this (1949:159). He even insists that progress in the cultural sciences occurs precisely through this perpetual reconstruction of concepts. That the concepts of the cultural sciences change with the conceptualizations of the social actors and the focus of investigators' interests is thus to be applauded, not deplored (1949:105). Weber does not, of course, suggest that the concepts of the social sciences are arbitrary; he makes the argument that the concepts of the social scientist must be historically and culturally specific. If the goal of the social sciences is elucidation of the meaning of cultural reality, it follows that this elucidation will be facilitated by the use of concepts specific to the society under investigation, rather than by a fixed conceptual scheme which is applied alike to all societies.

Weber's position on these issues is not quite as simple as may seem to be indicated in these passages. It could be argued that Weber's substantive research belies his insistence on the historical and cultural specificity of concepts. Indeed, the point of his monumental studies in *Economy and Society* is the comparison of societies through the use of "universal" concepts, that is, concepts which are not culturally specific. His comparison of various societies on the basis of their economic structure, religious beliefs, and structures of domination thus appears to be an instance of the approach he is attacking in these passages; but to conclude from this that Weber has been caught in a contradiction is premature. The object of Weber's attack is not universal concepts per se but comprehensive theoretical systems which offer universal explanations for the totality of social reality. Weber is trying to reveal the folly of constructing rigid theoretical systems designed to encompass all aspects of society in all historical periods. He is advocating, instead, an approach which is sensitive to the substantial differences in social systems, both cultural and historical. His advocacy of conceptual change is rooted in the belief that the social scientist's conceptual tools must be tailored to the characteristics of the society under investigation. His use of broad categories, such as "economy" and "society," can be accommodated to this belief because his use of these concepts is designed to take account of the peculiarities of the cultures he investigates. What cannot be accommodated to Weber's position, and is the object of his attack in this context, is an approach such as dogmatic Marxism, which attempts to explain all social systems in terms of a rigid theoretical framework that is much more inclusive than the system of concepts which Weber utilizes.

Closely related to the transitory nature of ideal-typical analysis is an issue that is frequently mentioned by critics of the approach: the possibility of eventually "transcending" ideal-typical analysis. Analysis that employs ideal types is always, to a certain extent, piecemeal. As the social sciences mature, however, it has seemed probable to many social theorists that at some point this piecemeal approach might be replaced by a comprehensive synthesis of ideal-typical concepts which would permit a more "sophisticated" theoretical stance. Again, Weber admits the apparent faults of ideal-typical analysis. He refers to ideal-typical concepts as "crude" in comparison to the laws of the natural sciences, admitting that the use of ideal types always indicates the "adolescence" of a discipline (1949:103). But, as in the previous issue, he turns what looks like a negative point into a positive one:

> There are sciences to which eternal youth is granted, and the historical disciplines are among them—all those to which the eternally onward flowing stream of culture perpetually brings new problems. [1949:104]

The concepts of the social scientist, because they must deal with their constantly changing subject matter, must be flexible rather than rigid, and ideal types fit this requirement perfectly. Although they are, in comparison to the concepts of the natural sciences, imprecise, such a comparison overlooks the important differences between the natural and the social sciences. In terms of the goal of the social sciences, which is elucidation of the meaning of concrete cultural reality, ideal types are far from imprecise. Rather, they are finely honed instruments, specifically adapted to the unique needs of the social scientist.

Weber's final comments on the theoretic status of the ideal type reveal a certain defensiveness. He is not, it seems, unaware of the appeal of comprehensive theoretical approaches and the concomitant disdain for the apparently ad hoc approach of ideal-typical analysis. In the end, however, he returns to his best and simplest arguments: ideal types are necessary tools of social-scientific analysis, and they best describe what social scientists actually *do*. This was the note on which Weber began his explication of ideal-typical analysis; it was also the excuse he offered for such an extensive exploration of methodological issues. He implies that his carefully elaborated theory is to be taken primarily as a description of his own research practices. This attitude is revealed by the fact that his objections to the theories of other social scientists in his methodological excursus are less concerned with their strictly methodological errors than with the consequences of these errors: the use of concepts which are ambiguous or vague.

It is this practical concern, finally, that reveals the essence of Weber's theory of the ideal type. His motto might be reduced to this: Since we must use ideal types to do social science, let us be clear about what it is that we are doing by making our concepts unambiguous (1949:43, 94).

3. Varieties of Ideal Types

A common criticism of Weber's theory of ideal types is the claim that he employs many different kinds of ideal types in his substantive work and that several of them violate the epistemology of types outlined in his methodology (Rex, 1971:18). These criticisms have taken two principal forms. First, Weber's critics have argued that although the ideal type, as outlined in his methodological works, adequately describes one of these varieties, the historical ideal type, it does not provide an epistemological basis for the general sociological ideal types, the ideal types of action, or the structural ideal types. Second, some of his critics have charged that Weber's use of ideal-typical analysis in his substantive work reveals a very significant, yet unresolved, tension between his ideal types of action and his structural ideal types. This latter criticism is of crucial importance to the present thesis and must be refuted if that thesis is to stand.

Against these critics, it will be argued that although it is undeniable that Weber employed a number of distinct kinds of ideal types in his empirical work, these types, when they are examined carefully, conform to the epistemological basis established in his methodology. The distinctive processes of selection and synthesis which set the ideal types apart from other kinds of concepts can be shown to be the basis of types as heterogeneous as the general categories of action in *Economy and Society* and the structural types of the comparative studies. To establish the argument for this conformity, consideration of Weber's use of ideal types in his substantive work will be divided into three areas: (1) the relationship between historical and general sociological types, (2) the epistemology of action types, and (3) the development of structural types from the general types of social action.

A. Historical and General Sociological Types

The most common criticism of Weber's historical and general sociological types is that his ideal type theory was formulated in the historical stage of his career, but never adapted to the sociological stage that evolved later (Burger, 1976:119). Critics of this aspect of Weber's work assert that his attempt to conflate the methodological tools of the historian and the sociologist must be seen as a failure because the two are not really comparable (Watkins, 1952; Rex, 1971:18). They argue that the historian must utilize concepts which are culturally and temporally specific while the sociologist must employ concepts which span different cultures *and* different time periods. Weber's "confusion" of these two types of concepts, his critics argue, is thus a serious flaw in his theory of the ideal type.

This line of criticism, at least in one sense, is a modern-day version of Rickert's position. Modern-day critics argue that because the historian's concepts are "unique" while those of the sociologist are "general," they cannot have the same epistemic base; but it was on precisely this point that Weber departed from Rickert's theory. Against Rickert, Weber argued that the sociologist's concepts are not "general," in the same sense that the concepts of the natural scientist are general, and that the historian's interest in the "unique" is not the only principle of synthesis which can serve as the basis for construction of ideal types. Rather, Weber understands the ideal type to be constructed on a principle of synthesis that is inclusive of both the historian's interest in uniqueness and the sociologist's interest in significant aspects of phenomena derived from many societies.

Because the epistemological analysis in the previous section specified this principle precisely, it can be maintained that Weber isolated two features of the ideal type which establish its distinctiveness vis-à-vis other concepts. First, the category of facts from which an ideal type is constructed is determined by "cultural significance," that is, by the meaning that social actors bestow on their actions. Second, once the investigator has chosen a certain group of these facts on the basis of theoretic interest, the principle that governs the synthesis of aspects of those facts is based on relationships of meaning and significance that are logically compatible with that theoretic interest and with the logic of the actors' concepts. Both features are clearly identifiable in construction of the ideal types of the historian and the sociologist. In constructing their conceptual tools, both begin with the subjective meaning of social actors and construct a synthetic concept that is determined by the logic of that subjective meaning as well as by the question posed in the investigation.

Matching this epistemological basis of the ideal type to the construction of historical ideal types is a simple process because (as Weber's critics have noted) the problems of the historian were of primary concern to Weber when he wrote his methodological works. In explicating Weber's understanding of the historical ideal type, however, an important point must be noted. Had Weber been concerned only with the formation of historical concepts, there would have been no necessity for developing his theory of the ideal type. Rickert's theory was more than adequate to describe the formation of these concepts, and that Weber had no objection to Rickert's understanding of the "historical individual" per se is evidenced by the fact that Weber's understanding of this concept is identical to Rickert's. The purpose of

Weber's development of the ideal type, then, was not to reject Rickert's understanding of this concept but to articulate a principle of synthesis that was more inclusive than Rickert's. Weber identified the characteristic principle of synthesis of historical ideal types, uniqueness, as only one variant of the principle of synthesis which defines the nature of ideal-typical concepts. Rickert's error was to identify uniqueness as the only possible basis for the concepts of the social scientist, and it was this restriction that prompted Weber to depart from Rickert's theory. This same restriction is echoed in modern criticism of Weber's ideal types.

Construction of a historical ideal type can be divided into three stages. First, like any social scientist, the historian begins with the distinctive subject matter of those sciences, the broad category of meaningful action as defined by social actors' bestowal of meaning. Second, the historian, because the interest that guides the investigation is, specifically, a *historical* interest, limits this category of meaningful action to a particular time period and, usually, a particular society. (This point may seem tautological, but from an epistemological perspective it is highly significant. Weber declares that the theoretic interest of the investigator is a key factor in guiding the synthesis of constructed concepts in the social sciences, and the theoretic interest of the historian is, quite simply, a historical interest.) Third, the historian selects particular elements of this selected group of facts and constructs a concept determined by the particular historical question which is posed in the investigation.

One of the primary goals of this synthesis is preservation of the uniqueness or peculiarity of the facts which are the basis of the concept under construction, a point made clearly by Rickert and reiterated in Weber's theory. This interest in uniqueness is instrumental in the formation of all historical ideal types and can be identified as the definitive variant of the principle of synthesis that is used to construct this particular ideal type. In somewhat simpler language, Weber's position is that if a historical question is posed, a necessary element of the synthesis by which the ideal type is constructed will be the historical context of the facts under consideration.

Because Weber identified a specifically historical interest as only one of a range of interests which may be utilized in construction of social-scientific concepts, it is not difficult to define an epistemological basis for general sociological ideal types which matches that of historical ideal types. The pattern for constructing the two variants, furthermore, is much the same, differing only with the nature of the investigator's interest. First, the category of facts from which a general sociological ideal type is constructed is identical to that of the historical type; something becomes a "fact" for analysis in both cases because the social actors bestow it with meaning. Weber makes this very clear when he states that the empirical material of sociology and history are "to a very large extent" the same (1968:19). Second, and in contrast to the historical ideal type, the category of facts that is of interest to the sociological investigator is not limited to one historical period or one society. On the contrary, the investigator who attempts to construct a general sociological ideal type will seek to gather information from as many historical periods and societies as possible. (Weber's almost obsessive desire to research widely divergent societies in numerous, different periods is certainly evidence of this.) Third, the sociological investigator synthesizes relevant aspects of the facts in this category according to the demands of the question at hand. But in contrast to the construction of a historical ideal type, in which the historical context of the facts is of primary importance, the historical context of the facts is only one of many relevant factors in construction of a general sociological ideal type, because these ideal types are constructed to answer questions concerning the nature of a social institution or practice in different societies in various periods. The sociologist's question will be posed with the specific aim of formulating an answer which transcends the historical and societal aspects of the institution under examination. Thus the variant of the principle of synthesis that guides construction of these ideal types is, in some sense, a-historical.[9]

It might be objected that this rendering of the similarities between historical and general sociological ideal types is insufficient because it ignores the fact (often mentioned in the critical literature) that general sociological ideal types are more "abstract" than historical types. They can be identified as more "abstract" in two senses: unlike historical ideal types, sociological types do not emphasize the uniqueness or peculiarity of the facts under investigation, and they are more selective; that is, they are a result of selection from a broader range of facts.

Weber himself points out this difference. General sociological types, he states, are "relatively lacking in fullness of concrete content" (1968:20). But he argues that general sociological ideal types are more precise than historical types because, in their construction, the investigator strives for the highest adequacy on the level of meaning. This might be interpreted to mean that the sociologist, to compensate for the removal of these ideal types from the uniqueness of historical reality, is more careful than the historian to construct precise concepts, which is certainly a significant difference between the two kinds of ideal types. But overemphasis on the abstraction of general sociological ideal types can lead to the error—quite common among Weber's critics—of assuming that a historical type is more "real" than a general ideal type.[10] To make this assumption is, however, to forget (again) that both types are constructed concepts and hence "unreal." Both are designed to explain a concrete, existing social phenomenon, as are all concepts of the social scientist. The significant difference between them is that historical ideal types are constructed to answer questions in which historical context is of primary importance, while general sociological ideal types answer questions in which this is only one of the relevant aspects. Thus the difference in abstraction between the two kinds of ideal types is one of degree, not kind.

Most importantly, this rendering of the similarity between historical and general sociological ideal types reveals the weakness of the position taken by Weber's critics. Weber defined a principle of synthesis for the ideal type that is more inclusive than the principle of uniqueness proposed by Rickert, and yet is distinct from the natural scientist's principle of commonality. It rests on meaning and significance determined by the logical relationships arising from both the actors' meaning and the investigator's question. The fact that many modern commentators fail to grasp this aspect of Weber's work indicates the subtlety of his reasoning on this point.

B. Epistemology of Action Types

Identifying the conformity of Weber's historical and general sociological ideal types to the epistemological basis established in his methodology is relatively simple, in comparison to the problems raised by his formulation of ideal, or "pure," types of action. The criticism of this aspect of Weber's theory has been most succinctly stated by John Rex, who argues that ideal types, in the sense of pure types of action orientation verified by probable courses of action, have little to do with ideal types, which involve artificial accentuations of reality in order to point out certain causal sequences (1971:24). This criticism raises two distinct problems, the first of which concerns whether the pure types of action that Weber presents at the beginning of *Economy and Society* violate the epistemology of types established in his methodology. The second problem involves the relationship between a pure type of motivation for action and the "probability" that a particular action will occur. The first question will be taken up in this section, the second in the next section, in the discussion of the development of structural types.

Weber's definition of the pure types of action arises from his discussion of the nature of social action at the beginning of *Economy and Society*. He defines action as social "insofar as its subjective meaning takes account of the behavior of others and is thereby oriented in its course" (1968:4). The pure types of social action that he develops on the basis of this definition represent different ways in which social action can be oriented—or what might be labeled the "motivational context" of that action. It was stated above that the two criteria which define the distinctive character of ideal types vis-à-vis other concepts are the category of facts from which the ideal type is drawn and the principle that guides the synthesis of the constructed concept. The first step in examining the epistemological basis of these pure types of action, then, is to determine from what category of facts the types are constructed. In his methodology, Weber clearly specified the category of facts that is definitive of the subject matter of the social sciences and from which all ideal types are drawn: the subjective meaning of the social actors. But in his discussion of pure types of action, Weber refers not to meaning but to "motivation" or "orientation." Thus the key to defining the category of facts from which pure types of action are drawn necessarily involves clarifying his distinction between meaning and motivation.

The most useful way of approaching the nature of this distinction is to place it in the context provided by Weber's definition of the two kinds of understanding which the social scientist may utilize to examine social action. The first is direct or observational understanding of the subjective meaning of a given act as such. The second is explanatory understanding, which Weber defines in terms of motive:

Thus we understand in terms of *motive* the meaning an actor attaches to the proposition twice two equals four, when he states it or writes it down, in that we understand what makes him do this at precisely this moment and in these circumstances. [1968:8]

He goes on to assert that rational understanding of motivation consists in placing the act in an intelligible and more inclusive context of meaning. Furthermore, this understanding, in terms of motive, is always in addition to direct observational understanding.

Definition of these two types of understanding clarifies how Weber interprets the category of facts from which the pure types of action are drawn, which is defined not simply by the meaning of an action but by its motivation. Understanding in terms of motive, Weber states, places the meaning of the action in a broader context; it involves the explanation rather than the mere observation of the action. The problem which must be confronted in this context, then, is whether shifting the definition of the category of facts from which a type is drawn from meaning to motivation invalidates the epistemology of ideal types which Weber developed in his methodology. And this problem, in turn, rests on what Weber means by the "understanding of subjective meaning." Since Weber has identified the subjective meaning of social action as constitutive of the basic category of facts from which the social scientist constructs ideal types, it is important to specify precisely how this subjective meaning is "understood" by the social scientist. Only then can it be determined how that understanding differs from motivational understanding.

These questions, however, raise the complex and much discussed issue of what Weber means by the term *verstehen*. (This problem will be dealt with at length in the next chapter because it involves issues which are central to the "subjective critique" of positivism, launched by phenomenologists and ordinary-language philosophers. At this point, then, several points will be briefly noted that will receive fuller discussion later.) The issue of *verstehen* has created great controversy among Weber's critics, but for many years the accepted interpretation was that advanced by Abel in his well-known article "The Operation Called *Verstehen*" (1948). Abel argued, in sum, that Weber was referring to some form of mental intuiting or imagining in his use of this term. In recent years, however, this interpretation has been challenged. A number of modern scholars have argued that Weber understood the "subjective meanings" of social actions to be publicly available data. They assert that Weber did not use *verstehen* to refer to the process of uncovering a hidden mental operation, but to the intersubjective meanings or socially constituted rules which define the meaning of action within a given society (Di Quattro, 1972; Tucker, 1965; Munch, 1975).

A second point that should be noted is that Weber was not as clear on this issue as he should have been. When he speaks of understanding the subjective meaning of social actors through "direct observation," he seems to assume that this is a straightforward, unproblematic activity which requires no explanation. (That it requires *much* explanation is evidenced by the extensive literature on this topic in recent years.) But although Weber is unclear as to how subjective meaning is apprehended by the social scientist, it is evident to careful students that he understands such meaning to be "directly observable" by the social scientist. Although Weber can be faulted for not adequately describing this process of meaning apprehension, the whole of his sociology depends on the public availability of subjective meaning.

The central problem under consideration here can now be addressed: If subjective meaning can be said to be publicly accessible, does the same apply to motivation? Or does determining the motive for an action necessarily involve a process of mental intuiting, even though establishing its meaning does not? This problem can best be dealt with by returning to the passage quoted above, in which Weber discusses what would constitute an "exchange" between two individuals. He concludes that an exchange can be said to take place only if the actors subjectively constitute that action as an "exchange." Furthermore, Weber assumes that subjective meaning-bestowal to be "directly observable" by the social scientist. Identifying this action as an "exchange" is thus an instance of his first definition of understanding, direct or observational understanding. The question at issue, however, is what would be involved if the social scientist, studying this exchange, were to inquire about the motivational context of the action; that is, attempt an explanatory understanding of the exchange? Would this necessarily involve delving into the mental operations of the social actors and intuiting their intentions?

It would not. By extrapolating from Weber's understanding

of the accessibility of subjective meaning, it can be argued that Weber also understands the motivation or orientation of an action to be publicly accessible. In the case cited above, establishing the motivational context of the exchange would involve examining the actions of each social actor which lead to participation in the exchange in order to determine the reason for which each performed the action. Thus explanatory understanding should be understood to involve placing the subjective meaning of a particular action in the context of the set of subjective meanings which led to that action. Understood in this way, it is clear that Weber's discussion of motivation does not entail a process that is fundamentally different from the apprehension of subjective meanings. It does not, in short, involve some form of intuition or empathy which reveals the motives of social actors to the social scientist. Weber's reference to motivation merely entails widening the context of the social scientist's observation to examination of a set or chain of subjective meanings, rather than identification of just one action.

Once it has been established that by examining the motivation or orientation of action Weber is merely shifting his attention to the larger context in which an action takes place, it is possible to be clearer about what is involved in his formulation of pure types of action. Weber sees both the meaning and the motivation of an action to be available to him as a social observer. The subjective meaning of the action identifies the action, defining the isolated event as one thing and not another. The motivation of the action has a broader scope, providing an explanation for the action's occurrence.

When Weber attempts to construct a pure type of action orientation, it is the motivation, rather than the subjective meaning, that occupies his attention. This is the category of facts from which the pure types of action orientation are constructed, a category not fundamentally different from that of the subjective meaning of a single action. The social scientist constructs an ideal type from this category by selecting certain aspects of the motivation for action and synthesizing them into an ideal type. The pure types of action orientation are the result of this synthesis. The principle that guides that synthesis, furthermore, is identical to that which guides construction of an ideal type: meaningful, relevant, logically compatible aspects are selected and synthesized according to the logical demands imposed by the investigator's question and the actors' concepts.

Specification of this outline of the construction of pure types of action clears up one of the principal confusions regarding the status of these types: the relationship between pure types of action and concrete occurrences of a particular action. In his description of pure types of action, Weber is careful to distinguish them from concrete cases of particular orientations of action (1968:8, 9). He insists that a pure type of action orientation does not establish, in every case of that action's occurrence, that the motives of the actors must be of the type specified. He also insists that pure types of action do not establish "averages"; they do not specify the motivation that *usually* accompanies a particular action. Rather, the pure types express the characteristic and significant aspects of the motivation of that particular action. They are limiting concepts which can be used to compare concrete instances of the action in question. This, of course, is also true of any ideal type, but in pure types of action, because they deal with what many commentators regard as the "intangible" realm of motivation, this relationship to concrete occurrences has raised questions that do not seem problematic in other kinds of ideal types.

Interpreted in this light, Weber's pure types of action fit the epistemological model of the ideal type very neatly, and perhaps the problems that have arisen with regard to them can be explained by the philosophical difficulties in defining what is meant by a "motive" for action. These problems have certainly been of much concern to modern philosophers of social science. Furthermore, Weber's rendering of how the understanding of subjective meaning and motivation is accomplished is, it must be conceded, seriously deficient and the subject of much criticism.[11] But from an epistemological perspective, there is no reason to conclude that pure types of action orientation contradict Weber's understanding of the distinctive features of ideal types. They are consistent with his epistemological understanding of the nature of ideal types with regard to both of the key features that he defines: the category of facts on which they are based and the principle of synthesis that guides their construction. But although this conclusion permits dismissal of most of the criticisms of this aspect of Weber's work, one aspect of these criticisms is undeniably accurate: the limited usefulness of pure types of action in concrete social-scientific research. Because of the extreme generality of these types, it is difficult to see how the social scientist's understanding of social action would be greatly enhanced by definition of these types of action.

It is significant that Weber himself rarely refers to these

pure types in his substantive research, but faulting Weber's formulation of the pure types of action on these grounds is not tantamount to questioning their epistemological foundations.

C. Development of Structural Types

In part I of *Economy and Society*, Weber touches on all the major varieties of ideal types under discussion here—not in haphazard fashion but in a very carefully structured discussion. Beginning with his definition of social action and pure types of action, he moves to a general definition of social relationship and then to examination of particular kinds of social relationships. Although the substantive analyses in part II were written before this conceptual exposition, the careful progression of definitions in part I, it will be argued, is consistent with Weber's use of structural ideal types in the substantive works. They also provide answers to a number of problems that have arisen with regard to these types, the first of which was mentioned above in connection with the pure types of action.

In his definition of "social relationship," Weber refers to the "probability" that a particular action will occur, and this reference has been particularly problematic for Weber's anti-positivist critics. It has been used to argue that he confuses a *verstehen* methodology with positivist techniques. Thus Winch accuses him of "checking" his *verstehen* explanations with statistics (1958:112) and Rex charges him with attempting—unsuccessfully—to reconcile *verstehen* sociology with positivist methodology (1974:53).

A second problem raised by Weber's use of structural analysis is how this analysis is to be assessed in terms of his theory of the ideal type. Rex suggests that Weber never developed a structural ideal type and that his structural analysis is completely divorced from the theory of ideal types presented in the methodology (1974:44). Other theorists have argued that Weber's structural analyses can be considered ideal typical, but that Weber never resolved the "tension" between his pure types of action, which are based on analysis of subjective meaning, and his structural ideal types. This criticism, from the present perspective, is the most serious, and it will be argued that Weber's relevance for contemporary social theory lies precisely in the fact that his approach avoids this "tension"—that is, it synthesizes the analysis of subjective meaning with the analysis of structural forms.

The argument that will be developed against both these sets of critics is that Weber saw subjective meaning and action as "two sides of the same coin." Although Weber does not present this thesis in a philosophically sophisticated manner, the order of his definitions in part I of *Economy and Society* establishes it. These definitions reveal that Weber saw a certain type of subjective meaning as linked to a certain type of action because the action is defined by the meaning bestowed on it—in other words, an action can be identified in a particular way through the meaning bestowal of social actors. This thesis of the correspondence between meaning and action provides the connection between the pure types of action with which the work begins and the structural analyses that comprise the bulk of the substantive studies. Furthermore, the argument in the previous section is closely connected to this thesis. That Weber saw subjective meanings as publicly accessible can be a first step in establishing that he assumed a necessary correspondence between meaning and action. The progression of definitions in *Economy and Society*, however, provides a more solid foundation for the thesis.

Weber began his catalogue of definitions with the statement that sociology is the interpretive understanding of social action, and thus with a causal explanation of its course and consequences (1968:4). This definition sets the stage for basic definitions of the conceptual exposition, as well as explanations of the "course and consequences" of social action, that is, the structural analyses. However, the pattern of Weber's sociological program can be glimpsed in this initial definition of his subject matter, where he asserts that he intends to present a program for social science which links the interpretation of subjective meaning to the course and consequences of social action—social structures. This program is revealed in the definitions which follow. His first step is to divide the interpretation of meaning into two kinds: analysis of concrete cases and construction of pure types. Initially, the pure types occupy his attention and are the subject of his subsequent definitions of social action and social relationship. The definition of social action has already been explored (above); his definition of social relationship, however, is equally significant:

> The term "social relationship" will be used to denote the behavior of a plurality of actors insofar as, in its meaningful content, the action of each takes account of that of the others and is oriented in these terms. The social relationship thus consists entirely and exclusively in the existence of a

probability that there will be a meaningful course of social action. [1968:26–27]

This definition is one of the clearest statements of the theme that runs through the conceptual exposition which opens *Economy and Society*: the link between subjective meaning and courses of action. Weber is saying, in effect, that actions which are oriented in a particular way—that is, are identified by a particular subjective meaning—result in particular courses of action. This definition appears to establish only a one-way determinism between meaning and action: certain kinds of orientations determine certain kinds of actions. But if this definition is placed in the broader context of the series of definitions, it becomes clear that Weber is asserting a two-way determinism between meaning and action. Weber always identifies an action by specifying its subjective meaning and by identifying the particular course of action that is linked to this meaning. Thus it is simply not the case that meaning determines action or vice versa; rather, meaning and action are linked, and both follow from identification of the action.

A fuller understanding of Weber's position on the relationship between meaning and action can be gained from his discussion of a particular kind of social relationship: domination. A few pages after his general definition of social relationship, Weber states:

Action, especially social action which involves a social relationship, may be guided by the belief in the existence of a legitimate order. [1968:31]

This definition, which introduces his discussion of legitimate domination, is in line with the preceding discussion of general categories of social action. The transition is simply to a particular kind of social action rather than the general category: social action guided by belief in a legitimate order. Weber then specifies four ways in which actors may "ascribe" legitimacy to a social order (1968:36), and his point is that a particular kind of ascription of legitimacy is tied to a particular kind of obedience. This is another instance of identification of action in terms of the linkage of subjective meaning and a course of action: ascriptions of legitimacy (subjective meanings) are linked to kinds of obedience (courses of action).

His subsequent definition of "domination," however, seems to contradict this approach:

> "Domination" is the probability that a command with a given specific content will be obeyed by a given group of persons. [1968:53]

It appears to focus attention exclusively on the "probability of action" and abandon the previous focus on subjective meaning as linked to action.

A key passage from the opening paragraphs of the sections on legitimate domination provides the answer to this apparent contradiction, as well as the necessary transition from definitions of meaning and action to the structural analysis that follows:

> Experience shows that in no instance does domination voluntarily limit itself to the appeal to material or affectual or ideal motives as a basis for its continuance. In addition every such system attempts to establish and to cultivate the belief in its legitimacy. But according to the kind of legitimacy which is claimed, the type of obedience, the kind of administrative staff developed to guarantee it, and the mode of exercising authority will differ fundamentally. Equally fundamental is the variation in effect. Hence, it is useful to classify the types of domination according to the kind of claim to legitimacy typically made by each. [1968: 213]

Weber effects an important terminology shift in this passage. In the previous discussion he was concerned with ways of "ascribing" legitimacy, but now he discusses "claims" to legitimacy. This change is crucial and must be carefully examined.

In the social relationship of legitimate domination, both ruler and ruled "ascribe" a certain subjective meaning to this relationship. Linked to this ascription is a particular kind of obedience, that is, a particular course of action. Weber is now asserting that the central aspect of this course of action is the "claim" of a particular basis for the legitimacy of the domination; other aspects of the course of action, he asserts, are dependent on the nature of this claim. Weber is asserting, then, that certain ways of ascribing legitimacy are manifest in certain kinds of claims to legitimacy and, conversely, that particular claims are necessarily based on particular ascriptions. In other words, ascriptions (meanings) and claims (actions) have a necessary correspondence.

For the purposes of his sociological analysis, Weber assumes this link between these claims and these ascriptions, but by shifting his attention from ascriptions to claims, Weber also effects an important transition: he shifts to the action side of the meaning/action nexus that he has assumed. In other words, he moves from a focus on the interpretation of meaning, which occupied his attention in the conceptual exposition, to analysis of courses of action, which will be the subject of the substantive analyses. However, in doing so he does not, in any sense, reject the correspondence between meaning and action. Quite the contrary. It is precisely his assumption of this correspondence which allows him to focus on courses of action without losing his grounding in subjective meaning.

An appreciation of Weber's position on this issue, furthermore, provides answers to both of the criticisms noted above. It can be argued that the confusion arising from Weber's reference to the "probability" of an action's occurrence stems more from the connotations of this term in modern social theory than from any confusion intrinsic to Weber's account, and two factors inform Weber's use of "probability" in this context. First, he uses the term to clarify his understanding of the relationship between meaning and action. He asserts that the "probability" that an action will occur can be established only by identifying the subjective meaning bestowed on that action by the social actors involved. Second, Weber uses "probability" in this context because his discussion is concerned with the pure types of action orientation rather than with concrete occurrences of particular actions. As was noted above, Weber is always careful to distinguish between an ideal type and a concrete case of the type; thus he cannot assert that a particular orientation *always* results in a particular course of action. He selects the term "probability" to convey his sense of the linkage between the ideal type and an actual occurrence in this particular kind of ideal type, the pure types of action. That this term is an unfortunate choice from the perspective of contemporary social theory is undeniable, but it does not follow that, by referring to "probability," Weber is retreating into positivism or behaviorism. Nor is he "checking" his meaning interpretations with statistics. Rather, Weber's discussion of the "probability" that certain courses of social action will occur is based on his formulation of pure types of action which involve "the highest possible degree of logical integration by virtue of complete adequacy on the level of meaning" (1968:20).

This understanding of Weber's position on the relationship

between meaning and action can also be used to refute the second set of critics, who question Weber's structural analysis. In the passage quoted above, Weber clearly states his understanding of the relationship between social structure and subjective meaning. He asserts that all significant aspects of structures of domination flow directly from the kind of legitimacy which is claimed by the social actors, claims which are based on ascriptions of subjective meaning. Because of this connection between claims to legitimacy and structures of domination, Weber finds it "useful" to classify structures of domination by the different kinds of claims to legitimacy. In other discussions of domination, Weber reiterates this understanding of the relationship between the subjective meaning of domination and the social structure which results:

> [Domination] refers to a meaningful interrelationship between those giving orders and those obeying to the effect that the expectations toward which action is oriented on both sides can be reckoned on. [1970:83]

Even more to the point:

> For a domination, this kind of justification of its legitimacy is much more than a matter of theoretical or philosophical speculation; it rather constitutes the basis of very real differences in the empirical structure of domination. [1968: 953]

On the basis of these passages and the definitions preceding them, it can be argued that Weber establishes a continuum between subjective meaning on the one hand and social structure on the other. This continuum is established in the careful progression of definitions which characterizes the discussion of legitimacy and domination, culminating in a definition of legitimate domination which serves as the basis of his structural analyses. Weber begins, quite clearly, with subjective meaning. He describes how actors ascribe legitimacy to their actions in a number of ways; then he asserts that these ascriptions are tied to certain courses of action, and central to these courses of action are the claims advanced by the social actors as to the basis for legitimacy. These various claims, in turn, serve as an organizing device for empirical analysis of structures of domination because the nature of these claims determines all key aspects of those structures. Thus the ideal types of legitimate domination that are the basis of some of Weber's most perceptive structural analyses are linked to particular subjective meanings which identify the patterns of action under examination.

It is not my intention to argue, however, that Weber does not analyze these patterns of action, the structures of domination, apart from the subjective meanings by which they are identified. In his sociology of domination, he rarely refers to these subjective meanings. What is argued, rather, is that the nexus between meaning and action that Weber establishes is crucial to these substantive analyses because it provides him a means of linking analysis of subjective meaning with that of structural forms. Also, the ideal type is revealed as the common method of analysis for both of these aspects of social phenomena.

Lack of such a continuum, however, has been the point of many criticisms of Weber's use of ideal types. A number of commentators have argued that Weber's use of structural ideal types is evidence of a tension, even a contradiction, in his analysis (Outhwaite, 1975; Turner, 1977). A representative and particularly useful example of this criticism may be found in a recent article by John Sewart (1978:348), where Sewart argues that Weber never resolves the tension between his analysis of social action and the interpretive understanding of social action, which is most evident in his *The Protestant Ethic*. It becomes evident in this work, Sewart argues, that Weber cannot adequately treat "objective realities" such as class and bureaucracy. He quotes Weber as asserting that such entities exist only "in the consciousness of an undetermined and changing plurality of individuals and in their minds assume multifarious nuances as to form, content, clarity and meaning" (Sewart, 1978:336).[12] However, Sewart does not agree with Rex's contention that Weber does not develop structural ideal types. He asserts that Weber does not resolve the tension between his interpretation of social action in terms of the conscious intentions of the social actors and that which is constituted by the system to which the action belongs and is external to the actors' consciousness (1978: 350).

Sewart's criticism of Weber's use of structural ideal types is important and challenging. In attempting to deal with this criticism, however, it must be pointed out that the conclusions Sewart derives from his analysis of Weber's structural ideal types are based on a faulty reading of Weber's methodology. The source of Sewart's error can be traced to the passage quoted above, for, contrary to his claim that Weber is discussing "objective realities" in this passage, Weber is discussing how the social scientist goes about studying a set of "ideas" (in this case, Christianity) which influence the social action of large numbers of people. It is worthwhile to quote Weber at length in order to clear up the distortion in Sewart's account:

> Those "ideas" which govern the behavior of the population of a certain epoch, i.e., which are concretely influential in determining their conduct, can, if a somewhat complicated construct is involved, be formulated precisely only in the form of an ideal type, since empirically it exists in the minds of an indefinite and constantly changing mass of individuals and assumes in their minds the most multifarious nuances of form and content, clarity and meaning. Those elements of the spiritual life of the individuals living in a certain epoch of the Middle Ages, for example, which we may designate as the "Christianity" of those individuals, would, if they could be completely portrayed, naturally constitute a chaos of infinitely differentiated and highly contradictory complexes of ideas and feelings. This is true despite the fact that the medieval church was certainly able to bring about a unity of belief and conduct to a particularly high degree. [1949: 95–96]

Two features of the discussion are crucial to an understanding of Weber's meaning in this context. First, Weber was *not* discussing the empirical structure of Christianity in this passage —that is, Church organization, the hierarchy of authority, the links between Church and State, etc. He was discussing the "idea" of Christianity, which he defined a few sentences later as

> a combination of articles of faith, norms from church law and custom, maxims of conduct, and countless concrete interrelationships which we have fused into an "idea." [1949:96]

Weber, of course, would argue that the idea of Christianity is inseparably linked to particular courses of action which constitute the structural aspects of Christianity, but he was not, in this passage, discussing those structural aspects, but the *ideas* to which they are linked. That Sewart does not see this seriously distorts his reading of the passage.

The second significant feature of this discussion, also overlooked by Sewart, is the reason for Weber's extensive examination of ideas in this context. Weber's purpose in this passage is to show that the idea of Christianity had no concrete reality in social life, which can be explained only by his intense animosity to collective concepts in social-scientific research. Weber was adamantly opposed to the Hegelian position that ideas are "real" forces in social life, and this passage represents Weber's attempt to define how the social scientist can utilize the "idea" of Christianity without imputing reality to this concept. Not surprisingly, his answer is that the "idea of Christianity" can be of use to the social scientist only if it is conceptualized as an ideal type.

Much of Sewart's argument against Weber collapses once the distortions of his interpretation are removed. However, Sewart's criticism raises important questions concerning two aspects of Weber's structural ideal types that constitute the central elements and, hence, the greatest strengths of these concepts. The first—the continuum Weber establishes between subjective meaning and social structure—has been discussed extensively above. Few critics have bothered to trace Weber's careful construction of this continuum through the progression of definitions at the beginning of *Economy and Society*, but if this progression is examined, it shows quite clearly that this "tension," which Sewart and others have referred to, is bogus. Indeed, Weber is very careful to ground his structural analysis firmly in subjective meanings. Against Sewart, it can be argued that Weber posits an interdependence between meaning and structure.

With regard to every structural analysis that he considers, Weber would argue that the structure would not be a particular type unless the dominant belief system were a corresponding type; and conversely, a particular kind of belief system is manifest in a particular structure. This interdependence is both the brilliance of Weber's account and the source of most misinterpretations of his analysis. If, like Sewart, Weber interpreted structural entities as "external" to the social actor's consciousness, the problem of tension between actors' meanings and social structure simply would not arise. Weber's desire to establish a connection between them creates the difficulty that Sewart and many other social theorists have sidestepped. The importance of Weber's work lies in his attempt to make this connection and his success in doing so.

The second question raised by Sewart's criticism is equally significant—that Weber cannot deal with structural elements which are "objective realities," external to social actors' consciousness. Sewart distorts Weber's meaning to "prove" his point, but even when his distortion is corrected, there is one sense in which his point still stands: Weber would not concede that either the "ideas" or the structure which constitute a social institution are an objective entity in the sense meant by Sewart. And Weber's point is well taken. The burden of proof is on Sewart, to show in what sense these objective entities are "real,"[13] and against this position, Weber asserts that neither the ideas nor the corresponding structure of a social institution can be conceptualized as "real." Such entities can only be grasped as ideal types, which must, according to Weber, always be distinguished from concrete occurrences of the type. Aron summarizes this nicely when he asserts that, for Weber, a structural ideal type refers to something which

> transcends individual consciousness, it was never lived in this way by any individual; it appears as the formalization and elucidation of the more or less obscure or implicit thought of historical agents. [Aron, 1969:307, trans. by Outhwaite, 1975:54]

The above analysis also permits refutation of Rex's criticism of Weber's structural analysis. Rex's claim that Weber never develops a structural ideal type rests on two grounds: (1) that Weber's structural analysis does not appear to fit neatly into the ideal type theory of the methodology, and (2) that Weber does not explicitly present his structural analyses as ideal typical. Both objections can be met by referring to the epistemic pattern of the ideal type developed from his methodology. The first requirement of that pattern is that the ideal type be drawn from the general category of facts available to the social scientist—facts endowed with meaning by the social actors. This requirement, which may seem an impediment to labeling Weber's structural analysis "ideal typical," can be removed by recalling Weber's continuum between subjective meaning and structural forms. When Weber considers the structural elements of a social institution, he may appear to be concerned with them only as objective entities; but for Weber, the structural elements of a social institution, the "courses of action" he refers to, are identified by their characteristic subjective meanings. Rex is correct in observing that Weber does not make this correspondence specific, but it was shown above that the sense of Weber's structural analyses depends on development of this correspondence.

The remaining elements of the epistemic pattern follow much more easily. The second step in construction of a structural ideal type involves selection of a particular group of these facts, determined by the theoretic interest of the investigation. In structural ideal types, this selection is determined by the goal of isolating the characteristic elements of the structure under consideration. In the third step, meaningful aspects of the selected group of facts are synthesized into a concept according to the logical demands of that theoretic interest.

Despite Rex's criticism, there is a sense in which Weber's structural ideal types illustrate the genius of the ideal-typical approach better than any of the other varieties, for his structural ideal types illustrate how each social institution exhibits a peculiar logic which is definitive of its elements. The ideal-typical approach reveals this logic very clearly through construction of a concept that specifies the meaningful interrelationship that is constitutive of the social institution. Weber's critics have generally acknowledged the valuable contribution of his structural analysis, but few of these critics have discerned the connection between these structural ideal types and Weber's stated sociological methodology.

The point of the foregoing has been to show that Weber's structural ideal types are not only consistent with the epistemic basis established in Weber's methodological works but intimately connected to the pure types of action which serve as the basis of his sociological methodology.

4. Conclusion

The purpose of the analysis of Weber's ideal type developed in this chapter is twofold. First, and most narrowly, it establishes the consistency of Weber's ideal-typical methodology. It has been argued that Weber's use of a variety of ideal types can be traced to a common epistemological basis which he elaborates in his methodology. The second purpose of the chapter, however, is broader and provides the motivation for this reassessment of Weber's theory of ideal types. It has been argued that, in the ideal type, Weber combines two elements which have figured prominently in contemporary antipositivist critiques of social-scientific methodology: subjective grounding of the facts of the social sciences and structural analysis. It is this combination of elements which makes Weber's methodology particularly relevant to contemporary controversies in the methodology of the social sciences.

The virtues of Weber's theory of the ideal type as a methodological tool can be summarized under four headings. (1) Weber's ideal type establishes that the category of facts, the "data" of the social scientist, is constituted by the social actors' bestowal of meaning. (2) Weber identifies the distinguishing feature of the ideal type as the principle of synthesis that guides its construction. Whereas construction of the concepts of the natural sciences is guided by the principle of commonality, the principle of synthesis, which is characteristic of ideal-type construction, is the meaningful, logical compatibility of concepts. (3) The epistemological basis which Weber provides for the ideal type allows him to develop and utilize a variety of ideal types that meet the range of research needs encountered by the social scientist. Historical, general sociological, action, and structural types are the major varieties. (4) In providing a structural ideal type, Weber supplies a means by which the social scientist can analyze the elements of social structure without relinquishing the subjective or meaningful grounding of its elements.

This understanding of Weber's theory of the ideal type will serve as the basis for the following examination of contemporary schools in the philosophy of social science, in which the major critiques of Weber, advanced by each school's adherents, will be considered. In some cases, these criticisms will be judged to be well founded; in other cases, theories developed by the schools will be utilized to bolster Weber's theory where it is weak or poorly articulated. But despite all these amendations and corrections, the basic strength of Weber's approach will be reiterated: Weber's theory offers a unified conceptual approach to analysis of both subjective meaning and structural forms.[14]

3. The Subjective Critique

1. Introduction to the Critiques

The foregoing analysis of Weber's ideal-type theory lays the groundwork for the central thesis of this study: with the ideal type, Weber provides a methodological tool for the structural analysis of social forms, which, at the same time, is grounded in the subjective meaning of the social actors. In the introduction it was suggested that these two elements of social-scientific analysis, the subjective grounding of the facts of the social sciences and the analysis of structural forms, are the principal foci of contemporary critiques of positivist methodology in the social sciences. It was also suggested that despite several efforts to achieve a synthesis between these two antipositivist camps, none has been forthcoming. This chapter (and the next) will employ Weber's synthesis as a means, first, of examining the positions taken by a number of contemporary antipositivist schools and, second, of outlining a possible synthesis of elements of these perspectives.

However, the direction of this examination must be clearly stated at the outset to avoid confusion. Initially, several approaches present themselves as possible strategies for organization of the analysis. The analysis could be concerned primarily with defending Weber against his many antipositivist critics. It can be argued that many of these critics have seriously misunderstood Weber's position and, as a consequence, have dismissed his theories too lightly. Or the analysis could be concerned with utilizing various elements of the antipositivist approaches to clear up ambiguities in Weber's theory. It should be evident from the preceding analysis that Weber's theory is in need of such assistance, and the philosophical and methodological support which Weber requires in a number of instances is available from contemporary theorists.

The strategy that will be employed, however, provides a broader scope than either of these approaches. In the following examination, Weber's synthesis of subjective grounding and structural analysis will be a point of departure for consideration of a postpositivist synthesis for contemporary social theory. Weber's synthesis, though successful in terms of his methodology, cannot simply be thrust into the context of contemporary social theory, because Weber's discussion of methodological issues is cast in terms of a vocabulary produced by the *Methodenstreit* of his day. Contemporary discussions, in contrast, are cast in terms of a vocabulary that to a large extent has been produced by philosophical and social-scientific fashions that have gained popularity since Weber's death. Although all the substantive issues that have been raised in contemporary discussions were also discussed in the *Methodenstreit,* the terminological differences between them obscure this similarity. And although the issues under discussion have not changed substantially, new philosophical schools have arisen to defend these positions in the contemporary debate. Thus if a synthesis is to be articulated which is relevant to the contemporary debate, it must be cast in terms of the issues as they are defined by these schools.

Using Weber's synthesis as a point of departure to outline a contemporary synthesis, however, serves a very practical purpose. In the following, each of the contemporary approaches under consideration will be examined from the perspective of the criticism of Weber advanced by that approach. This tactic facilitates the search for a contemporary synthesis because it provides a detour around the many critiques of positivism produced by these schools. It was argued in the introduction that, at this point in the discussion, exhaustive critiques of positivism do little to facilitate progress of the debate because articulation of a comprehensive postpositivist approach is required. Concentrating on the critiques of Weber's approach which are advanced by these schools, then, will move the discussion forward to constructing a postpositivist synthesis. It will also serve to isolate the strengths of each approach relative to such construction.

A few provisos are in order. From the perspective of the

theorists that will be considered below, this thesis will be unpopular on a number of counts. Most, if not all, of these theorists deny that Weber effected the synthesis which is here attributed to him. Further, many have rejected the possibility, even the desirability, of uniting subjective meaning and structural analysis in one approach. Thus arguing that Weber *has* effected such a synthesis and that a synthesis is necessary will contradict certain elements of all the theorists examined. Also, as was noted above, the major schools of contemporary social theory will be considered from the perspective of their critiques of Weber's methodology, rather than from their critiques of positivism, but it should come as no surprise that the critiques of Weber advanced by each of these schools are concerned with the same subjects as their critiques of positivism and, significantly, that many of these theorists attribute certain positivist tendencies to Weber. Thus the two schools that are considered under "subjective critique," phenomenology and ordinary-language analysis, fault Weber for improperly defining the subjective character of social action, while the two schools considered under "objective critique," structuralism and critical theory, fault Weber for failing to provide a critical assessment of structural forms.

Analysis of each of these four schools will be in two stages. In the first stage, each school will be examined from the perspective of the critique of Weber's methodology as advanced by its adherents. Sometimes this analysis will identify a weakness or explicit error in Weber's approach, sometimes it will defend Weber against an erroneous interpretation; but the goal, in all cases, will be to reveal the key issues, not merely to develop a narrow comparison to Weber's methodological approach. In the second stage, an attempt will be made to isolate the particular strengths of each approach and to discuss how these elements might be used to construct a contemporary postpositivist synthesis. As the discussion progresses, some of the serious philosophical and epistemological issues which divide these approaches and prevent emergence of such a synthesis will also be considered.

Although this pattern will be adhered to in analysis of both the subjective and the objective critiques, the course of the investigation of the two critiques differs significantly, due in part to the fact that the subjective critiques are much more sympathetic to Weber's approach than the objective critiques. Phenomenologists and ordinary-language philosophers tend to see Weber's approach as flawed, but essentially on the right track, while structuralists and critical theorists find Weber's approach to be barely distinguishable from that of the positivists. However, the principal difference between the analyses of the two critiques lies in the nature of the conclusions derived from the examinations. Examination of the subjective critiques leads to the conclusion that these approaches provide a clear understanding of the nature of subjective meaning in social analysis, and thus that these approaches contribute substantially to construction of a postpositivist synthesis. However, both approaches fail to provide a basis for structural analysis. The conclusion derived from analysis of the objective critiques, on the other hand, is that although they expose the need for structural and/or critical analysis of social forms, which is rooted in an understanding of what constitutes objectivity in the social sciences, the basis for that objectivity presented by each approach is logically flawed. Thus, rather than provide substantive contributions to the postpositivist synthesis, these approaches succeed only in defining a necessary element of that synthesis. This conclusion dictates the subject of the concluding chapter: the problem of objectivity in the social sciences.

2. Nature of the Subjective Critique

The ideal type, as Weber conceived it, is the methodological device by which the social scientist grasps the subjective meaning of social actors. In explicating the nature of ideal-typical analysis, Weber's attention is focused primarily on the manner in which the ideal type is synthesized into a constructed concept, but it is clear, particularly from the Stammler article, that the "raw data" from which ideal types are constructed are the subjective meanings of social actors. Two contemporary antipositivist approaches to the philosophy of social science, phenomenology and ordinary-language analysis, have developed perspectives which focus on how the social scientist analyzes the meaningful, or "subjective," action of social actors. The critiques of positivism advanced by these two schools are concerned with positivism's deficiency in this regard, and their critiques of Weber's methodology are similarly concerned with Weber's failure clearly to specify this aspect of social-scientific methodology. Although the two schools find fault with different aspects of Weber's theory of subjective meaning, both are engaged in what can be called a "subjective critique" of this methodology because they are primarily interested in the problem of social actors' understanding of the social world.

The similarities and dissimilarities between phenomenology and ordinary-language analysis have been the subject of a growing literature in the social sciences.[1] The similarity between the two approaches that is most commonly cited in this literature is that both emphasize social actors' understanding of their action and insist that this understanding must be the starting point of social-scientific analysis. But for the purposes of this examination, this similarity can be expressed more precisely in terms of a common rejection of the dichotomy between subjective and objective meaning which forms the basis of the positivist methodology of the social sciences. The positivist defines "subjective" meaning as the private understanding of the individual social actor, which is inaccessible to the social scientist. "Objective" meaning, on the other hand, is produced when social action is described in precise, "scientific" terms, defined by the social scientist and divorced from social actors' concepts. Phenomenologists and ordinary-language philosophers reject both definitions. They insist, instead, that the starting point of social-scientific analysis must be the understanding of social action in the terms provided by the social actors themselves. They insist, further, that this understanding is neither private nor inaccessible to the social scientist; it is public. It consists of the shared concepts of the social actors which are "intersubjective" or common. Both approaches also argue that because the subject matter of the social sciences is defined by the shared concepts of the social actors, analysis of social life that is not rooted in those concepts will fail to identify the subject matter that requires explanation. Thus the "objective" analysis, which is the goal of positivist social science (because it involves defining meaningful action in terms divorced from the actors' concepts), cannot be said to constitute an explanation of social action, because social action can only be identified, at least initially, in terms of the actors' concepts. In short, phenomenology and ordinary-language analysis show the subjective/objective dichotomy of the positivists to be totally inadequate to the problems of social-scientific explanation because it rests on a fundamental misunderstanding of how meaning is constituted in the social world.

This perspective will serve as an organizing device for the discussion of both the similarities and the differences between the two schools. Although rejection of the positivist definitions of

"subjective" and "objective" meaning is a notable similarity between the two approaches, it will emerge that the way in which
each approach conceptualizes the "intersubjective" world of the
social actor differs in significant ways. A second disagreement
between the two approaches is their very different understanding
of the manner in which the social scientist can legitimately
analyze this intersubjective world. It will be concluded that
although the two approaches start at the same point, the intersubjective world of the social actor, they move away from this
starting point along different paths.

3. Phenomenology

Although the label "phenomenology" has been used to
describe a number of approaches in both the social sciences and
philosophy, this analysis focuses on one theorist, Alfred Schutz,
and his understanding of social phenomenology. The reason for
this choice is twofold. Schutz is one of a very few social theorists
to take Weber's methodology seriously and devote considerable
effort to its explication, and of all the "phenomenologists" in the
social sciences, Schutz is the most thorough and careful. His approach, furthermore, can be shown to be the basis of most contemporary phenomenological theories in the social sciences.

Schutz's critique of Weber's theory of the ideal type is rooted
in his analysis of Weber's understanding of subjective meaning
constitution in the social world. He argues that because Weber
fails to clarify what he means by "subjective meaning," his whole
methodological approach, including his theory of the ideal type,
is not firmly grounded. Analysis of Schutz's critique of Weber,
then, must begin with an outline of Schutz's understanding of
meaning constitution and his definition of Weber's errors in this
regard.

In the first pages of *The Phenomenology of the Social
World*, Schutz states his central objection to Weber's
methodology: Weber accepts the meaningful act of the individual as an "irreducible primitive" in social-scientific analysis
(1967:7). Against this, Schutz argues that it is the task of the
social sciences to explain how the meaningful act of the social actor is constituted in the social world. Although Schutz approves
the basic orientation of Weber's methodology, he insists that this
oversight by Weber is so serious that it jeopardizes the whole

project. He thus defines his principal goal in *Phenomenology* as an attempt to rectify Weber's error on this point.

The implications of Weber's refusal to explore the problem of meaning constitution are revealed as Schutz attempts to clarify the basic elements of social action. He asserts that action is distinguished from behavior because the elements of an action are unified by the intention or "project" of the actor—in other words, that the elements which constitute an action are unified by the actor's bestowal of meaning (1967:61). Schutz agrees with Weber that the actor's bestowal of meaning *makes* action meaningful, and that interpretation of this "subjective" meaning is the goal of social-scientific analysis. But Schutz's definition of "meaningful action" reveals the liability of Weber's conception, and the problem is this: If an action's subjective meaning is supplied by the social actor's meaning bestowal, this meaning must be accessible to social scientists if they are to interpret subjective meaning. But since Weber refuses to explore the way in which subjective meaning is constituted, he closes off the realm in which subjective meaning is bestowed by the social actor. It is, for Weber, a "private" realm, which he makes no attempt to penetrate. But it follows from this that Weber's stated goal for the social sciences, interpretation of subjective meaning, becomes unobtainable. For if that which constitutes meaningful social action (the social actor's bestowal of meaning) is inaccessible to the social scientist, meaningful action cannot be interpreted, as Weber claims it must.[2]

Schutz discovers two errors in Weber's approach which led him to make this mistake. First, Weber's concept of subjective meaning encompasses two aspects which he failed to distinguish properly: the meaning which is constituted within the consciousness of the individual social actor and the meaning which is constituted in the process of social interaction. Schutz points out the serious difficulties created by Weber's collapsing of these two aspects of subjective meaning. Weber's second error, however, is equally important: he failed to specify that both of these aspects of subjective meaning are, in Schutz's words, constituted "intersubjectively." By this, Schutz means that the individual's constitution of meaning and the meaning constituted through social interaction are established in a meaning context that is defined by shared concepts. It is the intersubjectivity of meaning constitution on both these levels that provides the social scientist with access to what, for Weber, is a "private" realm.

The first level of meaning, which Schutz defines as meaning in its "primordial" sense, is constituted within the individual's consciousness (1967:45ff.). Exploration of this realm involves examining how the individual reflects on experience and how an experience becomes meaningful through the process of reflection. Schutz admits that there is one sense in which meaning on this level is "essentially subjective" and hence inaccessible to every other individual. Furthermore, he is not unaware of the dangers of this conception. In his discussion of this issue he notes:

> It might seem that these conclusions would lead to the denial of the possibility of an interpretive sociology and even more to the denial that one can ever understand another person's experience. But this is by no means the case. We are asserting neither that your lived experiences remain in principle inaccessible to me nor that they are meaningless to me. Rather, the point is that the meaning I give to your experiences cannot be precisely the same as the meaning you give to them when you proceed to interpret them. [1967:99]

But Schutz, turning to Husserl, goes on to argue that because meaning on the primordial level is constituted in an intersubjective context, it is accessible to other individuals in the social world.[3]

It is significant that Schutz asserts that meaning on this primordial level is not the goal of social-scientific analysis. Rather, it is meaning on a second level, in which social actors directly experience each other, that is the proper subject matter of the social sciences. Meaning on this level is constituted in the process of interaction between individuals in the social world. When two individuals share a single experience, the meaning which is constituted in that activity is intersubjective in a very literal sense. The subjective meaning of each individual is oriented toward the activity of the other and the constituted meaning is created through the interaction. As Schutz puts it:

> I see, then, my own stream of consciousness and yours in a single intentional Act which embraces them both. [1967:103]

Schutz uses this distinction between the two levels of meaning to organize his analysis in *Phenomenology*. His analysis of meaning on the primordial level is intended to serve as the foundation for his examination of the second level of meaning, the intersubjective understanding constituted by social interaction.[4]

His examination of the phenomenon of intersubjective understanding is concerned primarily with explaining how interaction between individuals in the social world takes place on many levels of anonymity. He points out that any experience that is shared by myself and another is always, to some degree, anonymous or "objectified," because the experience is no longer entirely *my* experience, but *ours*. But this anonymity can vary greatly. My experience with a close friend, for instance, is much less anonymous than my experience with a stranger. My intimate knowledge of my friend reduces anonymity while my ignorance of the stranger increases it.

Schutz uses this difference in levels of anonymity in social experiences to classify various kinds of encounters in the social world (1967:163–86). He asserts that the different levels of anonymity on which the individual experiences others in the social world create what he calls the structures or "regions" of that world. He employs a full range of conceptual tools which facilitate analysis of these structures: the face-to-face relationship; we and they relationships; worlds of predecessors and contemporaries. His definition of these terms allows him to present a clear picture of how social relationships vary in everyday life.

However, explication of this aspect of Schutz's work raises an issue which is crucial to his understanding of the nature of social-scientific analysis, and it should be clarified before discussing other elements of Schutz's approach. It should be clear that, thus far, Schutz employs the terms "subjective" and "objective" meaning in an unusual fashion. His first step is to define two separate understandings of "subjective meaning," as the phrase is used by Weber, but he makes it clear that neither conception is identical to the positivist's definition of the "subjective" as the "private" and, hence, that which is not accessible to observation. For Schutz, both conceptions are intersubjective, that is, constituted in the context of the shared meanings of the social realm. His understanding of "objectivity" also departs significantly from the positivist conception. For Schutz, any experience that is removed from the primordial realm of subjective meaning is to some degree anonymous or "objectified," and this leads him to assert that when social scientists study meaningful action in the social world, they are studying the "objectification of subjective meaning." Schutz's use of this terminology indicates that he finds the subjective/objective dichotomy of the positivists unacceptable, but instead of rejecting the terms he redefines them to suit his very different purposes.

Schutz's clarification of the ambiguities inherent in Weber's concept of subjective meaning has been widely acknowledged as a valuable contribution to modern social theory. His discussions of meaning constitution in the social world have provided the impetus for most of the studies which fall into the category "social phenomenology." But although this aspect of Schutz's work is undoubtedly significant, another aspect of his approach, which has received less attention, is also worthy of careful consideration. Schutz's explication of meaning constitution in the social world provides him a solid foundation for analysis of the manner in which the social scientist studies meaningful action. He discusses this topic in terms of the creation of the ideal types of the social scientist. The discussion, begun in *Phenomenology* and considerably expanded in a series of articles published later in his life, resulted in a comprehensive understanding of the activity of social-scientific analysis which, though rooted in Weber's understanding of the ideal type, is considerably more precise than Weber's theory.

Schutz's discussion of the ideal types of the social scientist is carefully connected to his explication of the nature of meaning constitution at the beginning of *Phenomenology*. In the course of this discussion he makes two points that are particularly relevant to his subsequent discussion of ideal types. (1) He notes that the second level of subjective meaning, intersubjective understanding, is always, to a certain extent, objectified because it is removed from the first (or primordial) level of meaning constitution. (2) He argues that intersubjective understanding is divided into "regions" on the basis of different levels of anonymity on which individuals interact in the social world. These two observations lead Schutz to formulate the thesis which serves as the point of departure for his analysis of ideal types: Social actors are able to understand and interpret the actions of their fellow human beings through a process of typification. Intersubjective understanding, which for Schutz constitutes the subject matter of the social sciences, necessarily involves typification because it entails reference to the shared set of meanings which constitute the social world:

> All our knowledge of the world, in common-sense as well as in scientific thinking, involves constructs, i.e., a set of abstractions, generalizations, formalizations, idealizations specific to the respective level of thought organization. Strictly speaking, there are no such things as facts, pure and

simple. All facts are from the outset facts selected from a universal context by an artificial abstraction or facts considered in their particular setting. . . . This does not mean that, in daily life or in science, we are unable to grasp the reality of the world. It just means that we grasp merely certain aspects of it, namely those which are relevant to us either for carrying on our business of living or from the point of view of a body of accepted rules of procedure of thinking called the method of science. [1962:5]

In this passage Schutz provides a summary of the principal elements of his theory of ideal types, and these elements can be categorized under two distinct headings. First, he asserts that the typifying activity of the social scientist is not radically divorced from the process of social understanding in the social world but is contiguous with it, because common-sense knowledge, like scientific knowledge, rests on typifications. He later reinforces and expands this thesis with the point that the ideal types of the social scientist are always based on the typifications of social actors. Second, he argues that although the ideal types of the social scientist are based on those of social actors, they are necessarily distinct from them:

There is a difference in kind between the type of naive understanding of other people we exercise in everyday life and the type of understanding we use in the social sciences. [1967:141]

Schutz's extensive discussions of the ideal types of the social scientist in his later work involve elaboration of these two themes: the social scientist's ideal types are both related to and distinct from the typifications of the social actor. He deals with these issues in two separate contexts: in his enumeration of the postulates which guide formation of the social scientist's ideal types and then in the explanation of his theory of multiple realities. In the first context, Schutz begins his discussion where he left off in *Phenomenology*, that is, with the observation that the social actor's common-sense knowledge is typified knowledge.[5] These typifications are the starting point of the social scientist's ideal types—the "raw data" of social-scientific analysis. Schutz is much clearer on this fundamental point than Weber; he states unambiguously that the social scientist *must* begin with the common-sense understanding of the social actors. He is also clearer on the steps in synthesis of the social scientist's ideal types which use these understandings as a base. His principal point is that the ideal types of the social scientist are "second-order constructs" because they are built on the social actors' concepts: they are thus "preselected and preinterpreted" by the social actors' understandings (1962:5).

Schutz then elaborates the elements that determine construction of the social scientist's ideal types, isolating three factors which place constraints on their formation. The first factor is the personal value or interest of the social scientist, which defines the problem and sets the parameters of the investigation. Once the problem has been defined by this interest, a second factor comes into play. The problem at hand creates, in Schutz's terminology, its own "system of relevances" that determines the precise nature of the ideal type which is constructed. Schutz describes in some detail the systemic web of relevances that emanate from a particular problem. Specification of this system of relevances provides the social scientist with a means of discriminating among the range of available data by supplying a clear-cut standard for judging the appropriateness of those data to the problem. The third constraint is imposed by the canons of scientific inquiry and subsumes both the agreed-upon rules of scientific method and the dominant theoretical presuppositions of the social-scientific community (1967:83).

Schutz organizes these constraints on the social scientist's ideal types under the heading of "postulates" that can be interpreted as guides for construction of these concepts. The postulate of *logical consistency* demands that the constructs be of the highest order of clarity and distinctiveness; the postulate of *subjective interpretation* demands that the constructs explain the observed facts as a result of the actor's bestowal of meaning; the postulate of *adequacy* demands that the constructs be understandable to the actors themselves (1964:43–44); and the postulate of *rationality* demands that the constructs assume that the action is performed with a clear and distinct (rational) knowledge of all the elements relative to it (1964:86). If these postulates are faithfully adhered to, Schutz concludes, they will provide the social scientist a model of the social world which is firmly rooted in the subjective meaning of the social actors, yet is removed from the mundane social world because of the logical rigor demanded by these second-order concepts (1964:18).

Informing Schutz's discussion of these postulates, however, is a particular concern which is not immediately apparent in the text but explains the meticulousness with which Schutz approaches the problem of the ideal types of the social sciences. In *Phenomenology* he states that the ideal types of the social actor have a distinct advantage over those of the social scientist: their accuracy is continually "checked" by participation in social action. This check, however, is not available to the social scientist. As observers rather than participants, social scientists have no means of guaranteeing the accuracy of their ideal types through social interaction (1967:205). Schutz is acutely aware of the problem posed by this situation: the social scientist's ideal types can easily lose touch with the subjective meanings of the social actors. Thus his attempt to carefully specify the postulates which guide formation of the social scientist's ideal types can be interpreted as an effort to preserve the subjective grounding of these concepts.[6]

The full implications of the difference between the ideal types of the participating social actor and those of the observing social scientist are more clearly revealed in the second context in which Schutz discusses social-scientific theorizing: his description of "multiple realities" or "finite provinces of reality." In this discussion, which is based on William James's theory of multiple realities, Schutz advances the thesis that all human experiences take place in one of a number of "finite provinces of reality," each of which is defined by a particular cognitive style that gives experiences in that province their particular "accent of reality." Schutz specifies several criteria by which the cognitive style of one province of reality is distinguished from another: each has its own "tension of consciousness," experience of self, form of sociality, and perspective of time (1962:230). Examples of these provinces of reality, which Schutz discusses, are the common-sense world of social action, the world of dreams, the world of religious experience, and the world of scientific theorizing.

Several elements of this discussion of multiple realities are central to understanding how Schutz conceptualizes the activity of social-scientific theorizing and the relationship between that activity and the world of social action. First, he argues that one of these finite provinces of reality, the common-sense world of social action, can be labeled "paramount reality" because it is the baseline to which we return after experiencing other realities. It is thus the standard by which we judge the nature of those other realities. For this reason alone, paramount reality is unique. But Schutz singles out another distinctive feature of paramount reality which is particularly relevant to his concerns: it is the only reality in which we directly experience other human beings, that is, in which we can participate in social action (1962:227). Second, Schutz argues that each of these provinces is "finite," by which he means that each is experienced separately and that transition from one to another always involves a "shock" (1962:232). Thus experiences in one province do not shade into those of another because of the distinctive cognitive style of each province.

For Schutz, the worlds of scientific theorizing in general and social-scientific theorizing in particular can be identified as finite provinces of reality. The cognitive style of the social scientist's province of reality is defined by the goal of the activity: observation and explanation of social life. The parameters of this reality are defined by the theoretical presuppositions of the social-scientific community as well as by the canons of scientific inquiry it shares with other scientific endeavors (1962:251). Further, defining the activity of social-scientific theorizing as a "finite province of reality" allows Schutz to formulate another perspective on the difference between pariticpation and observation, which has been of concern to him from the outset. The problem can now be cast in terms of the difference between these two provinces: the cognitive style of paramount reality includes participation in social action while that of the world of social-scientific theorizing specifically excludes it. The two activities, participation and observation, exist in separate provinces of reality and, more significantly, each activity is definitive of the cognitive style of the province to which it belongs. It follows from this that social scientists are prevented from "checking" the accuracy of their concepts through participation in social action, for if social scientists enter the world of social action, paramount reality, they are no longer observers but become participants, and in doing so they forsake the cognitive style that is definitive of social-scientific theorizing. Because this means of checking concepts is denied them, it is incumbent on social theorists to be very sure that the concepts they employ are (as Schutz puts it elsewhere) "subjectively adequate," that is, accurate representations of the social actors' concepts.

As Schutz sees it, the world of social-scientific theorizing is removed from the world of the social actor who participates in social action. The social scientist deals not with real actors but with ideal types who are "puppets," not with the real social world but with a model of it (1964:17). The parameters of that world are defined by the concepts of the social-scientific community, concepts that must be adhered to by individual social scientists if they wish to be intelligible to members of that community. Connection between the two worlds, finally, is facilitated by the social scientist's adherence to the postulate of subjective adequacy, that is, the insistence that social-scientific analysis begin with the social actors' concepts.

Schutz's description of the activity of social-scientific theorizing, particularly in the latter context, has been the subject of much discussion and criticism in the recent literature. Most of the criticism has centered around the charge that Schutz characterizes the activity of social-scientific theorizing too abstractly; that is, he overemphasizes the gap between social scientist and social actor. It is argued that he much too glibly admits that the social scientist does not make direct contact with the social world but deals with social actors as puppets. To some extent this criticism is justified, as the above account makes evident. Characterizing the world of social-scientific theorizing as a finite province of reality strongly emphasizes the abstractness of social-scientific theorizing and its removal from the common-sense world of social action. Stressing this abstraction to the exclusion of other factors leads to an erroneous conception of social science.

But against these critics it can be argued that Schutz's theory has several advantages over rival conceptions of this crucial relationship. Schutz specifies the nature of the difference between the activity of social actors and that of social observers. He insists that because the goal of social-scientific analysis is the observation and explanation of social action, the activity of the social scientist must be defined as distinct from that of the social actor who participates in social action. Schutz's distinction between participation and observation as definitive of different provinces clarifies this distinction. Although it may seem that this distinction is basic to any coherent social-scientific methodology, stating this distinction clearly is problematic for a number of contemporary antipositivist approaches in the social sciences. Because of their reaction against the positivist's conception of objectivity, several antipositivist approaches, and among them ordinary-language analysis, have failed to clarify the distinction between the activities of social actor and social scientist. Schutz's position avoids this problem by clearly articulating this distinction.

The second advantage of Schutz's theory is even more significant. It can be argued that the dominant theme of Schutz's description of the activity of the social scientist is not its abstractness but its intersubjectivity. As a whole, Schutz's discussion shows that the concepts of the social scientist are intersubjective in two senses. They are based on the intersubjective concepts of the social actors, which are the necessary foundation of all social-scientific analysis, and the social scientist's concepts are intersubjective with respect to members of the social-scientific community. They must conform to the theoretical presuppositions of the social sciences if the social scientist is to be intelligible to the members of that community. The concepts of social scientists, in short, must conform to two sets of intersubjectively constituted meanings: that of the common-sense world of the social actors on which they are based and that of the social-scientific community to which the observations are communicated. Schutz argues that the social scientist's concepts meet both of these criteria through adherence to the postulate of subjective adequacy, which states that the social scientist's concepts, though they derive from the world of social science, can be made understandable to the actors in the social world. Schutz's insistence on the intersubjectivity of social science on both these levels is perhaps the central contribution of his approach to social-scientific methodology.

It should be clear from the preceding that although Schutz's account of the formation of ideal types has much in common with Weber's account, it moves beyond Weber in important ways. Schtuz details and organizes the steps in construction of the social scientist's ideal-typical construct; and in doing so he fills one of the most significant gaps in Weber's account: specification of the role of the theoretical and methodological presuppositions of the social-scientific community. His extensive discussion of social-scientific theorizing provides a kind of phenomenology of social-scientific consciousness that far transcends the sophistication in Weber's account.

The difference between the methodological sophistication in the two accounts can of course be attributed primarily to the fact that Schutz is much more interested in methodological issues than is Weber. Schutz explicitly attempts to provide a coherent methodology for the social sciences while Weber was attempting merely to clear up conceptual confusions that stand in the way of empirical work. Both accounts, however, are unified by a common purpose: the desire to synthesize the subjective grounding of the facts of the social scientist with an objective or scientific method of analysis that facilitates empirical analysis. And it must be concluded that, at least on the methodological level, Schutz comes closer to doing this than Weber.[7] He shows that the "subjective" concepts of the social actor and the "objective" concepts of the social scientist are "intersubjective." This not only debunks the positivists' distinction between objectivity and subjectivity but defines the activity of social science as inherently intersubjective.

4. Ordinary-Language Analysis

The phenomenology of Schutz and the ordinary-language analysis of theorists such as Peter Winch and A. R. Louch are primarily concerned to criticize what has been identified as the subjective aspect of Weber's approach. Both Winch and Louch attempt to clarify what Weber meant by his insistence that the aim of social-scientific analysis is interpretation of social actors' subjective meaning. The critical literature on Schutz's phenomenology is focused almost exclusively on this aspect of Weber's approach, and the phenomenological tradition which his work has generated in the social sciences is also primarily identified with this issue. It was pointed out above that Schutz's agreement with Weber's approach lies not only in his similar desire to explicate the subjective aspect of social-scientific analysis but also in his desire to snythesize an analysis of subjective meaning with a "scientific" approach to the social sciences, but this aspect of Schutz's work has not received as much attention.

The approach of ordinary-language analysis differs from that taken by Schutz in two respects. The critique of Weber's understanding of subjective meaning, advanced by ordinary-language analysis, is rooted in a very different objection to Weber's concept than that propounded by Schutz, whose critique of Weber involves clarification of the two levels of meaning constitution which are confused in Weber's account. Winch and Louch, in contrast, are concerned exclusively with the social context in which social actors' concepts are apprehended by the social scientist. Also, ordinary-language philosophers, unlike Schutz, are not sympathetic to Weber's desire to synthesize the analysis of subjective meaning with a "scientific" approach to the social sciences. Rather, they devote considerable attention to revealing the inappropriateness of using "scientific" concepts in the social sciences. These two differences between the approaches will serve as a basis for comparison in the following analysis.

Because Peter Winch was the first theorist to make a serious attempt to apply the principles of ordinary language (as expressed by Wittgenstein) to the social sciences, this account will rely most heavily on Winch's approach, employing references to other theorists when appropriate. Winch's work also has the advantage of dealing explicitly with Weber's work. He states the objection of ordinary-language philosophers to Weber's understanding of how the social scientist apprehends meaningful (subjective) action in very simple terms, and begins by asserting that meaningful action always involves application of a rule. Rules, he argues, define action *as* meaningful. For example, unless playing softball can be distinguished from *not* playing softball through application of the rules which govern the use of the concept, the action cannot be said to be meaningful. But since it makes no sense to speak about rules outside a social context, action, to be meaningful, must be social (1958:50). Winch then makes the obvious point that the rules which define meaningful action are embodied in language. Putting all this together, Winch argues that meaningful action, social action, and social relations come to much the same thing, and all derive their meaning from rules expressed in language. It follows that the study of social relations is the same as the study of language:

> Our language and our social relations are just two different sides of the same coin. To give an account of the meaning of a word is to describe how it is used; and to describe how it is used is to describe the social intercourse into which it enters. [1958:123]

This formulation of the relationship between language and social relations leads Winch to his famous assertion that the problems of the social sciences are conceptual rather than empirical, from which it follows that sociology is more properly a branch of philosophy than of the empirical sciences. Social science, he asserts, is

> not a question of what empirical research may show to be the case, but of what philosophical analysis reveals about *what it makes sense to say.* [1958:72]

This sequence of arguments sets the groundwork for Winch's understanding of how the social scientist deals with the phenomenon of meaningful action. He insists that it is the task of the social scientist to examine the ordinary language of the social actors to determine "what it makes sense to say." Although this statement of the position of ordinary-language analysis may seem oversimplified, there is a sense in which these few statements constitute not just the essence of the approach to the social sciences but its totality as well. The simplicity of the approach contrasts sharply with the other social-scientific methodologies which Winch criticizes in his work; it also differs from the approach taken by Schutz.

From the perspective of Schutz's account, what is most notably missing from Winch's discussion is exploration of how the shared concepts expressed in ordinary language are constituted—that is, how these concepts come to be established *as* meaningful for the social actors. This exploration, as noted above, is one of the principal concerns of Schutz's critique of Weber. Although Winch is very willing to explore the nuances of meaning embodied in ordinary language, he explicitly avoids any reference to first-person experiences in the social context. He refuses to explore how the individual participates in the construction of meaning in the social world, beginning instead with the already constructed meanings of ordinary language.

This refusal to explore first-person experiences is not an oversight by Winch but is an integral part of his approach. It is rooted in his definition of meaningful action and the philosophical assumptions that inform that definition. If, as Winch argues, action can be called "meaningful" only by virtue of the fact that it is constituted by social rules, analysis of how the individual constitutes meaning (which occupies so much of Schutz's attention) is clearly unproductive because individuals, per se, do not constitute meaning. But for Winch there is more to this issue than the pragmatic exclusion of any discussion of individual meaning constitution. Discussion of this issue, he asserts, is not only unproductive but logically impossible. For Winch, exploration of individual meaning constitution entails probing the inner events of the mind, a task he sees to be radically mistaken.

Winch's understanding of the way in which the social sciences should approach the "inner events of the mind" is derived from his understanding of Wittgenstein's position on this issue. The clearest statement of that position can be found in Wittgenstein's discussion of private language in *Philosophical Investigations* (1953:155ff.), where he argues that it is difficult, if not impossible, to avoid falling into "conceptual confusion" in discussing the "inner events" of the mind. If such events exist, he says, we have no vocabulary with which to discuss them because the definition of our concepts depends exclusively on shared meanings. Thus his position on the existence of mental events is, technically, agnostic. Although he does not deny the existence of mental events, he insists that they cannot be discussed intelligibly and that, consequently, their existence or nonexistence cannot be discussed either.

Winch interprets this Wittgensteinian doctrine on mental events to mean that the realm of individual consciousness is "off limits" for social scientists, and this interpretation has important consequences for his conception of social-scientific analysis. It means, in effect, that the ordinary language of social actors is unassailable; it is, as Schutz said of Weber, the irreducible primitive of social-scientific analysis. The limitations that this position imposes on the social scientist are revealed very clearly in the account of another ordinary-language philosopher, A. R. Louch. In *Explanation and Human Action*, Louch attempts to examine "consciousness" from a Wittgensteinian perspective. His discussion consists of an attempt to find ordinary-language uses of the concept "mind" in order to explicate the notion of consciousness. This analysis leads him to assert, with Wittgenstein, that it is very difficult to specify what is entailed by the existence of "inner events."

> Whether there is something "within" or private that, from the agent's point of view, could be thought of as an occurrence or event, is irrelevant from the standpoint of explanation. [1966:139]

This issue of mental events is a crucial difference between the approaches of ordinary-language analysis and phenomenology. That it involves a fundamental disagreement should be clear from the above discussion. For Louch, mental events are "irrelevant"; for Wittgenstein, they are beyond the realm of the intelligible. For Schutz, on the other hand, the exploration of mental events is the foundation of his analysis. This issue has generated a great deal of acrimonious discussion between the two schools and undoubtedly stands in the way of any serious rapprochement between them. Since one of the aims of this analysis is to suggest such a rapprochement, this issue should be considered in detail. To come to grips with its exceedingly complex problems, the discussion of mental events will be organized around three central points which should reveal the major points in dispute.

The first and most obvious point is that this issue constitutes, at the very least, a sharp difference in focus between the two approaches. This is initially evident in the different terminology employed by the social scientists who subscribe to one or another of the two approaches. Social phenomenologists phrase their discussion in terms of various aspects of "meaning constitution" in the social world while ordinary-language philosophers concentrate on the "nuances of meaning embodied in ordinary-language concepts." The root of the difference between the two approaches, however, is far more than terminological; it stems from the very different philosophical orientations of the philosophers whose theories form the bases of these two approaches to the social sciences, Husserl and Wittgenstein.

The nature of this difference has been the subject of much discussion in recent philosophical literature. It has been phrased in a number of ways, but (for the purposes of this analysis) can be most succinctly stated in terms of the point of departure of the two philosophers. Wittgenstein clearly states the point of departure for his method of philosophical analysis: he begins with language, or more precisely the ordinary language of everyday life. Husserl's point of departure, in contrast, is not language but consciousness itself; his primary concern is to explicate the meaning-endowing act of the ego. Both philosophers, significantly, recognize the centrality of the other's point of departure. Husserl discusses the importance of language in the constitution of meaning; he insists, however, that we must "get behind" language to the intentional act of the ego. Wittgenstein, on the other hand, recognizes the existence of the ego; but he sees the "I" as the "border of the world of language" and avoids discussion of this issue on the grounds that it frequently results in conceptual confusion.

This fundamental difference in orientation is the principal cause of the disputes between advocates of the two camps. On the side of ordinary-language philosophers, the most frequent argument is that

> There is no evidence whatsoever for the sort of internal experience to which Husserl appeals. . . . Any supposed private experience, then, and in particular the internal experience of Husserl, is a fiction, or if it is held to do so without language, an absurdity, a meaningless receptivity. [Pettit, 1972:25]

The reply of phenomenologists is that exclusion of any discussion of consciousness or (as some have put it) "first-person experiences" seriously impoverishes philosophical analysis. Phenomenologists do not deny the significance of language, but insist that language derives its meaning from the meaning-intending act of the individual (Hems, 1976:81). What is demanded of philosophical analysis, they insist, is a serious attempt to understand this process of meaning constitution. Without an understanding of this process, philosophical analysis is deprived of its necessary foundation.

It is impossible to deny the importance of this difference between the two schools, but discussion of this issue need not end with the statement of this difference; a second aspect can be noted. It was observed above that Wittgenstein's position on the existence of mental events is, technically, one of agnosticism. He does not deny the existence of mental events; he denies only the possibility of an intelligible discussion of such events, if they, in fact, exist. Phenomenologists, clearly, have no doubt that such events exist, and furthermore are concerned to specify the conditions under which they occur. But in their attempt to explicate the process of meaning constitution, phenomenologists, and Schutz in particular, develop a position which provides another perspective on this issue, which was revealed in discussion of Schutz's understanding of the two levels of subjective meaning.

Schutz argues that on the primordial level as well as on the level of social interaction, meaning is constituted in an *intersubjective* context, that is, by reference to intersubjectively established meanings. It was argued that this is the basis for Schutz's conception of social analysis as inherently intersubjective. From the perspective of the problem of mental events as it is posed by Wittgensteinians, however, Schutz's theory has a different effect—of "opening up" discussion of this realm. Wittgenstein, by declaring all discussions of this realm to be unintelligible, has in essence closed the door to philosophical investigation of mental events. By disclosing the intersubjective character of this realm, Schutz *opens* that door. But—and most importantly—Schutz provides access to the realm of mental events not by relying on some ineffable process, such as intuition, but by showing that these events are constituted in an intersubjective context. It is this intersubjective context which makes this realm accessible to analysis, a point expressed very succinctly by Tugendhat:

> If we refuse to accept the assumption of a mental eye and if we insist that meanings are something essentially intersubjective, then the realization of the intention of a meaning must be, at least potentially, an intersubjective process. [1972:265]

This characterization of the way in which phenomenologists and ordinary-language philosophers approach the problem of mental events is significant for a number of reasons. It throws the dispute over mental events off dead center. It reveals that the discussion need not be abandoned with the observation that phenomenologists analyze what are, for ordinary-language philosophers, bogus entities. Comparison of the positions of Wittgenstein and Schutz does not warrant this conclusion; Wittgenstein does not deny the existence of mental events and Schutz does not rely on the services of a "mental eye." Also, these observations have the effect of reversing a common interpretation of the relationship between the phenomenological endeavor and that of ordinary-language analysis. Phenomenologists are frequently accused of probing the murky depths of consciousness in an unintelligible manner while ordinary-language philosophers are praised for remaining in the bright light of publicly accessible concepts. This interpretation reveals, however, that phenomenologists are bringing those "murky depths" to light by showing that mental events occur in an intersubjective context and are thus publicly accessible. Ordinary-language philosophers, in contrast, seal off the realm of mental events by labeling it "unintelligible." Phenomenologists replace this label with two quite opposite ones: "intersubjective" and "accessible."

The third point raised by these issues is essentially pragmatic, dealing not with the epistemological and philosophical points at issue but with the implications of this problem for the narrower interests of the social sciences. Although the philosophical and epistemological differences between the two approaches cannot be dismissed, it can be argued that these differences lose much of their significance from the perspective of the specific problems of the social sciences. The approach to social-scientific analysis that is advocated by these two schools is, in fact, remarkably similar. Both insist that the primary goal of social-scientific analysis is explication of social action in terms of the social actor's concepts; and this commonality has been frequently noted in the recent literature. Analysis of the *Lebenswelt* or life-world, which Schutz advocates, is commonly acknowledged to dictate the same kind of social-scientific analysis as analysis of the rules embodied in ordinary language, which is advocated by Winch and Louch (Wild, 1976:190–207). Both schools, further-more, reject the positivists' assumption that what Weber refers to as the "subjective meaning" of the social actor is private. Rather, both assume that social actors' concepts are public, accessible, and the necessary starting point of all social-scientific analysis. In the light of contemporary issues in the philosophy of social science, this commonality is important and deserves the serious attention which it has received.

The difference between phenomenology and ordinary-language analysis on the issue of mental events is not, however, the only dispute between the two schools. A second issue can be identified: understanding the manner in which the social scien-tist can legitimately study social action. Schutz's perspective on this problem can be summarized in his assertion that the social scientist must approach the analysis of subjective meaning with precisely defined concepts which, though preserving the subjec-tive grounding of those facts, allow for an empirical, scientific analysis of social action. Adherents of ordinary language ap-proach this issue in a quite different manner.

Once they have established that social science must focus ex-clusively on the publicly accessible rules of social action, rather than on mental events, both Winch and Louch place stringent limits on the kinds of concepts which can be legitimately utilized in social-scientific analysis. Their discussion of the issue falls into two distinct phases: insistence that the raw data of social-scientific analysis must be the conceptions of the actors themselves and the degree to which the social scientist can abstract from this realm in the course of analysis. The first phase of the critique occupies much more of their attention simply because Winch and Louch consider this the principal failing of positivist social scientists. Winch casts the problem in logical terms. He argues that to interpret social action in terms other than those of the social actors is to posit a reality that transcends the reality that is constituted by the concepts and rules of social reality. He advances two objections to this kind of approach to social-scientific analysis: (1) the social scientist who does not employ the actors' concepts cannot be said to be studying social action at all, because social action is *constituted* by the social actors' concepts, and (2) positing a reality beyond that of the social actors is epistemologically indefensible (1972:8–19).

Winch argues that Weber is also guilty of the positivists' error of ignoring the actors' conceptions of their actions.[8] However, it is not difficult to absolve Weber of this charge. In the foregoing analysis it was established that, for Weber, the raw data of ideal types are the actors' concepts; but the quarrel between Winch and Weber does not end here. In the second aspect of the ordinary-language critique of this issue, Winch advances another set of arguments against Weber on the degree to which the social scientist can legitimately abstract from the realm of the social actors' concepts. Winch's basic view on this question can be found in his statement that the study of society and social relations is the same as the study of language. It follows from this that the social scientist studies social action by studying the concepts of the social actors. Understanding social action, Winch asserts, is grasping the point or meaning of what is being done or said (1958:115).

Once the social scientist is satisfied that the action in question has been "understood," another set of questions arises: How does this understanding differ from the understanding of the social actor? If social-scientific analysis must begin with the actors' understanding, does this entail that it must end there? Winch deals with these important questions in two brief passages in *The Idea of a Social Science*:

> I do not wish to maintain that we must stop at the unreflective kind of understanding. . . . But I do want to say that any more reflective understanding must necessarily presuppose, if it is to count as geniune understanding at all, the participants' unreflective understanding . . . although the reflective student of society . . . may find it necessary to use concepts which are not taken from the forms of activity which he is investigating, but which are taken rather from

the context of his own investigation, still these technical
concepts of his will imply a previous understanding of those
other concepts which belong to the activities under investigation. [1958:89]

Later he notes:

The relation between sociological theories and historical
narrative is less like the relation between scientific laws and
the reports of experiments or observations than it is like that
between theories of logic and arguments in particular
languages. [1958:134]

From this it can be concluded that although Winch concedes that the "reflective student of society" can utilize concepts
not taken directly from the social actors themselves, these concepts cannot include natural scientific tools such as statistics and
causal laws. Later, Winch also excludes generalizations by arguing that social relations exist only in and through ideas, and ideas
are not the proper subject for generalizations (1958:133). He
justifies these exclusions by pointing out that the central concepts
of our understanding of social life are incompatible with those of
scientific prediction (1958:94), which is the origin of his sharp
distinction between conceptual and empirical analysis. Because
the empirical data produced by scientific analysis are at odds
with the actors' conception of their actions, it is inappropriate to
social-scientific analysis; only the conceptual analysis of the actors' concepts can be accepted as an appropriate form of analysis.
For Winch, then, the category of "legitimate tools of social
science" consists of conceptual analysis of actors' concepts and
reflection on these concepts that does not move beyond the realm
of what is understandable to those social actors. "Illegitimate
tools" includes all natural scientific concepts, and specifically
statistics, causal laws, and generalizations.

Louch's treatment of this issue follows much the same lines.
He points out that most of our ordinary-language explanations of
actions are ad hoc, yet sufficient for our purposes (1966:31). He
argues that these ordinary-language explanations—not the kind
of explanations utilized in the natural sciences—should provide
the model for the kind of explanations that are appropriate to the
social sciences. He sees the greatest danger in social-scientific
analysis to be the desire to erect general theories to explain the
totality of social life. To illustrate this point, he contrasts what he

calls "travelers' tales" with scientific theories. The former, he argues, contribute as much to human knowledge as the latter, but their form is infinitely more appropriate to the questions of social science than that of scientific theories (1966:160). Hypothetico-deductive accounts in sociology, he argues, are not only "grotesque parodies" of such sciences as mechanics, but are completely incompatible with social-scientific problems (1966:162).

The main point of Louch's book is to argue that conceptual analysis is the only kind of analysis that is appropriate to social science (Winch's point) and that the kind of conceptual analysis that is utilized in social relations is exclusively *moral* explanation. This is so because "talk about human institutions and practices is already a moral cutting of the empirical cake" (1966:171).

Louch then moves on to a brief but revealing discussion of Weber's ideal types. Like Schutz, Louch turns to Weber's ideal types because, in contrast to the other social-scientific concepts he discusses, Weber's ideal types are grounded in the social actors' shared meaning in the social world. But although these theorists approach ideal types from the same perspective, their treatment of them is notably dissimilar. Schutz utilizes Weber's theory to specify how the ideal types of the social scientist differ from those of the social actor: they are second-order concepts, preselected by both the social world and the world of social science; they must conform to the postulates of social-scientific method: adequacy, subjective interpretation, logical consistency, and rationality. Louch, in contrast, offers no explanation of how these concepts differ from those of the social actor, nor does he provide any guidance to how the social scientist might use ideal types in concrete analysis. He merely states that because Weber's ideal types are "characterizations or impressions of ways of thought and styles of living," they are useful for the purposes of social science (1966:172). Precisely how they are useful, however, is unspecified.

The point of this discussion of the ordinary-language understanding of the legitimate concepts and tools of social-scientific analysis should now be obvious: the theories of Winch and Louch in this regard are seriously deficient. Although both theorists clearly specify which concepts they consider to be illegitimate tools of social-scientific analysis, they are much less clear in specifying the tools that are legitimate. Brief references to "*ad hoc* explanations" and concepts which are "understand-able" to the social actors do not provide adequate understanding of the conceptual apparatus of the social scientist. And by failing to specify the conceptual tools of the social scientist, they incur another difficulty: they fail to draw a clear line between the activity of social-scientific analysis and that of the social actor in everyday life. If, as Winch argues, it is the goal of social-scientific analysis to "grasp the point or meaning" of social action, it is unclear how this understanding differs from the understanding of social action by the actors themselves.

It can be argued, furthermore, that the failure to clearly articulate a methodology for the social sciences, based on ordinary-language analysis, is not peculiar to the theories of Winch and Louch but is characteristic of all ordinary-language approaches to the social sciences. Several ordinary-language philosophers have sought to rectify some of the more obvious flaws in the accounts of Winch and Louch and, thus, to articulate a more coherent ordinary-language approach to the social sciences. Winch's account of "rule-governed activity" has been generally rejected as too narrow a conception of social action (MacIntyre, 1971:218). His distinction between conceptual and empirical analysis has also been set aside on the grounds that conceptual analysis *is* empirical analysis (Di Quattro, 1972:32–42).

Despite widespread discussion of the ordinary-language approach to the social sciences, this discussion has not resulted in a coherent "ordinary-language methodology for the social sciences." This is due, however, not to slothfulness or lack of insight on the part of ordinary-language philosophers; rather, the absence of an ordinary-language methodology for the social sciences can be traced to one of the fundamental presuppositions of ordinary-language philosophy. It was one of Wittgenstein's principal theses that the task of philosophical analysis is very specific and, in some senses, very narrow: to clear up conceptual confusions or, as he put it, to "let the fly out of the flybottle." He vigorously resisted the temptation to define a rigorous philosophical methodology on the basis of his theories or to grant philosophical analysis a privileged position with respect to ordinary language. It is not surprising, then, that the approach to the social sciences that emanates from Wittgenstein's philosophy has not resulted in the definition of a rigorous methodology or in a clear separation between social science and social action.

Hanna Pitkin, one of the most articulate advocates of ordinary-language analysis in the social sciences, goes so far as to suggest that ordinary-language analysis should not be interpreted as a methodological perspective at all. Rather, it should be seen as a supplement to more traditional methods of social-scientific analysis:

> The intention [of ordinary-language philosophy] is not to substitute the study of language for the study of politics or society. Ordinary language investigations are in order where conceptual puzzlement obtrudes itself and distracts us from our work. [1972:20]

These remarks also explain the difference between Schutz's discussion of social-scientific analysis and that of ordinary-language philosophers. On one level, at least, the two approaches are compatible. Schutz's understanding of the concepts of the social scientist as "second-order constructs" has distinct similarities to Winch's assertion that the social scientist employs "technical concepts" that are rooted in a prior understanding of the social actors' concepts. The difference between the two approaches arises from Winch's refusal to clearly specify the nature of these "technical concepts" which the social scientist may employ. But if Winch's refusal can be traced to Wittgenstein's philosophical assumptions, it is also the case that Schutz's rigorous efforts to precisely define the conceptual apparatus of the social scientist can be traced to the philosophical assumptions that inform his approach. Husserl's definition of the goal of philosophical analysis is closely tied to notions of "rigorous science" and "absolute certainty." Schutz echoes these concerns in his desire to specify the scientific character of social-scientific analysis and to set that activity apart from the mundane world of social action. Thus the contrast between Husserl's desire for rigor and Wittgenstein's refusal to reify philosophical analysis explains the different emphases of the approaches to the social sciences fostered by their positions.

Despite the weaknesses of the ordinary-language approach to the methodology of the social sciences, one aspect of that approach is a valuable contribution to the postpositivist understanding of the social sciences. Several ordinary-language philosophers have devoted themselves very profitably to a problem of crucial importance to the social sciences: specifying precisely what is meant by "public accessibility of subjective meaning." This problem is one which Weber, in particular, failed to treat adequately. In terms of his discussion, the problem can be stated as follows: If the ideal types of the social scientist are based on the subjective meanings of social actors, how are these meanings apprehended by the social scientist? Weber's answer, unfortunately, was virtually to ignore the question. He saw no great difficulty in apprehending the subjective meaning of social actors. Rather, he assumed that these meanings would be readily accessible to the social-scientific investigator.

This issue of how the social scientist gains access to the subjective meanings of social actors, however, is one which Weber should not have treated so perfunctorily. The dispute over how the social scientist "understands" social action—that is, the controversy over *verstehen* in the social sciences—has occupied a central position in the social-scientific literature since the time of the *Methodenstreit*, in which Weber was engaged. This question was by no means answered by Weber and his contemporaries, what Weber meant by *verstehen* has become one of the principal topics in subsequent discussions, and several aspects of this dispute have particular relevance for the present argument.

The dispute over *verstehen* in the social sciences can be roughly divided into two historical phases. In the first phase, or the "older" *verstehen* tradition, *verstehen* was understood to be the process by which the social scientist, through empathy and intuition, "relives" the experience of the social actor. Interpreting *verstehen* in this manner entails a number of distinct attitudes toward the nature of social-scientific analysis, for it follows that *verstehen* is the exclusive tool of the social sciences and sets them apart from the natural sciences because, unlike the tools of the natural sciences, *verstehen* is an inherently "subjective" process. *Verstehen*, in this interpretation, involves "getting inside" the actor's mind, a process far removed from "objective" apprehension of facts in the natural sciences.

In recent years, however, a "new" *verstehen* tradition has arisen to challenge this definition. Broadly, its aim is to show that the social actor's "subjective meanings" are publicly accessible and that grasping these meanings does not involve probing the hidden processes of the mind (Giddens, 1977:171–74). One result of this interpretation of *verstehen* has been (not surprisingly) a new interpretation of how Weber understood this term.

Early interpreters of Weber, most notably Theodore Abel, attributed to him the "older" interpretation of *verstehen*, but recent accounts have attempted to show this interpretation to be erroneous. A spate of articles has attempted to establish the empirical character of *verstehen* as Weber understood it (Tucker, 1965; Di Quattro, 1972; Munch, 1975). They established quite convincingly that Weber did not interpret *verstehen* as a process of intuition or reliving. Rather, these authors assert, Weber saw subjective meaning as publicly accessible. (It was this interpretation of Weber that was utilized in the previous chapter.) But although these studies have rendered a valuable service in clearing up this misinterpretation of Weber, they do not solve the fundamental problem in the dispute over *verstehen*. As Munch admits, Weber did not give this matter sufficient attention (1975:60).

A careful reading of Weber reveals that he saw *verstehen* as an empirical tool of social-scientific analysis. His approach to social-scientific analysis, furthermore, only makes sense if it is assumed that he saw social actors' meanings to be publicly accessible elements of the social world. But Weber failed to provide a philosophically sound basis for his assumption of the public accessibility of actors' meanings, and no amount of reexamination of his work will provide such a basis.

It is in supplying the needed philosophical basis for assumption of the public accessibility of subjective meanings that the approach of ordinary-language analysis makes its contribution. Theorists of this persuasion have argued cogently and with philosophical sophistication that interpretation of the subjective meaning of human action need not involve "getting inside" another's mind. Instead, they argue, the categories through which social action is made intelligible are public and, hence, accessible elements of the social world. This basic point is expressed from several perspectives, a number of which will be discussed below. Each variant, however, is similar in that it supplies a philosophical basis for the correspondence between meaning and action that Weber failed to provide.

The preceding account of Winch's theory reveals the basic themes of the ordinary-language approach to the problem of how the social actor's subjective meanings are made accessible to the social observer. Winch rejects Weber's distinction between meaningful and social action on the grounds that action can be said to be meaningful only in that it falls under socially defined rules of conduct. On the basis of this argument, Winch develops the position that it is the "rule governed" character of action which is definitive. Placing an action under a rule makes the action intelligible; it is the means by which we distinguish it from meaningless behavior. It follows from this that the study of human action—that is, social science—must focus on the nature and operation of these rules.

Winch's account of action as rule governed is, however, sketchy. He does not elaborate on how the social scientist might apply this perspective to the concrete problems of social analysis, but the work of R. S. Peters is more helpful in developing this approach. In his study of the concept of motivation, Peters asserts that asking for the explanation of an action involves asking for the reason it was done, and this involves placing the action under a rule-following, purposive model (1958:5). This entails that identifying an action, explaining it, and imputing a "subjective meaning" to it come to essentially the same thing. For the social scientist, this means the analysis of social action must begin with the assumption that

> human behavior is constituted by human beings maneuvering in a complex framework of purposes and rules that are appealed to both to identify and explain behavior. [1969: 138]

Although the rule-following model advocated by Winch and Peters essentially does the job of explaining how subjective meaning is made accessible to the observer, the approach is not entirely satisfactory. Critics have noted that to conceive of every action as falling under a rule stretches the notion of rule beyond acceptable limits. Understanding such an action as "going for a walk" by placing it under the rules that govern the concept of walking is, at best, an awkward formulation. Some deficiencies of the rule-governed approach have been remedied in the work of theorists who have come to be known as "action theorists," although they do not form a homogeneous group. Their theories range over a number of distinct positions with regard to the nature of human action, but their intensive examination of the issue has resulted in a number of theses that are relevant to the problems of the social sciences and particularly to how the social scientist interprets social action.

H. L. A. Hart's analysis of human action from the perspective of legal theories makes a point so simple that it has been almost universally overlooked by philosophers. In the law, judges and juries are routinely asked to impute motives or intentions ("subjective meanings") to human action, and unless these judges and juries thought they had access to actors' motives, the whole basis for our legal system would collapse. Proceeding on this observation, Hart argues that ascribing subjective meaning to the action of a fellow human being is not so mysterious as it has seemed to some philosophers. Making such ascriptions is something we do all the time, he says, in everyday life and in the law; and furthermore, it is something about which we have a great deal of confidence (Hart, 1948–49, 1961, 1968; Fitzgerald, 1968).

However, Hart's analysis has been criticized as superficial by other "action theorists." The root philosophical question, they argue, is *why* the description and interpretation of an action are so closely linked. This question has been explored in depth in the extended debate over whether reasons can be said to "cause" actions, and one of the positions that has emerged provides a clear formulation of the relationship between description and interpretation that is essential to the problem of how the social scientist studies human action. Several theorists who argue against the position that reasons can be identified as causes of action have developed the theory that reasons and actions are logically inseparable (Hamlyn, 1968:57; Melden, 1967). They assert that a reason cannot be distinguished from an action as its cause because actions cannot be described and identified apart from reference to particular reasons. The two are conceptually (that is, logically) linked in the description of the action.

This approach has important implications for establishing the identity of meaning and action in the social sciences. Like the definition of action as rule governed, it provides a means of linking the description of action to its subjective meaning. Blum and McHugh, two social scientists who have been particularly successful in applying this perspective to social-scientific analysis, argue that motives describe actions rather than provide knowledge of some kind of internal event. Thus to give the motive of an action is not to locate its cause but to assert how certain behavior is socially intelligible. Motives, therefore, are best conceived as descriptions of socially organized conditions which produce the use of certain motives (1971:100–103). Put somewhat differently, this means that we do not see people exhibiting angry behavior and impute an anger motive to their actions; rather, we see them *as* angry (Beck, 1975:64).

One further aspect of the literature generated by concern over the nature of human action should be mentioned, though it comes from a theorist outside the ordinary-language tradition. Paul Ricoeur, in an attempt to specify what he defines as the "hermeneutic" nature of the social sciences, advances the thesis that human action can be studied in much the same way as speech, because action, like speech, is a "statement" which can be objectified for the purposes of analysis. Just as speech, when objectified in a text, has a determinate range of meanings that is specified by the formal rules of language, action, which also can be objectified in this manner, has a range of meanings that are clearly specified by the social setting. This means that action, like language, can be explained through reference to shared rules of meaning. Like speech, action can be placed under typologies (such as Weber's ideal types) which specify the criteria of their proper application. These criteria establish the content of the rules which constitute different types of meaningful human action (1977:323).

Ricoeur's formulation of the identity of meaning and action is perhaps the clearest statement of the importance of this issue for the social sciences. All of the action theorists cited above are concerned to argue the thesis that the subjective meaning of action is not private but public knowledge. Ricoeur, by showing that the meaning of an action is accessible in the same way that the meaning of a word is accessible to speakers of that language, clarifies the implications of this position. An action has a certain determinate meaning in any society, and encompasses a range of meaning in the same way that words have a range of meaning. Thus the meaning of an action, like the meaning of a word, need not be seen as something hidden, inner, or inaccessible to scrutiny. The implications of this thesis for social-scientific analysis are clear: in daily life we routinely understand and interpret action simply by identifying it in terms of shared categories of meaning. There is no reason why the social scientist cannot do the same.

5. Conclusion

The preceding discussion of the accessibility of the "subjective meaning" of the social actor to the social scientist, though it provides a valuable insight into the problems of social-scientific analysis, again raises the issue which, more than any other, separates the perspectives of phenomenology and ordinary-language analysis: the status of mental events. From the above discussion, it could be concluded that the action theorists, as well as Ricoeur, Winch, and Peters, through their efforts to reveal the public accessibility of the "private" world of the actors' subjective meaning are, in effect, denying the existence of mental events. But if this interpretation is correct, the possibility of a rapprochement between the two approaches, which is here advanced, must be discarded. The task of the concluding section, then, will be to show that this judgment is premature, by revealing that phenomenology and ordinary-language analysis are more compatible on this issue than at first appears. Furthermore, reexamination of their positions on mental events will serve as a way of outlining a possible synthesis between the two approaches, which is the broader goal of the investigation.

The nature of the difference between phenomenology and ordinary-language analysis on mental events should now be clear. While careful examination of the structure of first-person experiences is the very foundation of the phenomenological approach, ordinary-language philosophers deny the possibility of discussion of this realm, and this contrast is particularly evident in Schutz's work. His discussion of the two levels of meaning constitution which emerges from his critique of Weber makes it clear that analysis of mental events is crucial to his approach. In attempting a final assessment of the positions of the schools on this issue, however, two elements of Schutz's theory should be reemphasized. First, Schutz argues that meaning constitution on the primordial level—that is, within the individual's consciousness—takes place in an intersubjective context. Thus, for Schutz, this realm, though private, is not inaccessible. The intersubjective context in which meaning on this level is constituted opens it to analysis. Second, and just as significantly, Schutz argues that meaning on this level is not the object of social-scientific analysis; meaning on the second level, meaning which is constituted through direct social interaction, is the subject matter of the social sciences.

Two elements of the ordinary-language position on mental events can also be reiterated for the purposes of this assessment, and these elements are evident in Wittgenstein's account of this issue—although they are sometimes obscured in the accounts of his less-than-faithful followers. First, Wittgenstein makes it clear that he does not deny the existence of mental events; rather, he sees first-person experience as the "border of language," as constituting the limit of what can be intelligibly discussed. Second, his position on the accessibility of supposedly private mental events, such as motives and intentions, is that we identify them through the shared concepts of ordinary language. In other words, such entities are accessible to us, both as social actors and social observers, through the public, "intersubjective" categories of ordinary language.

By comparing these central points of both approaches, several theses can be formulated about the relationship between these approaches and the significance of that relationship for the methodology of the social sciences. From the perspective of their appropriateness to the problems faced by the social scientist, it can be asserted that the overriding theme of both accounts is intersubjectivity. It is this aspect of the two accounts that is so frequently cited as the basis of the commonality of the two approaches. And since exploration of the intersubjective realm of social action is the starting point of all social-scientific analysis, it is not surprising that social scientists have been particularly cognizant of the compatibility of these two approaches.

But a second and much less obvious point can also be drawn from this comparison. In a strict sense, Schutz and Wittgenstein are discussing very distinct aspects of mental events. Schutz, almost exclusively concerned with the *constitution* of meaning in mental events, meticulously examined the levels on which meaning is constituted and the context in which this constitution occurs. Although he insists repeatedly that because this constitution of meaning takes place in an intersubjective context and hence is accessible to examination and interpretation, the virtue of his account lies in his explication of the constituting process, not in his description of exactly how these meanings *become* accessible. But it is on precisely this issue of accessibility that Wittgenstein focuses his attention. Conspicuously avoiding the question whether mental events occur at all, Wittgenstein ignores the issue of constitution, concentrating instead on how the actor's meaning is made intelligible in the shared world of ordinary language. His answer to the question of accessibility is, significantly, the same as Schutz's: We understand and identify mental events through public, intersubjective categories. But unlike Schutz, he clearly specifies how such identification occurs.

This distinction between constitution and accessibility provides the basis for the argument that phenomenology and ordinary-language analysis are not as incompatible on the issue of mental events as has generally been assumed. It also provides a means of identifying the particular strengths of the two approaches with regard to social-scientific methodology. Phenomenology, in sharp contrast to ordinary-language analysis, provides a vocabulary with which the first-person experiences of the social actor can be discussed. Schutz's position, that meaning, even on the primordial level of individual consciousness, is constituted in an intersubjective context, opens this private world to scrutiny. Ordinary-language analysis, on the other hand, provides the social scientist with a different tool of analysis. By discussing at length the way in which mental events are identified through the public categories of ordinary language, they provide a precise understanding of how such entities can be said to be accessible to social observation. Making this accessibility explicit is the unique contribution of the ordinary-language approach.

In short, these two approaches are complementary rather than contradictory. That integration of these two approaches, similar to that presented here, is at least a possibility has been suggested by a few contemporary theorists. The above argument is in close agreement with Ricoeur's advocacy of a "linguistic phenomenology." In his analysis of the two schools, Ricoeur argues that ordinary-language analysis and phenomenology operate at different strategic levels: ordinary-language analysis at the level of the articulation of discourse and phenomenology at the level of the meaning of the lived. What is needed, he insists, is not a choice of one of these two levels, but their integration into a single approach (1975:184–93).

The point of the foregoing has been to argue that such an integration is both necessary and possible. Habermas also indicates that he sees integration between what Ricoeur defines as the two levels of analysis to be possible. In his analysis of the role of linguistic analysis he remarks:

Language functions as a kind of transformer, because psychic processes such as sensations, needs, and feelings are fitted into structures of linguistic intersubjectivity, inner episodes or experiences are transformed into intentional contents. [1975:10]

Finally, a further issue relevant to comparison between these two approaches should be noted: the degree to which each approach supplies the social scientist with conceptual tools and methodological procedures, thereby providing a clear notion of what constitutes the activity of the social scientist. This issue was mentioned briefly above, but because it serves as a necessary introduction to the concerns of the next chapter, it should be stated more explicitly. The judgment of phenomenology on this issue should be evident from the account of Schutz's work, for he supplies the social scientist an extensive set of conceptual and methodological tools with which social reality can be analyzed. In doing so, he also provides a clear notion of the activity of the social scientist and how that activity is distinct from social action in the everyday world. His lengthy discussion of typification clarifies both the similarities and the dissimilarities between social action and social science.

It was argued above, furthermore, that Schutz's analysis of the ideal types of the social scientist is superior to Weber's in this respect; that is, he offers a clearer account of the constitution and function of the concepts of the social scientist. But an important reservation must now be added. In another respect, Schutz's account of ideal-typical analysis is distinctly inferior to Weber's. Unlike Weber, Schutz fails to use the ideal-typical methodology to develop a method by which social structures can be analyzed and assessed. Although Schutz's ideal types supply a theoretical foundation that is capable of supporting the analysis of social structures, he fails to develop this theoretical potential. In his posthumous *Structures of the Life-World* (1973), co-authored by Thomas Luckmann, Schutz seems to be moving in this direction; but even in this work, which by its title would seem to be concerned with analysis of social structures, Schutz, on the contrary, was concerned exclusively with the sociology of knowledge. "Structures" in this work refers to patterns of knowledge and their dissemination—not, as for Weber, to patterns of action that have been objectified in social institutions. Although Schutz occasionally refers to the need for analysis of the institutions that structure the social and cultural life of the individual (pp. 83, 299), nowhere is there any reference to the economic, political, and religious structures that occupy Weber in *Economy and Society*.

It might of course be argued that Schutz had no intention of matching Weber's structural analyses and thus cannot be faulted for failing to do so. But particularly in the context of the present analysis, this excuse is insufficient. The fact that neither Schutz nor his followers have engaged in structural analysis of this sort is highly significant in the context of contemporary social theory. In theory, Schutz's approach provides the basis for structural analysis, but Schutzian phenomenology has in practice never moved beyond the analysis of meaning constitution. Phenomenologists have been so occupied with meaning constitution that they have neglected the equally important empirical analysis of social structures and, as a result, have failed to produce the kind of structural analysis that Weber supplies so liberally. This failure has a serious consequence. It must be concluded that the synthesis that Schutz attempts between analysis of meaning constitution and scientific, empirical analysis of social structures is successful on the theoretical level only. In practice, Schutzian phenomenology fails to move beyond the limits of the subjective critique.

The judgment of ordinary-language analysis with regard to this issue is even harsher. Unlike phenomenology, ordinary-language analysis fails to supply either a set of conceptual tools and methodological procedures or a clear distinction between the activity of the social scientist and that of the social actor. Although Winch and Louch indicate that such concepts and tools are legitimate if they are based on a prior understanding of the social actors' concepts, this theme is not developed; nor is it developed in the work of other ordinary-language philosophers. The approach supplies, at best, only a vague indication that the social scientist may employ concepts and procedures that are not available to the social actor. What these might be, however, remains unclear. As a result, ordinary-language analysis blurs the distinction between social science and social action, a distinction which, it seems obvious, is crucial to a coherent methodology of the social sciences.

This chapter has argued that phenomenology and ordinary-language analysis have remedied one of the major deficiencies of the positivist approach: ignoring social actors' definition of their action. By rejecting the positivist distinction between subjective and objective meaning and replacing it with a clearly articulated understanding of the intersubjective, public character of social actors' meanings, they supply the social scientist with a clear understanding of how those meanings are to be interpreted. They *fail* to provide, or in the case of phenomenology provide only in theory, a means of analyzing and assessing social structures, a deficiency that is of primary concern to the two schools that will be considered under the heading "objective critique."

4. The Objective Critique

1. Nature of the Objective Critique

In the previous chapter it was argued that the commonality between phenomenology and ordinary-language analysis lies in their rejection of the positivist dichotomy between subjective and objective meaning in the social sciences. Specifically, it was asserted that both schools reject the positivist definition of subjective meaning as private and inaccessible and replace it with a conception of social actors' concepts as intersubjective, public, and accessible. Thus labeling these positions the "subjective critique" is misleading in one respect: these schools do not discuss subjective meaning in the sense of the commonly accepted positivist definition. Use of the term "subjective" in discussion of these two schools is justifiable, however, because both schools continue to employ this term, even though they radically alter the positivists' definition. It is also justifiable on historical grounds. In discussions in the social sciences extending back at least to the time of Weber, the problem which these two schools address has been most commonly labeled "subjective meaning."

The same kind of qualifications must be extended to "objective critique" as it is applied to the two schools of thought discussed in this chapter, structuralism and critical theory. One justification for this label is, again, historical: both schools' principal critique of positivism involves issues which have traditionally been placed under the heading "objectivity in the social sciences." However, "objective" in the present discussion does not entail that either structuralism or critical theory adheres to

101

the positivist definition of objectivity. On the contrary, both reject that definition as radically flawed. Further, although significant differences can be identified between the antipositivist definitions of objectivity offered by each school, placing these schools under the label "objective critique" can also be justified on the grounds that their definitions of objectivity have important similarities which provide a common core for their analyses.

Both structuralism and critical theory define objectivity in the social sciences in terms of four key elements of social-scientific analysis. Although their positions with regard to these elements vary, they agree that "objective" analysis in the social sciences is linked to a correct understanding of these elements. For both schools, "objectivity" involves what social scientists have generally labeled "macroanalysis." Both assert that "objective analysis" involves the assessment of social forms, structures, and institutions on the societal rather than individual (or "micro") level. For both schools also, the definition of "objective" in the social sciences is tied to the definition of "scientific." But because defining the "objective" as the "scientific" is a key element of the positivist conception of objectivity, defining an antipositivist conception of objectivity involves, for both structuralism and critical theory, redefining the positivists' conception of "scientific analysis."

Also, both schools define "objective" in the social sciences in opposition to "ideological," which can most easily be explained by the fact that both schools have their roots in the Marxist tradition of social thought. Although the interpretations of Marx's thought that are accepted by each school are distinctively different, their Marxist roots dictate a common concern to separate the "objective" from the "ideological" in social-scientific analysis. For both schools, finally, "objective" is defined in opposition to "culturally relative." For both schools, relativism is one of the key problems of the social sciences, which must be overcome in any attempt to formulate a comprehensive social-scientific methodology.

The commonality between the two schools under the heading "objective critique," then, lies in their identification of the principal problem that confronts the social scientist, the nature of "objective" analysis in the social sciences and their definition of this problem in terms of these four elements. Although structuralists and critical theorists are not unconcerned with the problems addressed by the subjective critique—that is, the methodological and epistemological problems in apprehending the meaning of social actors—their primary concern is to articulate a methodology which will enable the social scientist to assess social life from an "objective" standpoint, defined in terms of the elements discussed above.

The different ways in which the two schools approach the problem of objectivity in the social sciences will not be ignored in this analysis. Althusser's definition of the objectivity of social-scientific analysis is rooted in his understanding of the process of scientific conceptualization while Habermas' is informed by his very different understanding of the relationship between theory and practice. An even more important difference between the two schools is their definitions of structural analysis. Althusser defines structures as objective realities that "create" subjects; Habermas, who defines his approach as radically opposed to that of structuralism, discusses structures under the "objective framework" of social reality, which he defines as constituted by the language of the social actors as well as by the "real factors" of labor and domination. In light of these differences, no attempt will be made to suggest a rapprochement between the two schools. Rather, it will be argued that their commonality is that their primary objection to positivist social science is its failure to properly define the objectivity of social-scientific analysis.

In the introduction to chapter 3 it was stated that although the pattern of analysis employed in examining the subjective and objective critiques would be similar, the conclusions would differ significantly, and what was meant by this statement can now be expressed more precisely. As in the subjective critique, analysis of the two schools, under the label "objective critique," will begin with an outline of the basic elements of each approach, then examine the treatment of Weber's methodology that is characteristic of each school. But the conclusions from this analysis will be fundamentally different than those from the analysis of the subjective critique. The conclusion in the previous chapter was that phenomenology and ordinary-language analysis provide substantive solutions to one of the necessary elements of social-scientific analysis: apprehension of the meaning of social actors. These solutions, it was argued, can be utilized in construction of a contemporary postpositivist synthesis for two reasons: the contributions of the two schools can be shown to complement, rather than contradict, each other, and together they solve the major problems raised by the attempt to define what is involved in the social scientist's understanding of social actors' meanings. These two schools, in short, offer a positive contribution to the postpositivist synthesis.

The contribution of the schools under the label "objective critique," in contrast, can best be characterized in negative (rather than positive) terms. It will emerge that both structuralism and critical theory identify a signficant weakness in the positivist conception of the social sciences and that both schools clearly identify the need to redress this weakness, that is, to define an antipositivist conception of objectivity in the social sciences. But it will be concluded that these two schools exhibit at least one irreconcilable difference and that neither of them offers substantive solutions to the problems posed by the need for a coherent conception of objective analysis in the social sciences. Rather, it will be shown that the conceptions of objectivity defined by both schools are logically flawed. This conclusion will be argued more forcefully of structuralism than of critical theory. (Certain epistemological elements of Habermas' position on objectivity will be assessed in a more favorable light in the final chapter.)

The principal goal of the analysis in this chapter will be to establish that the overall contribution of these approaches is not a positive solution to the problem of objectivity but a clear negation of the positivist position. In sum, by revealing the deficiencies of the positivist conception of objectivity and outlining the parameters of a correct conception, they define what would constitute a solution to the problem, even though they fail to supply such a solution.

2. Structuralism

Analysis of social structures has occupied a major place in the tradition of social-scientific analysis since long before the present controversy over positivist methodology in the social sciences. It has also, significantly, occupied a major role in the positivist tradition that is now under attack. It will be necessary at the outset, therefore, to clarify the structural analysis that will be examined in this section and to explain how it differs from analysis of social structures in the positivist tradition. For the positivist, analysis of social structures involves gathering empirical data about the permanent, nonindividual character of society. This "structural analysis" rests on the same epistemological foundations as the other elements of the positivist tradition and involves inductive analysis of discrete "facts," informed by a conception of scientific activity identical to that in the natural sciences.

However, the term "structuralism," as it will be used below, denotes a significantly different approach to analysis of social structure: the search for abstract principles which determine the organization of social relations. This definition of structuralism describes the movement which, in recent years, has had such impact on a great many areas in the social sciences. Structuralism in this sense is nonempirical and concentrates on methodological and epistemological problems.[1] Structuralists who adhere to this definition, furthermore, identify their position in opposition to the positivist tradition, and this approach to structural analysis has resulted in a methodology for the social sciences which rivals the positivist conception.

The advent of the structuralist movement can be identified as one of the major events of the social sciences in the twentieth century. As a distinctive approach to social scientific problems, structuralism has affected nearly every variety of social-scientific discipline. In the following, no attempt will be made to survey its broad impact; rather, the analysis will concentrate on one theorist whose work has been particularly influential in the anti-positivist critique in social theory: Louis Althusser. Although Althusser is a French Marxist and his work, as a consequence, has been discussed most thoroughly by Marxist social scientists, it has also had significant effect outside the Marxist circle. Particularly among British social theorists, the work of Althusser has generated great controversy and resulted in serious reassessment of the traditional problems of the social sciences which are raised in his work. Assessment of Althusser's impact and the formidable social theory on which it rests is the goal of the following discussion.

The principal thrust of Althusser's work is investigation into the nature of scientific activity, and his work provides a sweeping critique of the epistemology of Western science and philosophy. His aim, in the broadest sense, is to show this epistemology to be fundamentally misconceived and to take the first steps toward its replacement. He defines this epistemology, in all its manifestations, as "empiricism" and claims that all empiricist epistemologies are based on two central dichotomies: the real–abstract dichotomy and the subject–object dichotomy. Althusser places a number of different approaches in science and philosophy under his label of empiricism, and he justifies this categorization by arguing that all these approaches accept these two dichotomies. Adherence to both dichotomies, furthermore, dictates a particular understanding of scientific knowledge that Althusser identifies as the root problem of empiricism. The first dichotomy dictates that scientific knowledge be understood as an abstraction from the real, the second that it be understood as resulting from the opposition of subject and object. As a result of these attitudes, he concludes, all empiricists necessarily conceive of knowledge as a part of its object—or, as he puts it, "a real part of the real object in the real structure of the real object" (Althusser and Balibar, 1970:38).

This empiricist conception of scientific knowledge is the principal object of Althusser's attack. He advances the thesis that we must reject this empiricist epistemology by making an "epistemological break" with its fundamental premises, and this conception of such a break (or "rupture") is crucial to Althusser's theory. The term is not, however, his own, but is borrowed from Bachelard, for whom an epistemological break occurs when a tradition of thought encounters an obstacle that is a product of the contradictions inherent in the tradition itself. In Bachelard's terminology, such an "epistemological obstacle" is encountered when an existing organization of thought is in danger. Such an obstacle is a "resistance of thought to thought" and appears when the epistemological presuppositions of a tradition of thought create problems that cannot be solved with the theoretical tools provided by that tradition (Lecourt, 1975:135).

Applying Bachelard's theory to contemporary empiricist thought, Althusser argues that empiricism has encountered an epistemological obstacle and, consequently, that an epistemological break with this tradition is both imminent and necessary. To reveal the nature of this obstacle, Althusser turns to a close analysis of the work of Marx. For Althusser, Marx is the only theorist who had even begun to lay the groundwork for the necessary epistemological break with empiricism—but Marx had only *started* the required, comprehensive work. The nature of Marx's breakthrough is his realization that knowledge is the result of a process of production which is analogous to production in the material world. Althusser identifies two theses in Marx's work which provide the basis for this theoretical breakthrough: the objects we call "knowledges" (as well as material objects) are a result of a process of production, and a rigid distinction must be drawn between the process of production in the realm of thought and in the real world. Whereas production of a real object takes place entirely in reality, production of a thought object takes place entirely in thought. Discovery of this distinction between thought and reality, Althusser argues, allowed Marx to transcend the sterile dichotomies of empiricism (Althusser and Balibar, 1970:41).

Building on this interpretation of Marx, Althusser examines the process which results in the production of scientific knowledge. Because he takes the position that knowledge is analogous to production in the material world, it is incumbent on him to identify the elements: raw materials, instruments, processes, and finally the product. He does this in a systematic fashion; however, specification of the first element in this process of production, the raw materials employed, immediately brings him into direct conflict with the empiricist tradition.

Because he asserts that production of knowledge occurs entirely within the realm of thought, it follows that the raw materials of this production must also be found in this realm. Althusser complies with this stipulation by identifying the raw material of knowledge production as the concepts supplied by the scientific community at the time of the knowledge's production—concepts that can be defined as either abstract or concrete. Abstract concepts refer to (or "bear on," in his terminology) formal entities; concrete concepts refer to singular objects. Althusser insists, however, that even concepts which he identifies as concrete are not to be mistaken as elements of the real world. Rather, abstract and concrete concepts are both defined as instruments that belong wholly to the realm of thought and are utilized in production of entities which come to be identified as "knowledges." He goes so far as to assert that abstract concepts, precisely because they designate formal entities in the real world, are more "concrete" than concrete concepts that designate singular objects in the real world:

> Every abstract concept therefore provides knowledge of a reality whose existence it reveals: an "abstract concept" then means a formula which is apparently abstract but really terribly concrete, because of the object it designates. [1976:76]

Although it may appear that the aim of Althusser's theory of the production of knowledge is merely to wreak havoc with traditional definitions, his goal is much broader: to transform the relationship between the real-concrete and the abstract that is at the basis of empiricist epistemology. His assertion that concrete concepts are not more "real" than abstract concepts, because both exist in the realm of thought and are, as such, rigidly separated from the real world, calls for a radical redefinition of the nature of scientific activity.

Empiricists define scientific analysis as a careful movement from real-concrete concepts, which are elements of the real world, to the formulation of abstract concepts, which are the tools of scientific analysis. They define these abstract concepts, furthermore, as the means by which the essence of the real is revealed (1976:192). Althusser's understanding of the production of scientific knowledge, however, completely reverses this conception. Because he defines the raw materials of the production of scientific knowledge as the concepts of the scientific community, he defines scientific analysis as the manipulation of past and present scientific concepts. The end result of this process is something the scientific community regards as "knowledge." But Althusser makes it clear that this knowledge does not reveal the essence of entities in the real world; it is entirely a product of the world of thought. It is this redefinition of the nature of scientific knowledge, then, that constitutes the epistemological break that is both the essence of the contribution that Althusser attributes to Marx and the core of his own theory.

But this radical break necessitates, as Althusser fully appreciates, a new definition not only of scientific activity but also of the relationship between scientific knowledge and the "real world." For the empiricist, whether or not something is granted the status of scientific knowledge depends entirely on whether it is an accurate representation of some element of the real world, but for Althusser this test no longer has meaning. By his rigid separation of the worlds of thought and reality, he removes the possibility of any form of comparison between knowledge and reality. His position entails that all questions about the nature of scientific knowledge can be answered only within the realm of thought. Thus empiricists, by posing the question in terms of comparison between scientific knowledge and the real world, are posing a question that is fundamentally misconceived and unanswerable; therefore the question must be restated in terms which avoid empiricist assumptions.

Althusser offers the following formulation: By what mechanism does production of the object of knowledge produce the cognitive appropriation of the real object existing outside thought in the real world? (Althusser and Balibar, 1970:56).

Althusser's answer to this question takes him into the details of his theory of the process by which scientific "knowledges" are produced—but it is important at this point to distingiush the nature of this question and the implications which arise from the fact that Althusser poses the question in these particular terms. Traditionally, philosophers of science have put the question of scientific knowledge in terms of "grounding"; thus their inquiries have been directed to discovering the *foundations* of scientific knowledge. Posed in these terms, the question of the nature of scientific knowledge naturally leads to comparison between scientific concepts and the real world, but this is precisely the formulation to which Althusser objects. He puts the question in quite different terms: he inquires after the *mechanism* by which knowledge is produced in the sciences. This phrasing leads the discussion into the internal workings of the scientific community, which is precisely where Althusser thinks it should lead. The answer to the question of scientific knowledge lies, he says, in the realm of science and analysis of the activity of scientists. We learn about the nature of scientific knowledge, in short, by following the dictum of Bachelard: "Go to school with the scientists" (Lecourt, 1975:110).

Thus Althusser's treatment of the nature of scientific knowledge and, hence, of the intimately related question of objectivity is exclusively in terms of the production of scientific knowledge. He contends that the theoretical practice of science contains definite protocols which validate or "guarantee" the product which emerges. Productions which have been validated according to these protocols have the "knowledge effect," which he defines as the peculiar quality possessed by those special products which are "knowledges" (Althusser and Balibar, 1970:62). He insists that definition of the "knowledge effect" must be the goal of the effort to guarantee scientific theories, not the bogus comparison to reality employed by empiricists, because the "knowledge effect" is produced by rigid adherence to the criterion of scientificity, a criterion supplied entirely within the province of science (Althusser and Balibar, 1970:67). (Althusser's contention that both the method and the content of science are internally given, as well as the inevitable circularity of definitions which this position entails, have often been criticized [Glucksmann, 1974:96], but these criticisms will be postponed until the full extent of Althusser's position has been examined.)

On the basis of his epistemological critique of empiricism, Althusser articulates two theses which are directly relevant to the problems considered in this study. The first concerns the implications which his altered view of the nature of scientific activity have for the theory of concept formation in the social sciences; the second concerns his understanding of the role of the individual human actor in social-scientific analysis. Having rejected the empiricist conception of scientific activity as the movement from the real-concrete to the abstract, Althusser develops the position that production of scientific knowledge can more accurately be portrayed as a movement from the abstract to the concrete. To show how this is possible, he divides scientific concepts into three categories: Generalities I, II, and III.

Generalities I are the raw material of theoretical production; they are the body of concepts made available to scientists by the prevailing scientific tradition of the time. Generalities II are the broader corpus of concepts which form the problematic of a particular tradition of thought, a corpus which, at present, is constituted by the basic epistemological assumptions of empiricism. Generalities III are the "knowledges" produced by the work of Generalities II on Generalities I. Employing these definitions, Althusser maintains that it is erroneous to assume, as do the empiricists, that the result of scientific investigations (the "knowledges" of Generalities II) reveals the "essences" of the raw material from which they are drawn (the concepts of Generalities I). Nor are these results more abstract than the raw material. Rather, he describes the process as one in which the "knowledges" of Generalities III transform the raw material provided by Generalities I into new forms which are *more* concrete than these original concepts. This process of reasoning allows Althusser to call this transformation a movement from the abstract to the concrete (1969:182; also Callinicos, 1976:54–57).[2]

Quite obviously, this theory has important implications for an understanding of the nature of scientific activity per se, but it has particular significance for an understanding of the nature of social-scientific concepts. Applied to the social sciences, Althusser's theory has the effect of denying one of the principal theses of the two schools analyzed in the previous chapter. Both phenomenologists and ordinary-language philosophers assert unequivocally that the social scientist's analysis must begin with the concepts of the social actors themselves; these concepts are identified as the necessary raw material of the social sciences.

Althusser's position, however, is that the production of scientific "knowledges" must always begin with *scientific* concepts—that is, concepts which belong to a particular scientific tradition. On this point, then, Althusser is clearly at loggerheads with the subjective critique.

The opposition between these positions emerges most clearly in Althusser's discussion of the distinction between scientific and ideological concepts. One of his principal aims in presenting his theory of scientific activity is to distinguish between these two kinds of concepts (1971:164), and his distinction relies on the theory of scientific concept formation outlined above, in which he defines scientific concepts on all three levels as wholly internal to the activity of science. The raw materials, methods, and conclusions of science are entirely in the world of thought and are divorced from the real world. In opposition to this definition of scientific concepts, ideological concepts are defined as products of the real or material world; they are the mechanism by which individuals are "plugged into" the institutional structure of a society. And the pivotal ideological concept, Althusser asserts, is the category of the subject, or "man." He identifies this category as constitutive for all ideology; it functions as the means by which subjects are "recruited" from the individuals who constitute a society (1971:170–76). The concept of the subject is (in his words) a "bourgeois myth" and the conception of "man" as the absolute point of departure for all science and philosophy is a radical misconception (1976:52).

The primary goal of Althusser's attack on the concept of the subject is to discredit humanist interpretations of Marx, but the thesis he develops is significant for more than an internal dispute among Marx's interpreters. Althusser argues that the ideological conception of "man" can be countered only by utilizing Marx's discovery that history is a process without a subject. Against the humanist view that social actors' intersubjective actions are constitutive of social reality, Althusser interprets Marx as saying that individuals are agents in history; they are the supports or "bearers" of the social structure, not its constituent elements (1976:95; Althusser and Balibar, 1970:32). It follows that the only proper object of social analysis is not individuals but the structure which individuals support. The self-understandings of social actors must be explicitly rejected because those understandings are necessarily discontinuous with the scientific understanding of the structure that transforms them into subjects.

Althusser's controversial thesis concerning the subject has been attacked on a number of fronts. Humanist Marxists have labeled his interpretation of Marx "anti-humanist" and one which does violence to Marx's intent. Other social theorists have accused him of formulating a theory which "loses" man; that is, it fails to account for what appears to be the undeniably fundamental element of social life, the individual. Althusser replies to these criticisms by asserting that the humanist interpretation of Marx denies his epistemological break with empiricism and hence misses the essence of his contribution to social theory. More broadly, he argues that the humanist conception of man, because it transforms individuals into subjects, distorts their essential qualities. He asserts, in other words, that it is the humanists, not he, who "lose" man, and that the bourgeois ideology of humanism ultimately obscures the existence of living individuals (1976:205).

This outline of Althusser's approach is a necessary basis for assessment of his position and for examination of the structuralist critique of Weber's methodology. In the course of his work, Althusser does not deal explicitly with Weber's methodological position; he assumes that Weber's approach to the social sciences is rooted in an empiricist epistemology and hence can be dismissed within his critique of empiricism.

Weber, in fact, makes explicit use of the two dichotomies which Althusser identifies as the foundation of the empiricist problematic. With regard to the subject–object dichotomy, Weber is very clear that all social analysis must begin with the subject. He identifies the subjective meanings of the social actor as the raw data of analysis. He further asserts that interpretation of the subjective meaning of social action is the basis for the conceptual tool that is fundamental to all social-scientific analysis, the ideal type. This alone is a radical misconception, from the structuralist perspective, but by interpreting society as the product of the intersubjective meaning constitution of social actors. Weber commits an even more serious error: he argues that ideal types, based on intersubjective meanings, can be utilized in structural analysis. Weber's adherence to the abstract–real dichotomy is also explicit. He defines the activity of science as a process of abstraction and specifies his primary goal in discussion of the ideal type as identification of the particular kind of abstraction which is peculiar to the social sciences.

Although Althusser has not undertaken a specific analysis of

Weber's approach, a structuralist critique of Weber's methodology has been formulated by other social theorists who share that
perspective, most notably Paul Hirst and Barry Hindess. These
theorists, furthermore, have concentrated on one aspect of
Weber's approach which is of particular interest in the present
context: the "ideological" nature of the concepts he employs.
However, this interest in Weber by structuralist theorists is, in
some senses, curious. From the perspective of Althusser's theory,
Weber is as guilty of the errors implicit in the empiricist
epistemology as any positivist; yet structuralists take great pains to
refute Weber's position specifically, rather than subsume it under
their general critique of positivism, and this attention is not acci-
dental. It is indicative of the complex relationship between
Weber's methodology and the structuralist approach, a complexity which is not immediately apparent in Althusser's account.

Paul Hirst's critique of Weber's theory of concept formation
is one instance of his thesis that the forms of classification in a
sociological theory cannot be independent of the forms of
theoretical explanation. He develops the position that within any
social theory the objects to be classified are constituted by the
concepts provided by the theory itself. Hirst, who demonstrates
his thesis by showing how this connection between categories of
classification and theoretical presuppositions operates in the
work of a number of social theorists (among them Max Weber),
begins his critique of Weber with the assertion that the
"transcendental presupposition" of Weber's sociological theory is
the valuing human subject (1976:60). This transcendental
presupposition, Hirst argues, is the constitutive element of his
social theory and thus the basis for the categories of classification
in his empirical analyses. But it is a presupposition, Hirst claims,
which leads Weber into a series of methodological difficulties,
and the first is relativism. Because Weber denies the existence of
absolute values, he is forced to treat the values of the subjects he
studies as equivalent. He cannot, therefore, make comparative
judgments among these values, which results in his adoption of
radical relativism. Weber's second problem is nominalism. Hirst
asserts that because social-scientific investigators choose subjective meanings on the basis of their personal values, "the subjective meaning of the actor is in the hands of the interpreter of
action" (1976:74). And since these subjective meanings are the
basis of social scientists' ideal types, it follows that Weber's ideal-
typical methodology rests on nominalist grounds (1976:75).

Hirst applies this critique of Weber's sociological theory to specific aspects of his thought. Turning to Weber's concept of social action, he argues that Weber's presupposition of the valuing human subject entails the assumption that this subject acts rationally. For Weber, he asserts, the category of rational action is primary and thus he categorizes all nonrational action as "subhuman" (1976:73). This interpretation of Weber's theory of action is unwarranted, but Hirst propounds an even more bizarre thesis about Weber's ideal-type theory. Hirst interprets the ideal type as a means of selecting the facts which the social scientist studies and as a mechanism for specifying the significance of those facts. Ideal types are formed by combining the values of those who produce the concrete action (social actors) and the values of the scholar.

The problem with this procedure, Hirst argues, is that it results in the "total relativism" of theory in the cultural sciences (1976:77). He illustrates what he sees as the serious consequences of the relativism of ideal typical analysis through examination of the ideal types of legitimate domination. Weber, he asserts, defines domination as a "personal relationship" constituted by the meanings endowed on it by ruler and ruled. This definition is relativistic, Hirst argues, because it follows that legitimacy, which is a product of those subjective meanings, cannot be judged apart from the social setting in which it occurs. Hirst moves from this statement to his conclusion: Since it is the ruler and not the ruled who establishes the parameters of the social setting and thus controls the definition of legitimacy, Weber's theory glorifies the ruler or (as Hirst defines it) the *Übermensch*. The *Übermensch* creates the conditions of domination and, as such, is the "hero" of Weber's theory of legitimate domination (1976:87).

The structuralist critique of Weber's methodology by Barry Hindess follows similar lines, although its conclusions are less sweeping. Like Hirst, Hindess points to Weber's reliance on the valuing, purposeful human subject as the fundamental presupposition of his methodology (1977:29). He argues that Weber sees the essence of human action to be the ultimate choice of values by the human subject; but, like Hirst, Hindess draws some unfounded conclusions from this observation. He begins by labeling the basic presupposition of Weber's methodology a "religious conception," then argues that Weber sees the meaning of an action to be a "transcendent entity" not subject to empirical observation (1977:34). This entails two problems for Weber's ideal-typical methodology. It follows that ideal types, based on subjective meanings, cannot be considered empirical tools of social-scientific analysis; rather, they are "unreal" because the social observer can only postulate subjective meanings (1977:35). Also, the individualistic basis of ideal types creates a problem for analysis of nonindividual social phenomena. To explain social phenomena on a supraindividual level, the Weberian social scientist must necessarily abandon the individualistic basis of ideal types. This, Hindess insists, results in a serious methodo-logical contradiction (1978:170).

The critiques of Weber's methodology by Hindess and Hirst raise a number of important issues. First, both critiques are, in a strict sense, derivative of the epistemological critique implicit in Althusser's position. Weber's "errors" with regard to his transcendental presupposition of the valuing subject are, from the structuralist perspective, a product of his larger "error" with regard to the two dichotomies of empiricism which Althusser reveals. Second, the critiques of Hindess and Hirst can easily be shown to rest on erroneous interpretations of Weber's theory. It can be argued against Hirst that Weber does not in any sense in-terpret nonrational action as "sub-human"; such a conclusion reveals misunderstanding of Weber's entire sociological pro-gram. Against Hindess, it can be argued that Weber does not regard the subjective meanings of social actors as a "transcendent entity" not subject to empirical observation. The empirical basis of ideal types is rooted in his assumption of the availability of subjective meanings in the social world. Furthermore, the nature of the conclusions they adduce from their analyses of Weber's work is evidence of the polemical intent of those analyses. Their conclusions are not a result of careful analysis of Weber's position but of a preconceived desire to expose a fundamental error in Weber's methodology, whether or not that error exists.

The primary significance of the critiques of Hindess and Hirst, however, is in another aspect of their work: both theorists expose the essential problem between Weber and the struc-turalists, which does not emerge as clearly in Althusser's strictly epistemological account. The arguments of Hindess and Hirst are designed to show that Weber's fundamental presupposition of the valuing human subject skews his analysis in a particular direction or, in other words, deprives it of "objectivity." The result is a social theory which interprets social structure as a product of subjective meaning bestowal. This, clearly, is anathema to structuralists. But although rejection of the Weberian approach to social structure is the object of the structuralist critique, the presupposition that informs this critique should be clearly specified. A critique which points to lack of an objective basis for analysis in a particular theorist logically entails belief in such a basis in the theorist who makes the critique. In other words the structuralists, by faulting Weber for not providing an objective basis for analysis, must at the same time assume that an objective basis *can* be defined.[3] The importance of the critiques of Hindess and Hirst, then, is that they reveal this presupposition of objectivity, and this is the fundamental issue between Weber and the structuralists.

If it is asserted that the structuralist critique of Weber presupposes the possibility of "objective" social-scientific analysis, then the next step must be to explore the structuralists' definition of objectivity, which is no easy task. Presupposition of an objective basis is an element of the structuralist methodology but is nowhere stated explicitly, and a number of factors may be cited for their reluctance to discuss this issue directly. First and most significantly, repudiation of the naive positivist position on objectivity has created a situation in the social sciences in which any discussion of objectivity is suspect. Discrediting the positivists' thesis that the facts of the social sciences are as "objective" as those of the natural sciences has cast a shadow over all discussions of the topic. Structuralists, furthermore, are particularly sensitive to the difficulties incumbent on an antipositivist understanding of objectivity because they themselves have been instrumental in exposing the fallacies of the positivist position.

Second, the failure of structuralists to formulate a theory of objectivity may be attributed to the simple fact that it is much easier to criticize other theorists' lack of objectivity than to formulate an alternative conception. Structuralists' exposures of the nonneutral, ideological character of the concepts of other social scientists are brilliantly executed and in most cases completely accurate, and this applies to their critique of Weber as well. The structuralists' argument that Weber's basic values (his "transcendental presuppositions") determine the concepts and categories of his sociological theory and, furthermore, that these concepts cannot be taken to be neutral because his values determine the direction of his analysis is irrefutable; but it should be

noted that Weber would have absolutely no quarrel with this indictment. It should be clear from the present analysis of Weber's
theory of concept formation that he does not deny that values
play a constitutive role in the construction of social scientists'
ideal types. Weber does not claim neutrality for his concepts,
however, because he argues that no concepts can be neutral in
the sense of free from values. But in their critique of Weber,
structuralists assume a rather different position. By exposing the
lack of neutrality of Weber's concepts, they imply that neurtral
concepts can be formulated—without specifying how this might
be done.

In their critique of Weber, then, structuralists seriously
misinterpret Weber's concept of "value neutrality" and this
misinterpretation distorts their assessment of his position. Weber's
famous and widely misunderstood concept of value neutrality
refers to his position that the analysis of the social scientist cannot
be used to scientifically establish the superiority of one value position over another. Structuralists seem to miss this definition entirely; they also confuse the discussion by failing to distinguish between the theoretical presupposition of scientific analysis and the
specific, normative commitments of the researcher. It was noted
above that Weber is less aware of this distinction than he should
be, but this criticism applies to structuralists as well. Finally, the
structuralist critique glosses over the extent to which adherence to
the canons of science can be considered a "value." This was an
issue of deep concern to Weber, and his answer is very clear: Pursuit of scientific truth is definitely a "value" position. Structuralists
not only confuse the complex issues in this question, but fail even
to identify it as a significant question.

A third reason for the difficulties in the attempt to define the
structuralists' position on objectivity can be traced to Althusser's
perspective. It was noted above that Althusser argues that empiricists, because of their fundamental misunderstanding of the
nature of scientific knowledge, have cast the question of objectivity in the wrong terms; so Althusser seeks to rectify this error
and thus redefine objectivity by reformulating the question.
Instead of dealing with objectivity in the empiricists' terms, he
poses it in terms of the relationship between the world of thought
and the real world. As he puts it, objectivity is achieved by
discovering the "mechanism" by which the "cognitive appropriation" of the real object can be achieved in the realm of thought.

Careful reading of the passages in which Althusser discusses this problem leads to two conclusions of paramount importance to understanding his definition of objectivity: the world of thought and the real world are strictly separate, and the production of scientific concepts is not dependent on a relationship between these two worlds. In sum, Althusser concludes that the "mechanism" by which scientific concepts appropriate objects in the real world is found wholly within the realm of thought. Thus the principal error of empiricism is the assumption that the gap between the realms of thought and reality can be bridged.

Althusser arrives at these conclusions concerning the relationship between thought and reality in his discussion of the production of scientific concepts, that is, of Generalities I, II, and III. This theory was discussed above, but its full implications have yet to be examined. Briefly, Althusser argues that scientific "knowledges" are produced by the operation of Generalities II, the epistemological assumptions of a particular tradition, on Generalities I, the scientific concepts supplied by that tradition. It follows from this theory that significant advances in science have nothing to do with "better" conceptualization on the level of Generalities I, if "better conceptualization" is defined as construction of concepts which are truer representations of the real world. Rather, the "epistemological breaks" which Althusser identifies are the result of the discovery of logical contradictions between the concepts of Generalities I and the methodological presuppositions of Generalities II.

This position is nicely illustrated by Althusser's analysis of the nature of the revolution accomplished by Marx, who began his analysis of capitalism with the concepts of classical economists, which constituted the category of Generalities I in his time. But as Althusser interprets it, Marx made no attempt to reconstruct these concepts so that they reflect social reality as it exists in capitalist society more accurately. He interprets Marx as attempting to discover logical contradictions between these concepts and the methodological presuppositions, the "problematic" of classical economics, and his success allowed him to break away from this problematic and open what Althusser refers to as a new "continent" of thought which did not exist prior to his theoretical work. As Althusser sees it, Marx's breakthrough is not that he reveals the "objective reality" of capitalism in the sense of exposing the true, empirically accurate facts of capitalist society. Rather, Althusser identifies Marx's breakthrough as revealing the logical contradictions inherent in the scientific enterprise of the classical economists.

The way in which Althusser transforms the traditional approach to objectivity in the social sciences should be clear from this analysis of his treatment of Marx's work. Questions of the objectivity of social-scientific concepts have usually been cast in terms of the correspondence between those concepts and the "real" world. The problem of objectivity is thus seen as making scientific concepts more accurate reflections or representations of that reaity, which Althusser specifically rejects. He argues that, due to the rigid separation between the realms of thought and reality, the traditional heading "objectivity" involves problems which must be conceived as wholly internal to the world of thought. He asserts that the objectivity of scientific concepts is determined through analysis of the logical relationship among concepts on the three levels of conceptualization (Generalities I, II, and III), an analysis that is completely divorced from the real world.

Several conclusions regarding the structuralists' approach to objectivity can be deduced from Althusser's position. It follows that discussions of objectivity which revolve around the correspondence between scientific concepts and the real world are ruled out of consideration. It also follows that another traditional concern under the heading "objectivity," the effort to make the social scientist's concepts "neutral," must also be rejected. If the social scientist begins with concepts supplied by the scientific community and the validity of the analysis is dependent solely on the internal relationship of these concepts, any attempt to ensure the "neutrality" of these concepts becomes irrelevant. Hindess puts this point succinctly:

> If we were to send into the field a team of ideal observers, stripped of all concepts (to avoid the possible influence of alien categories), they would return with nothing to report and no vocabulary with which to report it. [1973:40]

Althusser's radical transformation of the question of objectivity has not gone unnoticed by his fellow social theorists, and two principal criticisms of his position have been advanced. It is argued that Althusser's absolute separation of the realms of thought and reality is untenable. Criticis have noted that establishing a viable relationship between these two realms is a necessary prerequisite of any adequate social theory, and Althusser's failure to supply this is a fundamental flaw in his analysis (Benton, 1977:186; Glucksmann, 1972:74; Callinicos, 1976:110). It also is argued that Althusser's denial of universal criteria of scientificity, on the one hand, and on the other hand his assertion of epistemological concepts of universal applicability involves him in a contradiction (Glucksmann, 1974:96).[4] Both of these criticisms are certainly valid, but despite these serious flaws in Althusser's theory his transformation of the question of objectivity can be interpreted as a valuable contribution to the philosophy of social science. It can be maintained, in other words, that various aspects of Althusser's theory of objectivity offer valuable insights which are not provided by the traditional approach.

The strengths and the weaknesses of Althusser's theory of objectivity can best be illustrated by comparing that theory not with the empiricist theory he criticizes but with the theory of concept formation advanced by Weber. Although Althusser sees Weber as falling prey to the real–abstract dichotomy of empiricism, and the two theories seem to be diametrically opposed, close examination reveals significant commonalities.[5] In the discussion of Althusser's theory of objectivity it emerged that, for Althusser, the production of scientific knowledge begins and ends in the realm of thought. Although he claims that this process moves from abstract concepts (Generalities I) to concrete ones (Generalities III), his definition of "concrete" must not be confused with "real" (in the sense "part of the real world"). Rather, his "concrete" concepts are transformations of the raw material from which they are drawn. Althusser is very clear, furthermore, on the nature of this raw material: the historically evolved concepts of the scientific community. These concepts are manipulated according to the principles of scientific logic and method and are thereby transformed into scientific knowledge.

Weber's theory, in contrast, begins with what Althusser would call the empiricist understanding of scientific knowledge as abstraction from the real. With respect to the social sciences, this entails that Weber see social-scientific concepts as abstractions from the raw material of social-scientific analysis. But it was noted in the analysis of Weber's theory of concept formation that he defines the raw material of the social sciences as the social actors' concepts, and these concepts are "real" in the sense that they are constitutive of social reality. But Weber makes it clear that this "reality" is of a different order than the "reality" to which the natural sciences refer. Actors' concepts represent a reality which is preselected by the social actors' bestowal of meaning. Thus, for Weber, the raw material from which social-scientific knowledge is "produced" is concepts supplied by the social world. Further, Weber defines the process by which these concepts are transformed into ideal types, and hence tools of social-scientific analysis, as logical manipulation that adheres to the rules of logic and scientific method. Thus Weber's theory reveals two commonalities between his approach and that of Althusser: both see concept formation in the social sciences as beginning with preselected concepts, and both define scientific knowledge as produced by manipulation of those concepts according to the rules of logic and scientific method.

Thus the relationship between the two theories is more complex than it at first appears. Comparison, furthermore, pinpoints what can be identified as Althusser's principal contribution to an understanding of objectivity in the social sciences, and his theory offers one clear advantage over Weber's: he describes, much more completely than Weber, the precise nature of the production of scientific concepts. By dividing the process into Generalities I, II, and III, Althusser clarifies aspects which are, in Weber's account, sometimes vague or confusing. His specification of the raw materials, methods, and results of scientific analysis provides clear guidelines for concept formation in the social sciences.

But juxtaposition of the two theories also reveals the principal liability of Althusser's theory. Despite their commonalities, there is a serious disagreement which cannot be ignored. Althusser claims that the raw materials of scientific knowledge are the concepts of the scientific community, Weber that they are the concepts of the social actors. Althusser's position on this issue stems from his insistence on separation of the realms of thought and reality, but his failure to provide an understanding of the relationship between these two realms is the Achilles' heel of his elaborate theory. To give Althusser his due, it must be conceded that he is not unaware of this difficulty. He does not deny that specifying the relationship between theory and reality is a central problem for social science. However, his position that these two realms are absolutely separate seems to imply that positing *any* relationship between the real and the theoretical must fall back into the empiricist problematic. This, it seems, is the principal reason for Althusser's refusal to define any relationship between the two realms.

What Althusser's theory comes to, then, is that social theory has two options: reliance on the empiricist understanding of the relationship between the real and the theoretical realms, or denial of any relationship. But there is a third option, implicit in the work of phenomenologists and ordinary-language philosophers. Both schools argue that the raw material of concept formation in the social sciences is the actors' concepts, not the concepts of the scientific community. Further, they argue that the actors' concepts are constitutive of social reality, and if the aim of social-scientific analysis is to study social reality, it must begin with the actors' concepts. It does not follow, however, that the reality created by actors' concepts is the same reality to which the positivist social scientist refers. The positivist defines reality as a realm of "objective facts" which are methodologically indistinguishable from the facts of the natural sciences. The reality defined by phenomenologists and ordinary-language philosophers, in contrast, is created by the concepts of the social actors. By declaring that the actors' concepts are the raw material of concept formation in the social sciences, these approaches provide a clear connection between social theory and social reality, but this connection avoids reification of reality along positivist lines and is, hence, an alternative to both the positivist position and Althusser's rigid separation of these two realms. The positions of these two schools would of course be anathema to Althusser, but they provide precisely the element which his theory lacks: understanding the relationship between social theory and social reality that avoids the positivists' presupposition of a realm of "objective facts." Althusser's failure to specify the relationship between theory and reality leaves social science in a nether world of concepts which have no reference point.

Althusser's contribution to the philosophy of social science is that he very clearly reveals the liabilities of the positivist understanding of objectivity and he outlines a comprehensive theory of concept formation in the social sciences. But his theory fails to provide what was identified at the beginning of this book as the primary requirement of contemporary social-scientific methodology: a conceptual apparatus which can unite analysis of the subjective world of the social actor with analysis of the structural forms of society undertaken by the social scientist. Instead of providing such a conceptual apparatus, Althusser "solves" the problem by declaring the two worlds to be absolutely separate. Unfortunately, this turns out not to be a solution at all.

3. Critical Theory

The critique of positivism which has been posed by the group now commonly referred to as "critical theorists" has many similarities to that of Althusser. Both have their roots in the Marxist tradition and both are primarily concerned with positivism's inability to provide an objective basis for social-scientific analysis, but within these broad limits the nature of the two schools' critiques differs significantly.

The emphasis of Althusser's critique is primarily episte-mological. Because his attack on positivism focuses on the epistemological assumptions embodied in the empiricist prob-lematic, his approach to the problem of objectivity is cast in epistemological terms and his solution, rigid separation of the worlds of thought and reality, is dictated by his epistemological perspective. Critical theorists, in contrast, see the gap between thought and reality—or, as they put it, between theory and prac-tice—to be the central problem of social theory. They define their critique of positivism as having a "practical intent" which determines its theoretical inquiries. Like Althusser, they are con-cerned with the empiricist dichotomies and, furthermore, ex-plicitly reject Weber's position because of his adherence to these dichotomies (Wilson, 1976:299). But in contrast to structuralism, their principal theme is explicitly normative. Their critique of positivism emphasizes the negative effects of sociological theories based on the empiricist problematic. They define the technical manipulation made possible by the empiricist approach to social-scientific analysis as one of the principal problems of contem-porary social theory.

The present examination of critical theory will focus on Jürgen Habermas, with particular emphasis on his early work. For most contemporary social scientists, Habermas' early work is definitive of the approach of critical theory. The theses in his ear-ly work, particularly in *Knowledge and Human Interests*, have been extensively discussed in the social sciences and thus have had the greatest impact on the thinking of social scientists. Also, it is in his early work that Habermas deals most explicitly with the methodological problems of the social sciences. Finally, although Habermas has in recent years been occupied with themes quite distinct from those of his early work, his recent works have not yet received much attention among social scientists (in large part because they have only recently become available in English).

In his early work, Habermas' principal concern was to reveal the errors of positivist social science and to detail the detrimental effect of positivist thinking in the social sciences. But his point of departure is not immediately apparent; it is, at the same time, very contemporary and deeply historical. Habermas insists throughout that his analysis is motivated by a "practical intent" that is revealed in his definition of a concern that is a principal theme of these works: the technical manipulation of society facilitated by positivist social science. However, Habermas' understanding of the error of positivist social theory that leads to this manipulative capacity is rooted in his historical examination of the role of theory which goes back, ultimately, to Aristotle. Habermas advances a historical argument against positivist social science which rests on the assertion that it has abandoned the proper relationship between theory and social reality that was first articulated by the Greeks. The analysis begins, then, with this historical argument.

Habermas defines the Greek understanding of the relationship between theory and practice from several perspectives. He argues that Greek theory served a liberating function with regard to practice, defining theoretical activity as a means of separating knowledge from opinion and thus liberating individuals from the false appearances of the social world. But the Greeks also defined theory and practice as two different spheres of being, a distinction that is particularly important for politics because the Greeks defined political questions as partaking of both the theoretical and practical spheres. Aristotle, who is particularly clear on this point, defines politics as a "practical science," asserting that it cannot assume the stature of a rigorous, purely theoretical science because it deals with "prudent" understanding of practical situations. Furthermore, because politics is concerned with human action, it is inseparable from moral questions. And he insists that prudent understanding, characteristic of politics, calls for a form of reasoning distinct from that in the rigorous sciences (1973a:41ff.).

Habermas claims that positivist social science violates all these understandings of the relationship between theory and practice established in Greek thought. Positivists replace the liberating function of theory with a technical function; they define the relationship of theory to practice exclusively in terms of technical manipulation of social life facilitated by theoretical inquiries. Habermas directs this aspect of his critique at what he calls "Weberian social science," which, he claims, "allots to the social sciences the task of producing knowledge capable of being utilized technically" (1977a:66). But positivists also reject Aristotle's definition of the character of theoretical inquiries into political and social questions; they declare that politics can and should be a "rigorous" science, methodologically indistinguishable from the natural sciences. They further assert that the reasoning appropriate to the social sciences is identical to that in the natural sciences. For the positivist, only the form of reasoning that is characteristic of the natural sciences can be labeled "scientific"; thus this form alone is appropriate to any activity that aspires to the status of science. Finally, positivists claim that this definition of scientific reasoning is completely divorced from evaluative considerations (1973a:254ff.).

It is Habermas' intention to reveal the errors of positivism on each of these points. His goal, most broadly conceived, is to restore the critical or liberating function of social theory as it was defined by the Greeks. Crucial to this accomplishment is definition of a form of reasoning appropriate to the social sciences, one which is tailored to the evaluative concerns of these disciplines. However, he must first reveal the errors of the positivist attitude toward values. He argues that positivists err by claiming that social science can be free of value concerns and by asserting that it has no value component. Against this, Habermas says that positivists conceal a commitment to technical rationality behind a facade of "value freedom." His intent to establish this argument informs his consideration of the broader question of the relationship between knowledge and interest.

The conviction that guides Habermas' analysis in *Knowledge and Human Interests* is that the positivist assumptions that inform contemporary philosophy and social theory must be refuted before substantive alternatives can be offered. In his "Postscript," he states this purpose very clearly: "In my book I have summarily traced the history of ideas by dealing with these problems up to the critical point where the conception of a new and transformed transcendental philosophy became necessary" (1973b:165). He also states what he sees as the principal defect of the positivist position that he attacks in the book: Positivism "gave up entirely the demand of a reflexive foundation in the interest of objectivism" (1973b:164). Thus his principal concern is not an extended critique of positivism nor explication of his "transformed conception of transcendental philosophy," but analysis of a number of eighteenth-and nineteenth-century thinkers who, in Habermas' view, can be useful in formulating an alternative to the positivist perspective.

It should be noted, however, that although Habermas identifies significant positions of the post-Enlightenment thinkers that comprise the studies in *Knowledge and Human Interests*, he concludes that none of them provides the epistemological perspective which he is seeking for the social sciences. The book begins with an analysis of Hegel, and although Habermas has much praise for Hegel's perspective, he argues that his transcendental philosophy fails on two counts: it is preoccupied with the postulates of the philosophy of identity and it ultimately relies on the conception of absolute knowledge (1971:5–21). In the next chapter he takes up Marx's perspective, and again, though Marx gets high marks in many regards, his approach is also found wanting: "The philosophical foundation of [Marx's] materialism proves itself insufficient to establish an unconditional phenomenological self-reflection of knowledge and thus prevent the positivist atrophy of epistemology" (1971:42). Subsequent discussion of Peirce and Dilthey reveals that these thinkers contribute an element that is missing in both the Marxist and positivist approaches: a self-reflection of the sciences. But ultimately these approaches are also found to be seriously deficient. Habermas argues that both are so under the spell of positivism that they cannot escape its demand for objectivism (1971:69).

In the second half of his book, Habermas analyzes three thinkers whose work—in combination, not singly—provides an outline of the proper methodological perspective for the social sciences. Kant and Fichte, he states, developed the concept of "interest of reason" which reveals the connection between knowledge and interest. The importance of Kant's work, in particular, is that his analysis of the necessary subjective conditions of possible experience provides exactly what Habermas is seeking: a "nonobjectivist foundation for knowledge" (1973b:164). But Habermas is careful to avoid the temptation of arguing that a return to Kant is the solution to the problem posed by positivism, because "the dimension of self-reflection cannot be rehabilitated as such by a mere return to the historical phase of the philosophy of reflection" (1971:189). What is needed is a methodological example that will demonstrate that this element of self-reflection has emerged in conjunction with positivism.

The example Habermas chooses is Freudian psychoanalysis. His discussion of Freud is central not only to his analysis in this work but to his quest for an alternative to the positivist epistemology that informs his subsequent works. Freudian psychoanalysis provides an example of synthesis between two elements that, it emerges, Habermas defines as necessary elements of social-scientific method: the self-reflective or hermeneutic element found in the interpretive approaches but missing from the positivist position, and the nomological, causal analysis that is characteristic of the methods of the natural sciences. Freud's approach, Habermas asserts, is unique in its combination of these two elements:

> A final peculiarity of the logic of general interpretation results from the combination of hermeneutic understanding with causal explanation: understanding itself obtains explanatory power. [1971:270]

Because it combines these elements, Freudian psychoanalysis provides a model of the proper relationship between the social theorist and society, a model that is consonant with the Greek conception of theory that informs Habermas' analysis. Methodologically, Freudian psychoanalysis accomplishes this by integrating the search for nomological knowledge with self-reflection. In a broader sense, however, it is successful because the goal of psychoanalysis is identical to that of a properly critical social science: the emancipation of the subject.

The full significance of his analysis of Freud is revealed in Habermas' theory of the relationship between knowledge and interest. His argument centers on the assertion that the points of view from which reality is apprehended have their roots in the "natural history of the human species," and he identifies three such points of view or "cognitive interests": the technical, the practical, and the emancipatory. Habermas attempts to establish that these interests are common to all human social life and can be identified with particular aspects of our natural history. His more immediate concern, however, is that each corresponds to a particular form of knowledge in modern social analysis:

technical interest generates the knowledge produced by the empirical-analytic sciences; practical interest produces the knowledge characteristic of the historical-hermeneutic sciences; but only the third interest, the emancipatory, is tied to the form of knowledge which, in his defintion, is the proper aim of theoretical inquiries: critical knowledge, which, his analysis shows, has been abandoned by modern social theorists due to the influence of positivism. It was interest in emancipation, Habermas states, which informed the Greeks' attempt to separate appearance from reality and thus liberate individuals from the false appearances of the social world, and only the renewal of emancipatory interest can reinstate the proper role of theoretical inquiries (1971:308ff.).

Shortly after the publication of *Knowledge and Human Interests,* Habermas published an extensive analysis of the major contemporary approaches to the methodology of the social sciences, *Zur Logik der Sozialwissenschaften* (1970c). In a sense, this book completes the task he began in *Knowledge and Human Interests:* examining the alternatives to positivism for contemporary social science. In the first work, Habermas assessed the alternatives to positivism in post-Enlightenment philosophy in an attempt to find the basis for a "transformed transcendental philosophy." In the second, he altered his focus in two ways: he is interested in the narrower question of the methodology of the social sciences and he turns almost exclusively to contemporary positions, many of them specific reactions to the rise of positivism in the social sciences. But taken together, the two books form a unity; they provide a comprehensive survey of post-Enlightenment thought from the perspective of the problematic created by positivism.

Habermas begins his analysis with the sweeping statement that only two positions are considered in contemporary methodological discussions: positivism and hermeneutics. Noting that adherents of neither position are attentive to the arguments of their opponents, he defines his role in the dispute as uncovering the confusions in both positions with the aim of "bringing the social sciences under one roof" (1970c:73). The manner in which he proposes to accomplish this is an echo of his assessment of Freud's method in *Knowledge and Human Interests:* integration of the analytic and hermeneutic methods (1970c:97), which provides the central theme of the extensive discussions that comprise the work. Habermas' analyses of both sides of the methodological dispute follow distinct patterns. He finds fault with approaches that search for nomological explanations in the social sciences for ignoring the historical conditions of action. These approaches, he repeatedly asserts, are too abstract; in their search for universal laws they miss the historical reality of social life. But those who adopt a hermeneutic or interpretive approach are also criticized. These approaches, Habermas declares, are relativistic and unsystematic. The social sciences must be able to go beyond the mere description of social action; they must be able to systematize their observations and offer critical standards of judgment.

Habermas does not present a clear picture of what his integration of the nomological and hermeneutic approaches would entail, but in his analysis of the interpretive approaches he presents a number of arguments that are particularly relevant to this analysis. His critique of Winch and ordinary-language analysis is especially pertinent. Instead of attacking Winch on the well-known grounds of relativism, Habermas argues that Winch errs in proposing a methodology for the social sciences which his position cannot accommodate. Winch advocates analysis of social life in terms of the "language games" of the social actors, but fails to take account of the status of the game by which such an analysis would be accomplished. In other words, he proposes a "metalanguage" of analysis without justifying or explaining its status (1970c: 236–44).

This critique of Winch is both accurate and insightful, but in his critique of another interpretive approach, hermeneutics, Habermas reveals his principal objection to what has been referred to as the "subjective critique." Habermas sees hermeneutics, and in particular the hermeneutics of Gadamer, as superior to the Wittgensteinian approach in one respect: unlike Wittgenstein, Gadamer does not interpret language games as monadic unities but as "inwardly and outwardly porous." Despite this advantage over the Wittgensteinians, Habermas argues that Gadamer, like Winch, fails to take account of the "power of reflection developed in understanding" (1970c:283). The right of reflection, Habermas claims, "calls for a reference system that goes beyond the framework of tradition" (1970c:285). Gadamer is bound to the limits of tradition, just as Winch and the Wittgensteinians are bound to the limits of the social actors' concepts, but both kinds of limits, Habermas argues, are illegitimate.

An interpretive sociology that hypostasizes language to the subject of forms of life and of tradition ties itself to the idealist presupposition that linguistically articulated consciousness determines the material practice of life. But the objective framework of social action is not exhausted by the dimension of intersubjectively intended and symbolically transmitted meaning. The linguistic infrastructure of a society is part of a complex that, however symbolically mediated, is also constituted by the constraint of reality—by the constraint of outer nature that enters into procedures for technical mastery and by the constraint of inner nature reflected in the repressive character of social power relations. These two categories of constraint are not only the object of interpretations; behind the back of language, they also affect the very grammatical rules according to which we interpret the world. *Social actions can only be comprehended in an objective framework that is constituted conjointly by language, labor, and domination.* [1970c: 289][6]

In opposition to this position, Habermas calls for a "hermeneutically clarified and historically adjusted functionalism" (1970c:306).

The position that Habermas advocates for the social sciences can now be more accurately located in terms of the concerns of this analysis. Habermas, unlike Althusser, sees one of the principal tasks of social theory to be clear definition of the relationship between thought and reality. Also in contrast to Althusser, Habermas is very attuned to the issues raised by what has been identified as the "subjective critique" of positivism: phenomenology and ordinary-language analysis (and also, for Habermas, hermeneutics). The upshot of Habermas' concern with subjective meaning is that, unlike the structuralists, he does not dismiss the meaning-endowing role of the social actor as irrelevant to the rigorous kind of analysis required by a comprehensive social theory. Rather, he accepts the basic thesis of these schools: social actors' meanings play a constitutive role in the construction of social reality. Thus the project which Habermas undertakes is more complex than that of Althusser: he must establish an understanding of the relationship between thought and reality which avoids the pitfalls of positivism, and he must establish an "objective framework" for critical social theory which takes account of the meaning-constitutive role of the social actor.

Since Habermas insists that social reality is constituted not only by language but also by work and domination, which distinguishes his approach from the subjective critique discussed above, this aspect will be the focus of the following analysis. Habermas' departure from these approaches can be addressed by attempting to answer the following question: How does Habermas explain and justify the "objective framework" of social action in terms of a method for social-scientific analysis?

In the course of his work, Habermas offers two models of how the social scientist comprehends social action: the psychoanalytic model in *Knowledge and Human Interests* and the model of "communicative competence" in his more recent works. Thus examination of these models should reveal his understanding of how the social scientist comprehends social action in terms of an "objective framework." The psychoanalytic model rests on a straightforward analogy between the relationship of the psychoanalyst to the patient and the relationship of the social scientist to society. As Habermas understands it, in the therapeutic process the psychoanalyst's first task is to attempt to understand the statements of the patient in the context of the meaning system created by the patient's mental disorder. In this he is consistent with one of the first tenets of Freudian psychoanalysis: the complex of meanings which creates "reality" for the patient must be uncovered before therapy can begin. Only after the psychoanalyst has fully comprehended the patient's definition of reality can the goal of therapy be realized: bringing the patient's conception of reality into line with reality as it is defined by the larger society (1971:220ff.).

Habermas identifies two aspects of this understanding of the therapeutic process which can be used as a model to explain the relationship between the critical social theorist and society. The first is the psychoanalyst's attempt to comprehend the patient's definition of reality. Applying this to the situation of the social scientist, Habermas argues that it is necessary for the social scientist to fully comprehend the reality created by the concepts of the society under investigation. It is in this stage of social-scientific analysis that Habermas sees the tools of the ordinary-language philosopher, the hermeneutic investigator, and the phenomenologist to be valuable. Their methods of analysis allow the social theorist to comprehend the social actors' concepts and thus to communicate in terms of the reality created by the social actors. Habermas then develops a corollary of this principle which is also derived from the psychoanalytic situation. The psychoanalyst cannot claim to have "explained" the patient's disorder unless that explanation is cast in terms of the patient's definition of reality, and the same is true of the social theorist: unless the explanation of social reality offered by the social scientist is understandable to the social actor, it fails as an explanation. This corollary, it should be noted, is one of the principal theses of the approaches of both Schutz and Winch.

In his identification of the second aspect of the psychoanalytic process which can be employed in his model, Habermas moves away from the perspective provided by these schools. In psychoanalysis, the patient is "cured" when the psychoanalyst brings the patient's reality into line with reality as it is defined in the larger cultural context. Using this aspect of the psychoanalytic process as a model to explain the relationship between the social theorist and society entails that the reality created by the concepts of social actors be brought into line with another conception of reality which is, in some analogous sense, more objective. In the psychoanalytic situation, the patient's reality can be defined as "subjective" in the sense that it is solitary, while the definition of reality supplied by the culture is "objective" in the sense that it is shared. In the social theorist's analysis of society, this means that the social actors' definition of reality must be labeled "subjective" and, hence, must be brought into line with "objective" reality, created, as Habermas puts it, conjointly by language, labor, and domination. In other words, Habermas argues (through this therapeutic model), that the social actors' subjective meaning must be completed or, better, corrected by juxtaposing it to the objective framework that is constitutive of social action.

The second model which Habermas proposes as a guide for the social scientist's analysis of society is developed in his discussion of "communicative competence." In recent years, Habermas has concentrated increasingly on this issue, which many commentators refer to as his "linguistic turn." The distinction which serves as the starting point of Habermas' discussion of communicative competence is between communicative and linguistic competence. He asserts that every act of speech necessarily presupposes both of these competencies. He defines linguistic competence as that which provides the speaker the basic qualifications for speech and symbolic interaction. Communicative competence, in contrast, is a more encompassing concept:

> Communicative competence is defined as the ideal speaker's mastery of the dialogue-constitutive universals, irrespective of actual restrictions under empirical conditions. [1970a:369]

Central to Habermas' understanding of communicative competence is his definition of the "ideal speech situation." After asserting that all speech acts necessarily presuppose communicative competence, he states that communicative competence, in turn, presupposes that all speech is potentially oriented to the idea of truth (1970a:372). What Habermas means by this statement is revealed most clearly in his distinction between distorted or repressed speech and speech that is oriented toward the idea of truth, that is, ideal speech.

> No matter how the intersubjectivity of mutual understanding may be deformed, the *design* of an ideal speech situation is necessarily implied in the structure of potential speech. [1970a:372]

The repressive institutions of society thus produce distortion of the ideal speech situation which is implicit in all speech, so that the "true consensus" created by ideal speech is replaced by a "false consensus" engineered by those repressive institutions (1970b:131).

With these definitions of communicative competence and ideal and distorted speech, Habermas constructs a model for the activity of the critical social theorist. On the basis of this theory, he can assert that every society will exhibit either a true consensus, based on realization of the potentiality of ideal speech, or a false consensus, which is a product of repressive institutions. The task of the critical social theorist, on this model, is to reveal the design of the ideal speech situation and thus to distinguish between a false and a true consensus.

To show how this model can be implemented and, more specifically, to present a theory in which a distinction between false and true consensus can be made, Habermas attacks a central tenet of positivist social science: the separation of facts and values and the exclusion of values from rationality. He deals with this problem in a discussion of contemporary theories of truth (*Wahrheitstheorien*), and his aim in this analysis is twofold: to refute the "is–ought" dichotomy, central to positivist thought, and to establish the rational character of normative discussions.

The basis of Habermas' argument is his rejection of the positivists' correspondence theory of truth, which dictates that statements are true because they correspond to facts in the world and thus only statements about facts can be declared true or false. The truthfulness of evaluative statements cannot be assessed because such statements do not refer to factual states; so it follows that they are excluded from the realm of rationality. Habermas counters the correspondence theory by arguing that the radical distinction between the epistemology of factual and evaluative statements, assumed by positivists, cannot be substantiated, and that any claim, whether factual or evaluative, is justified discursively, that is, by argumentation (1973c:211–65).

The most important consequence of Habermas' attack on the correspondence theory of truth is his conclusion that evaluative as well as factual statements have a rational basis. For the positivist, evaluative statements are excluded from the realm of rationality because the truth of statements can only be tested by their correspondence to the "real world." But Habermas, by rejecting the correspondence test through his argument that statements are justified discursively, then by rejecting the epistemological distinction between facts and values, removes the impediments to considering the rationality of evaluative statements. This position is essential to his theory of communicative competence. His theory of discursive justification of factual and evaluative statements allows him to move into a realm that positivists had declared off limits: rational justification of evaluative statements.

Also central to this discussion is Habermas' identification of the principle by which evaluative statements are subjected to the test of rationality. He argues that the rational basis of norms depends on their "generalizability." Norms that fail to meet this criterion cannot be discursively redeemed and hence are not rational. The test of generalizability completes Habermas' refutation of positivists' fact–value dichotomy and the resulting restriction of the concept of rationality. And his alternative view has important consequences for the social sciences:

I have sought to prove that practical questions *can* be treated discursively and that it is *possible* for social scientific analysis to take the relation of norm systems to truth methodically into consideration. [1975:117]

In recent years Habermas' discussion of communicative competence has been cast in terms of a subject he labels "universal pragmatics." "The task of universal pragmatics," he declares, "is to identify and reconstruct universal conditions of possible understanding" (1979:1). He advances the thesis that anyone who acts communicatively—that is, anyone who performs speech acts—must raise universal validity claims and suppose that they can be vindicated. This thesis lays the groundwork for a more complete definition of "repressed speech." Speech is repressed, he asserts, when social actors are prevented from realizing validity claims about the institutional arrangements of their society. Every society attempts to justify its institutional arrangements discursively, but when such justification is impossible—that is, when institutional arrangements cannot be justified according to universally valid claims—it can be concluded that speech is repressed.

Habermas' exploration of universal pragmatics provides a more complete statement of the task of critical social theory on the model of communicative competence. It reveals that (1) critical social scientists must uncover the ideal speech situation implicit in all speech, and (2) they must pursue the validity claims of repressed speech and reveal the falseness of these claims. When speech is repressed, the speech acts of social actors create a false consensus through which the validity claims of the society appear to be justified. However, it is social scientists' task to distinguish false consensus from true consensus, which exists when the universal validity claims implicit in all speech are vindicated. Habermas argues that ability to make this distinction is available not only to the social theorist but to all native speakers of a language:

> Reaching an understanding is a normative concept; everyone who speaks a natural language has intuitive knowledge of it and therefore is confident of being able, in principle, to distinguish a true consensus from a false one. [1973a:17]

On the basis of these discussions, it can be concluded that Habermas' aim in both models is to provide a means by which the social scientist can distinguish appearance from reality in the social world. This goal, which the Greeks defined as the basic function of any social theory, informs Habermas' articulation of both models. In the psychoanalytic model, the distinction between appearance and reality is cast in terms of the reality created by social actors' concepts and that created by the objective framework of language, labor, and domination. In the model of communicative competence, it is cast in terms of the distinction between a false and a true consensus. It is clear, in both models, that Habermas is seeking an "objective" basis for analysis by the critical social theorist.

Up to this point, the presentation of Habermas' theory has been largely uncritical, but the broader aim of the examination can now be addressed: the success of Habermas' approach and, consequently, his contribution to the antipositivist critique. To this end, we will examine Habermas' critique of Weber and, in the final chapter, several aspects of Habermas' most recent discussions, to further assess the epistemological significance of his position on objectivity.

Habermas' methodological critique of Weber is in *Zur Logik der Sozialwissenschaften*, where he faults Weber for failing to distinguish clearly between understanding and explanation in the methodology of the social sciences (1970c:84–91). Although Habermas is highly critical of Weber's methodology, his criticism reveals an affinity between Weber's position and the stated goal of Habermas' work. As noted above, Habermas asserts that the purpose of this methodological examination is to integrate a hermeneutical perspective, which focuses on the problem of understanding, with a perspective that allows for nomological, causal analysis of social action. But although Habermas does not acknowledge it, this goal is nearly identical to the goal of Weber's sociological work. Thus, although Habermas dismisses Weber's integration of these two elements as unsuccessful, his criticism should be interpreted in terms of their common methodological purpose.

Habermas' most thorough account of the errors of Weber's perspective is presented in *Legitimation Crisis*, in which he formulates several objections to Weber's concept of rationality that he uses as the basis of his critique of Weber's concept of legitimacy. Weber's concept of rationality is judged to be flawed because it is a strictly instrumental conception. Weber defines rationality as concerned only with the efficient organization of means to ends, which excludes any normative elements (1975:65ff.). This exclusion is shown to be problematic when Weber attempts to develop his conception of legitimacy. Habermas argues:

> If belief in legitimacy is conceived as an empirical phenomenon without an immanent relation to truth, the grounds upon which it is explicitly based have only psychological significance. Whether such grounds can sufficiently stabilize a given belief in legitimacy depends on the institutionalized prejudices and observable behavioral dispositions of the group in question. If, on the other hand, every effective belief in legitimacy is assumed to have an immanent relation to truth, the grounds on which it is explicitly based contain a rational validity claim that can be tested and criticized independently of the psychological effect of these grounds. [1975:97]

A number of important arguments are condensed in this passage, but most immediately, Habermas is making a definitional point against Weber. Weber's concept of legitimacy, he asserts, is flawed because it is a purely empirical and hence psychological concept that erroneously excludes all normative considerations. But a second, more inclusive argument is implicit in the passage. Habermas claims that Weber accepts the positivist separation of facts and values and that this is the root of his erroneous definition of legitimacy. In other words, Weber's acceptance of the positivist dictum that values are not subject to rational judgment leads him to exclude values from his definition of legitimacy and, hence, distorts the meaning of the concept.

Although Habermas' critique of Weber on this point is correct in a strict sense, he glosses over several relevant elements of Weber's approach to the problem of values. In Habermas' terminology, Weber adopts a "decisionist" approach to problems of value in general and the concept of legitimacy in particular. However, the implications of Weber's position are not specified very clearly in Habermas' discussion. Weber's theory of legitimacy rests on the thesis that different kinds of normative commitments are definitive of the different forms of legitimacy. His decisionist approach to norms was dictated by the belief that there is no scientific way of adjudicating opposed normative commitments. This position does not exclude the possibility that the social scientist might argue that one form of legitimacy leads to a type of social arrangement more preferable than another, it dictates that such a preference cannot be granted the status of scientific truth. This view resulted in Weber's conviction that value positions are the outcome of individual decisions rather than scientific judgments.[7]

Against Weber's definition of legitimacy, Habermas asserts the basic principles of his theory of truth: the exclusion of evaluation from the realm of reason is illegitimate and the rationality of normative claims rests on their generalizability. Central to his argument, in this context, is his definition of "rational will." Rational will, he argues, is based on a consensus that emerges as a result of agreement that is free of force; it is rational because the consensus arises from generalizable interests. This definition, he claims, reveals the implicit irrationality of the (Weberian) decisionist theory that rests on the plurality of interests (1975:108).

Finally, Habermas objects to Weber's concept of legitimacy on the grounds that it restricts the proper role of the social scientist. Because Weber's concept is relativistic—that is, because it excludes the possibility of critical assessment of social arrangements—it in effect limits the social scientist to a purely descriptive role. In another context, Habermas states his alternative position on this point:

> Generalizable interests and norms which must be justified in discourses have a nonconventional core in that they are neither empirically *found to exit*, nor simply *posited* by a decision. Rather, they are at once *shaped* in a noncontingent manner and *discovered*. This must be so, if there is any meaning in saying that something like a *rational* human will exists at all. The cognitive purpose of discursive decision-making consists in attaining a consensus about the generalizability of proposed interests. [1973b:177]

In terms of the specific points that Habermas advances against Weber's conception of legitimacy, it can be concluded that his assessment of Weber's position is accurate. Although he does not sufficiently emphasize Weber's departure from the classical positivist position on values, Habermas' central point against Weber is correct: Weber's separation of facts and values leads him to exclude the possibility of the rational resolution of value conflicts. The difficulty with Habermas' approach, however, lies not in his assessment of Weber's position but in his justification of the movement away from the Weberian perspective. By arguing that normative claims and, among them, the claim to legitimacy have universal validity because of their generalizability, Habermas raises a difficult question that Weber carefully avoids: What is the epistemological status of these claims? To assert the universal validity of truth claims is to imply that these claims have a transcultural, if not transcendent, status. But how can such claims be justified?

In the course of *Legitimation Crisis*, Habermas deals with this problem in a number of contexts. At the beginning of the work he discusses what he identifies as the "universal properties" of social systems. Implicit in this discussion is the position that these properties provide a transcultural standard by which social arrangements can be assessed. On the basis of this discussion, he can, for example, conclude that class societies necessarily exhibit "fundamental contradictions" (1975:27). At other points he implies that social arrangements can be assessed on the basis of whether they meet basic human needs. Thus he refers to specific human needs that are not met in bourgeois society (1975:78) and, further, to at least one universal prerequisite of human life: the autonomy of adult subjects (1975:89).

These references suggest that, in opposition to Weber's "relativism," Habermas is proposing substantive normative principles that are universally applicable, but a number of other references throughout *Legitimation Crisis* belie such a conclusion. Habermas frequently refers to the difficulties incumbent on such a view:

> But from a systematic point of view as well, the assumption of basic *material* norms capable of being justified leads to the difficulty that certain normative contents must be theoretically singled-out. Hitherto, philosophical efforts to rehabilitate traditional or—as Winckelmann himself seems inclined—modern natural law, in whatever version, have proved as unavailing as attempts to found a material value ethics. [1975:100]

Other statements throughout the book reinforce this position. He declares that the only norms that can claim generality are those on which *everyone affected* could agree in unfettered discussion (1975:89) and, further, that "the expectation of discursive redemption of normative-validity claims is already contained in the structure of intersubjectivity and makes specially introduced maxims of universality superfluous" (1975:110).

These passages suggest a very different conclusion: the truth of normative claims is dependent on culturally specific normative beliefs, not on universal principles.

Although in *Legitimation Crisis* Habermas does not resolve this ambiguity, in a later work, which develops his theory of legitimacy, he states his position on this issue more succinctly (1979:178–205). He locates his conception with respect to other conceptions of legitimacy. Beginning with the assumption that the classical conception of legitimacy relied on an appeal to "ultimate grounds," he argues that such grounds can "no longer be made plausible" (1979:184). Replacing the theories of ultimate grounds are the transcendentally oriented theories advanced by theorists from Kant to Karl-Otto Apel, in which the "formal conditions of possible consensus formation" possess the legitimating force rather than appeal to ultimate grounds. And it is in this tradition that Habermas places his own theory:

> Thus by *levels of justification* I mean formal conditions for the acceptability of grounds or reasons, conditions that lend to legitimations their efficacy, their power to produce consensus and shape motives. [1979:184]

As Habermas conceives it, this transcendental conception of legitimacy can be clearly distinguished from other contemporary conceptions of legitimacy; further, it offers a number of advantages to the social sciences. In opposition to the Weberian "empiricist" approach, it has the advantage of giving the sociologist "the possibility of systematically checking the truth of an assertion independently of whether or not it is held to be true in a specific population" (1979:200). In contrast to the metaphysical or "old European" theories, it is historically sensitive. And in opposition to the "hermeneutic" path taken by Gadamer and Wittgenstein, what Habermas calls his "reconstructive" concept offers standards of judgment that allow the social scientist to rationally distinguish legitimate from illegitimate domination (1979:202–4).

What this comes to is that Habermas attempts to carve out a position between the extremes of relativism, on one hand, and universal substantive moral principles on the other, a position he thinks is made possible by positing formal conditions of consensus formation. But it is also clear from his attempt to counter Weber's relativistic, decisionist approach with a theory that allows him to render cross-cultural judgments on the rationality of social arrangements that—in the parlance of contemporary social theory—he is seeking an "objective" basis for social-scientific analysis that is exempt from the variability of cultural definitions. Both Habermas' argument against Weber and his presentation of the two models discussed above point to this conclusion. But this conclusion leads back to the question posed at the beginning of this section: How successful is Habermas in justifying the conception of objectivity that he advances in these different contexts?

The foregoing survey of Habermas' work reveals three distinct varieties of arguments in defense of his conception of objectivity: (1) a historical argument, concerning the relationship between theory and practice; (2) a methodological argument, based on the two models of psychoanalysis and communicative competence; and (3) an anthropological argument, based on universal attributes of societies and individuals.

The first of these arguments, the historical, is undoubtedly the weakest of the three. Habermas' appeal to the Greek relationship between theory and practice, although accurate in a historical sense, does not constitute an epistemological defense of his position on objectivity. Merely claiming that the Greeks originally conceived of theoretical activity as a device to liberate individuals from the relative truths of their society fails to establish the difficult thesis that social theory can accomplish this task. Aristotle's conception of this relationship, in addition to his understanding of the division between the natural and social sciences, is certainly compelling; nevertheless, it implies a conception of an Archemedian point from which the relative conceptions of society can be assessed. But it is precisely this conception, which in twentieth-century terms would be labeled a conception of "objective analysis," that has come under such vigorous attack in contemporary thought. The epistemological critiques of such a conception of objectivity which have been advanced in recent years have, at the very least, seriously undermined the legitimacy of this conception of the role of social theory. Habermas is not, of course, suggesting that the problems of contemporary social theory can be solved by simply adopting the Greek conception of the relationship between theory and practice; he realizes that such a move is neither possible nor desirable. He is suggesting, however, that the Greek conception of the role of theory is a legitimate model for contemporary social theory. In light of twentieth-century critiques of "objective analysis," however, this suggestion requires more defense than he provides.

The defense provided by the two methodological models is more substantive, but does not establish the epistemological legitimacy of Habermas' approach. His model of psychoanalysis provides a useful analogy, but it raises a crucial question which Habermas fails to answer. The explicit goal of the therapeutic process is to bring the patient's conception of reality into line with reality as it is defined in the broader cultural context. When this therapeutic model is applied to the social theorist, however, a particular problem is raised: What is the origin of the conception of reality which the critical social theorist utilizes and, more importantly, what is the epistemological status of that reality? For the psychoanalyst, this question does not arise because the culturally defined reality of the society can be accepted as a given; but the social theorist is in a very different position. It is precisely this culturally defined reality that is the task of social theory to question. Habermas deals with this problem by asserting that social reality is not defined by the actors' concepts alone but must be completed by reference to the other constitutive elements of the "objective framework" of social action. But again, his assertion that these "real factors" conjointly constitute social reality is not sufficiently justified. He readily admits that transposition to the world of social reality from that of the therapeutic situation is problematic, but he fails to offer a convincing epistemological justification for the "objective framework" utilized by the social theorist (1971:274ff.).[8]

Habermas' model of communicative competence is more satisfying because it deals directly with the key issue of social theorists' relationship to the actors' conception. But, ultimately, it also is flawed by the lack of epistemological justification for the conception of objectivity which is utilized. On one level, Habermas' discussion of communicative competence can be understood in the same light as Winch's discussion of the rules of ordinary language or Schutz's understanding of intersubjective meaning constitution. But there is a fundamental difference between Habermas' conception and these two theories. Winch and Shutz appeal to intersubjective understandings which are culturally specific and thus, in Habermas' sense, relative. Habermas, however, defines the "idea of truth" which is implicit in all speech acts as a universal criterion. He appeals to a potentiality of vindication based on "universal validity claims." But this again raises the crucial problem of epistemological justification for what amounts to an Archemedean point existing outside cultural definitions. To claim that the "idea of truth" is a formal criterion of all speech begs the question of epistemological justification.

The third argument, Habermas' appeal to characteristics of individuals and societies which, on the basis of anthropological evidence, can be shown to be universal, would seem, on the surface, to offer a solution to the problem of epistemological justification. For if he can show that certain characteristics of individuals and societies are, empirically speaking, universal, then the identification of those characteristics would provide a basis for the Archemedean point to which he appeals in the other two arguments. Habermas sees his recent work on social evolution and historical materialism as fulfilling this role precisely (1979: 205).

The problems raised by this line of inquiry, however, are very different, and Habermas encountered the first problem in his formulation of the theory of knowledge and interests. Critics of *Knowledge and Human Interests* pointed out that the status of the cognitive interests is confused; they can be interpreted in either empirical or transcendental terms. In an attempt to make sense of Habermas' position on this issue, it has been suggested that the cognitive interests are "quasi-transcendental" (McCarthy, 1978:59) or even "meta-empirical" (Dallmayr, 1981:221). Adding to the confusion is the fact that, at various points, Habermas appears to make a distinction between the status of the emancipatory interest and that of the technical and practical interests. The emancipatory interest, he claims, has a special status because it can be apprehended a priori:

> It is no accident that standards of self-reflection are exempted from the singular state of suspension in which those of all other cognitive processes require critical evaluation. They possess theoretical certainty. The human interest in autonomy and responsibility is not mere fancy, for it can be apprehended a priori. [1971:314]

It has been argued that the difficulty of justifying the status of the cognitive interests led Habermas into his later studies of social evolution and historical materialism (McCarthy, 1978:59); but the problem of epistemological status plagues these studies as well. Habermas' ventures into philosophical anthropology have not solved the problem of the status of the universals which he posits; on the contrary, it has given the problem new importance. It has also raised another difficult issue: Of what use to the social scientist are the findings of this philosophical anthropology? Habermas admits that the universal elements he identifies are formal rather than substantive; that is, they define only the formal conditions, not the substantive content, of human social life. He contends, however, that positing these formal conditions makes it possible for the social scientist to evaluate social arrangements critically. And since critical evaluation is, for Habermas, the essence of social theory, these conditions are, by definition, necessary to the practice of social science. This argument is central to Habermas' later work and to the concerns of this essay. Consideration of this argument, however, raises a number of complex and far-reaching issues, and thus discussion of this aspect of Habermas' work will be postponed to the concluding chapter.

But a definite conclusion can be drawn from the arguments advanced in the present context. The intention of the foregoing has been to establish that, in his examination of the role of the social theorist vis-à-vis society, Habermas fails to offer an epistemological justification for the Archemedean point he accords to the analysis of the social theorist. Thus far the argument has been expressed in terms of contrast to the arguments advanced by Winch and Schutz. This contrast between the position of Habermas and what has here been referred to as the "subjective critique," however, has an echo in another context that has gained notoriety in contemporary social theory: the debate between Habermas and Gadamer. I will not attempt to assess the complex issues in this debate, but a brief reference to Gadamer's position will highlight the significance of this argument.

Gadamer's principal thesis is what he calls the "universality of hermeneutic understanding." Against Habermas, he argues that all understanding takes place in language, and thus for Habermas to posit "real factors" outside the scope of language is "absolutely absurd" (1976:31). Thus his argument against Habermas is very similar to the Wittgensteinian position. Where, he asks, do these "real factors" come from, if not from language? (1971a:71). He claims that Habermas, by positing factors outside of language, reveals a dogmatic objectivism which distorts the concept of hermeneutical reflection (1970:85). For Gadamer, in short, Habermas' move beyond the realm of language is illegitimate. This is precisely the position that was argued above in different terminology: Habermas' positing of these "real factors" entails that his theory lose its necessary grounding in the language of the social actors.

My conclusion, then, is that Habermas does not establish the epistemological legitimacy of the objective social-scientific analysis for which he argues. However, the importance of Habermas' account, from the perspective of an examination of contemporary antipositivist critiques, lies in the fact that he comes so close to achieving a synthesis of the subjective and objective critiques of positivism. Unlike the structuralists, Habermas accepts a key aspect of the subjective critique: the social actors play a constitutive role in the definition of social reality. For Habermas, it follows that these concepts must play a part in construction of a viable social-scientific methodology. But Habermas is acutely aware of the liabilities of the subjective critique, specifically its failure to provide the social scientist with tools for the analysis of social structure and a viable conception of objectivity. His attempt to formulate a conception of objectivity in the social sciences can be seen, in part, as an attempt to remove these liabilities. His goal is to avoid the errors of the positivist conception of objectivity, and to take account of the constitutive role of the social actors' understandings.

It is the argument of this book that this is precisely the understanding of social-scientific methodology that is called for in contemporary discussions. Thus it is disappointing to conclude that Habermas' project ultimately falters because he fails to provide the necessary epistemological justification for his conception of objectivity.

4. Conclusion

It was stated at the outset that the primary contribution of structuralism and critical theory to the postpositivist synthesis is their emphasis on the need for a coherent conception of objectivity in the social sciences, rather than their substantive provision of such a conception. On the basis of the foregoing analysis, this statement should now be qualified in two ways. First, this analysis of the two approaches reveals that although neither solves the problem of objectivity, each makes significant contributions to understanding the problem. Thus particular elements of both theories can be identified as important additions to the understanding of social theorizing. Second, the emphasis of these schools on the need for a definition of objectivity in the social sciences is by no means an insignificant contribution. If a viable postpositivist methodology of the social sciences is to be constructed, it must include a coherent, epistemologically justifiable understanding of "objective analysis" and, furthermore, it must supply a clear understanding of the distinction between such analysis and the everyday understandings of the social actors. Both the structuralists and the critical theorists illustrate the need for such a conception, and in doing so they reveal the key deficiency of the subjective critique.

Althusser's contribution cannot be noted without, at the same time, mentioning the liability of his conception. Although Althusser brilliantly explains the process by which scientific concepts are "produced," he pays a high price for the neatness of his theory: radical separation of the worlds of thought and reality. By positing an absolute separation of these two worlds, Althusser is able to avoid many errors of the positivist conception, but he cuts off the process of social-scientific theorizing from any connection to the world of the social actors' concepts. For Althusser, as a result, "the human subject is definitively abolished" (Geras, 1972:76). By arguing that social-scientific analysis begins with the concepts of the scientific community, rather than those of the social actors, Althusser severs the connection between social science and the social reality constructed by the social actors' concepts. On Althusser's account, objectivity is achieved by adherence to the canons of scientific inquiry and the rules of logic, criteria supplied wholly by the scientific community.

But if the structuralist contribution can be said to be flawed by the radical separation of thought and reality, the contribution of critical theory can, in contrast, be defined as an explicit attempt to close this gap. Habermas, unlike Althusser, agrees with the principal thesis of the subjective critique: social actors' concepts play a constitutive role in the construction of social reality. He is also persuaded that the first task of social-scientific analysis is to explicate the meaning of the social actors' concepts. It is Habermas' attempt to integrate analysis of the social actors' conceptions with a conception of objective analysis in the social sciences which constitutes critical theory's most significant contribution to the antipositivist critique. Habermas' conviction that the first step in sociological analysis must be interpretation of subjective meaning dictates the definition of "objective social-scientific analysis" which he attempts to formulate. He insists that objective analysis in the social sciences entails movement beyond the actors' concepts but that this movement must not lose sight of these concepts. This conception of objectivity informs his models of psychoanalysis and communicative competence. It has been argued, however, that he does not entirely succeed in this attempt to justify his conception of objectivity in the explication of these models. By positing "real factors" outside of language, his theory loses its necessary grounding in the actors' concepts. Thus the contributions of these models lie in the fact that they clearly identify what is involved in an attempt to formulate a conception of objectivity which seeks to integrate these two aspects of social analysis.

In the previous chapter's discussion of subjective critiques a synthesis between the two approaches was suggested by emphasizing the commonality of the two schools and reassessing the epistemological issue which separates them; the approach to objective critiques in this chapter is similar only with respect to the former point. This analysis has revealed that structuralism and critical theory are concerned with a common problem: a conception of objective social-scientific analysis that provides a perspective from which the social scientist can critically assess the structural arrangements of social life. Both critiques formulate their conceptions of objectivity with respect to the four central issues identified at the outset: structural analysis, the nature of scientific investigation, the contrast between science and ideology, and the universal basis for social analysis; and the foregoing analysis details the different ways in which the two schools approach these issues.

Althusser defines structures as objective entities that "create" subjects; he defines scientific investigation as analogous to, but radically separate from, production in the material world; he distinguishes between scientific and ideological concepts in terms of their adherence to the rules of scientific production; and he identifies the criterion of objective analysis as internal to science. Habermas' position on each of these points differs significantly. He analyzes social structures in terms of the "objective framework" constituted by language, labor, and domination; he defines scientific analysis in the social sciences in terms of the Aristotelian model of the social sciences; his distinction between science and ideology rests on the separation between appearance and reality; and he identifies the universal basis for objective analysis in terms of a philosophical anthropology. No attempt was made to gloss over the differences in these accounts. The similarity between the two approaches, however, lies in the similarity of the issues which both feel compelled to address.

This discussion of the objective critiques reveals an issue which constitutes a sharp difference between the two schools: the relationship between the worlds of thought and reality. Rather than attempt a reconciliation between the two schools on this point, it was concluded that Althusser's radical separation of these two worlds is simply untenable. His denial that social actors' concepts are constitutive of social reality and, therefore, that analysis of those concepts is the necessary first step in social-scientific analysis cannot, ultimately, hold up against the arguments of Weber, the subjective critiques, and Habermas. Cutting off social-scientific analysis from any connection to social reality, in short, cannot provide the basis for a viable social theory.

The conclusions of this chapter, however, are in an important sense incomplete. It has been argued that both Althusser and Habermas point to the need for a definition of objectivity in the social sciences but that both fail to provide an epistemologically justifiable definition of that concept. This dictates two lines of inquiry which will constitute the subject matter of the next chapter. First, an argument must be advanced to substantiate the need for a conception of objectivity in the social sciences. Although it has been argued that, together, the subjective critiques provide adequate understanding of this aspect of social-scientific analysis, no explicit argument has been advanced to establish that this understanding must be supplemented with a conception of objectivity. Second, an outline of a viable postpositivist conception of objectivity must be supplied. If the conceptions offered by Althusser and the early Habermas are rejected, at least an indication of what is entailed by a correct conception is certainly called for. That providing such a formulation is not an easy matter should be obvious. The principal argument in the next chapter, however, will be to show that the theories of objectivity in the social sciences, developed by a number of contemporary critics of positivism, provide perspectives which can be used to formulate a postpositivist conception of objectivity.

5. Logical Status of Social-Scientific Analysis

1. Introduction

At the beginning of this examination of contemporary discussions in the philosophy of social science it was asserted that the most important requirement of a successful postpositivist synthesis is that it provide a connection between analysis of actors' subjective meanings and social scientists' assessment of institutional structures. It has been argued that schools of the "subjective critique" fail to meet this requirement because, in practice, they do not move beyond analysis of actors' subjective meanings. Further, it has been argued that Althusser and the early Habermas also fail to meet this requirement, because in attempting to make the social sciences "objective" they either lose sight of the actors' meanings (Habermas) or ignore them completely (Althusser). A conception of the activity of the social scientist that could meet this requirement would have to show (1) how analysis of social actors' concepts can be synthesized with structural analysis and (2) how social scientists' knowledge relates to the actors' everyday understandings. Some of the issues addressed in this context are normally placed under "objectivity in the social sciences," but in the present context this label is misleading. As will be discussed below, the problem can more properly be defined as the logical status of the analysis of social life by the social scientist.

I argue that clear understanding of the logical status of social scientists' concepts is prerequisite to effecting a synthesis between interpretive and structural analysis. Before assessing contemporary discussions of this issue, however, a preliminary problem must be addressed: justification for these requirements for understanding the logical status of social-scientific analysis.

The issue can best be approached by examining two unsatisfactory conceptions of the logical status of social-scientific analysis that arose in the foregoing discussion. Both conceptions solve the central problem of the relationship between the concepts of the social scientist and the social actor, but each does so in a way which negates a major aspect of social-scientific analysis. The first conception is frequently attributed to ordinary-language philosophers: the social scientist does no more than reproduce the concepts of the social actors. This solves the problem of the relationship between the concepts of the social actor and social scientist very neatly by asserting that although the latter's concepts may be more self-conscious than those of the former, they are not fundamentally different. It will be argued below that this is an erroneous conception of the ordinary-language position; nevertheless it is commonly attributed not only to ordinary-language analysis but to phenomenology as well. However, this conception is inadequate because it cannot accommodate the social scientist's structural analysis; it does not permit development of social-scientific concepts which do more than clear up ambiguities in everyday concepts. In the terminology employed here, it ignores the objective side of the antipositivist critique.

A second conception of the logical status of social-scientific analysis is offered by Althusser. He asserts, quite simply, that it is not necessary to establish *any* connection between the social scientist's concepts and those of the social actor. The social scientist operates in an autonomous realm which has no connection to the reality created by the concepts of the social actors. This solution, however, is unacceptable for a very different reason. It clearly defines the logical status of the social scientist's analysis, but it obviates the possibility of a synthesis between the two necessary elements of social-scientific analysis: analysis of subjective meaning, on one hand, and of structural or institutional forms on the other. By declaring that subjective meanings are irrelevant to social-scientific analysis, Althusser makes such a synthesis impossible.

These two conceptions of the logical status of social-scientific analysis can be identified as the two extremes in contemporary discussion of this issue. In keeping with the Weberian spirit of this study, the following will develop a position somewhere between these extremes. This perspective relies on two arguments which have been alluded to above but must now be elaborated. The first argument has its roots in Wittgenstein's thought, but its relevance for the social sciences has been most succinctly stated by Winch, who argues that social action is constituted by the meanings which social actors give to their actions and that those meanings are conceptualized in ordinary language. It follows that unless social scientists begin with assessment and understanding of the social actors' concepts, they will miss the object of their analysis: social action. This argument, expressed in many forms in the foregoing discussion, is accepted by all who fall under the heading "the subjective critique," as well as by Weber. The argument, furthermore, has important implications for social-scientific analysis. Fay and Moon state these implications nicely:

> If social scientists wish to go beyond those self-understandings by introducing concepts and principles which may be at variance with them, they face the problem of relating these new principles to those employed by the actors themselves. Failure to make this relationship would result in the scientists' failing to capture the phenomena they wish to explain, since the events in question would slip through the conceptual net the scientists had constructed. [1977:221]

The second argument which defines this perspective is rooted in Habermas. It was noted above that, in his critique of Winch and Gadamer, Habermas argues that analysis of social life demands a "metalanguage" which can mediate the various language games that are constitutive of social life. This is the case, he argues, because implicit in the activity of social-scientific analysis is the intention to inquire behind the apparent meaning of everyday language. This argument contains an important insight into the nature of social-scientific analysis: a clear statement that the aim of social-scientific analysis, its raison d'etre, is to *explain* social activity. Habermas' point is that if social-scientific analysis is conceived as a language game which is simply different from that of everyday life, the meaning of that analysis as an explanatory activity is negated. That the activity of the social scientist is constituted by explanation, analysis, and critical assessment of social life entails that the language game of social science afford a clearer perspective than that provided by the language game of everyday life. Thus, unless it can be shown that the activity of the social scientist assesses and explains social life, that activity is purposeless.

Contemporary critics of positivism regard Habermas' argument with a good deal of skepticism. Since a major thrust of the critique of positivism has been to reveal the error of positivists' unquestioned belief in the superiority of social scientists' concepts, any argument which appears to repeat that error is quite rightly viewed with suspicion. Although that suspicion is warranted and this issue must be approached with care, the issue cannot be ignored, for one aspect of Habermas' argument is correct: Social-scientific analysis derives its meanings from its definition as an explanatory activity. "Explanation," in this context, cannot mean the mere reproduction of actors' concepts; it entails assessment of those concepts and a clearer perspective than is provided by those concepts alone. What is entailed by this notion of explanation, furthermore, must be articulated without falling back on the positivist understanding of the transcendent nature of the social scientist's ideal language.

The following discussion of the logical status of social-scientific activity will be within the parameters created by the two arguments by Winch and Habermas. The arguments do not, in themselves, offer complete justification for this perspective, and thus additional arguments will be offered as the discussion develops. The aim will be to define a conception of social-scientific analysis which begins with actors' conceptions of their actions yet grants social-scientific understanding an explanatory status vis-à-vis those concepts. The examination will begin with a discussion of Weber's theory of objectivity, which is useful not only because his arguments have set the tone for many subsequent discussions of these issues but also because Weber's attempt to define a conception of objectivity which avoids the pitfalls of both positivism and subjectivism is highly relevant to contemporary discussions.

The analysis will then move to the contemporary debate on objectivity, which will be organized under three headings that are central to the definition of the logical status of social-scientific activity: the relationship between the social scientist's understanding and that of the social actor; the relationship among rival social-scientific theories; and the status of the social scientist's analysis of other cultures. Various contemporary perspectives on these three topics will be considered, but the argument will focus on the theories of Wittgenstein, Habermas, and Toulmin. It will be argued that they offer the most coherent understanding of the logical status of social-scientific analysis and, further, that elements of their theories provide a foundation for a synthesis of antipositivist perspectives on this issue.

2. Weber's Concept of Objectivity

The theory of objectivity which Weber elaborates in his methodological works is a product of the same set of concerns which motivated his development of the ideal type. His principal goal is to develop a theory which avoids the errors of the two dominant schools of his day, positivism and subjectivism. Specifically, his aim is to develop a conception of objectivity which preserves the scientific nature of social science and avoids the relativism implicit in the subjectivist perspective, while at the same time encompassing the analysis of subjective meaning.

Weber's treatment of objectivity in the social sciences can be organized into three distinct themes. The first two are tangential to the previous discussion of the ideal type and so will be summarized; the third, however, is new to the discussion and thus will be treated in more depth. It is also the theme most relevant to the contemporary debate on objectivity. Although the discussion will be divided into these three themes, Weber's treatment does not lend itself to such neat organizational devices. His treatment of objectivity is typical of his treatment of all methodological issues: rather than boldly set forth his theory, he devotes much attention to the errors of others. Thus a theory of objectivity on the basis of Weber's critique of his contemporaries must be accomplished through a careful process of reconstruction rather than simple exposition.

Weber's first theme is the relationship between science and ethics, and his discussion revolves around two issues which were of great interest to his contemporaries: the extent to which university professors should advocate particular values and the distinction between the normative validity and empirical existence of particular values. Weber deals with both issues from the same theoretical standpoint. It is beyond the powers of social science, indeed of any science, he argues, to establish the normative validity of a particular position. Thus for the university professor or the social-scientific investigator to claim scientific validity for value positions is a fundamental error (1949:39).

Weber's discussion of science and ethics has been discussed at great length in the social-scientific literature on objectivity, and although it is of historical interest, it will be dismissed in the present context. Weber makes it clear that he accepts the positivist distinction between the epistemology of factual and evaluative statements—a position that, as Habermas' critique reveals, is untenable. Weber concedes that the distinction between facts and values is difficult to make; nevertheless, he makes this distinction the cornerstone of his discussion. No attempt will be made to defend Weber on this point; it can be argued, however, that despite Weber's acceptance of the distinction, his treatment of the role of values in the formation of ideal types and his understanding of the complex relationship between social-scientific analysis and personal or cultural values are accurate and useful. But since this relationship was discussed extensively above, it will not be repeated here.

One aspect of Weber's discussion, however, is both valid and relevant to the contemporary discussion of objectivity. He asserts that examining a norm empirically and examining its moral validity are different "spheres" of analysis. In terms more compatible with contemporary discussion, Weber's point is that the task of the moral philosopher who examines the normative validity of a value is quite different from that of the social scientist, who examines the functioning of a society predicated on acceptance of that value.

Weber's point in this regard has become one of the central themes of the contemporary discussion, particularly in the work of Toulmin, who casts the issue in terms of the different varieties of logical argument in analysis of the two spheres. Weber's discussion differs from the contemporary debate, however, in more than terminology. Although he recognizes the distinction between these two spheres, he fails to articulate the related point which has been emphasized in contemporary discussion: investigators who espouse different sets of values will almost certainly gather different sets of facts (Taylor, 1969).

The second theme of Weber's treatment is his refutation of the erroneous conceptions of objectivity advanced by positivists and subjectivists. His method of revealing the errors of both positions follows the same pattern: he reveals that adherents of these schools misrepresent the kind of facts that the social scientist studies; then he shows that this error leads them to a misconception of the goal of social-scientific analysis. Weber disposes of the first task quite easily, because, curiously, both the positivists and subjectivists argued for what appears to be the same position: the facts of the social sciences are "presuppositionless." Each school, however, defined presuppositionless in a different way. Positivists meant to assert that the facts of the social sciences are as readily accessible as those of the natural sciences (1949:76); subjectivists meant that the facts of the social sciences are the "given" facts of immediate experiences (1975:160). Weber shows both positions to be untenable in his discussion of the ideal type. He argues that part of existing, concrete reality becomes an object of social-scientific investigation only insofar as it is related to value concepts. Thus these facts cannot be presuppositionless in the sense meant by either positivists or subjectivists.

What is particularly relevant about Weber's discussion, however, is the manner in which he refutes each school's definition of the distinctive goal of social-scientific analysis—a definition which matches that school's conception of the nature of facts the social scientist studies. Positivists asserted that, like the natural sciences, the social sciences should formulate universal laws from which reality is "deduced" (1949:80). Subjectivists asserted, in contrast, that social scientists must reproduce the feelings of social actors in immediate experience, which they defined as distinctly different from the natural scientist's "objective" analysis (1975:160). To refute both positions, Weber employs an indirect but highly effective argument: positivists and subjectivists were led to their misconception of the goal of social-scientific analysis as a result of their misleading conception of "natural" and "social" sciences. Both schools conceived of the basic division of the sciences in terms, on one hand, of "objectifying" sciences which deal with causal laws and universal uniformities of objective facts and, on the other hand, "subjectifying" sciences which deal with the subjective elements of human cultural life (1975:130). This understanding of the division of the sciences led them to the conclusion that the social sciences, because they fall into the "subjectifying" category, are "irrational" and "illogical," while the natural sciences are "objective." On this understanding, positivists tried to make the social sciences more "objective" by mimicking the methods of the natural sciences. This same understanding led subjectivists to embrace the "subjectivity" of the social sciences and to proclaim this "subjectivity" as the distinctive hallmark of those sciences.

Weber rejects both conclusions by proposing a different conception of the division of the sciences: between the sciences of "concrete reality" and the sciences which formulate universal laws. He defines the aim of the sciences of concrete reality as the explanation of events as concrete occurrences in the world. These events can be part of either the human or natural worlds. The sciences which study concrete *human* events, he asserts, are necessarily concerned with elucidating the cultural significance of those events. But central to Weber's theory is his argument that the sociocultural sciences are not the only sciences of concrete reality. A number of sciences concerned with aspects of the natural world are also concerned to explain the meaning of concrete events. (He mentions meteorology as an example.) The sciences in the second category, however, those which formulate universal laws, have an entirely different orientation. They regard concrete events as heuristic instruments which are utilized in the formulation of universal laws. Investigations in these sciences are thus not interested in uncovering the meaning of events as concrete occurrences but are interested in those events only as illustrations of the functioning of universal laws (1975: 64–69).[1]

This division between the sciences allows Weber to sidestep many difficulties encountered by positivists and subjectivists. It allows him to reject the assumptions that the social sciences are inherently "subjective" and irrational, that the natural sciences are "objective" and rational. By shifting the emphasis from subject matter to the purpose of investigations, he can maintain that the meteorologist's logic of analysis has much in common with that of the historian: the goal of both kinds of investigations is to elucidate concrete "historical" events. Likewise, the physicist's attempt to formulate universal laws that govern the natural world can be identified as similar to the physiologist's attempt to establish universal laws relating to human beings. Significantly, he can also conclude that the reason why no attempt is made to formulate universal laws in some of the social sciences has nothing to do with the inherent irrationality of their subject matter. Rather, it stems from their distinctive aim: explanation of concrete events.

This alternative conception of the division of the sciences allows Weber to dispose of both the positivist and subjectivist definitions of the goal of social-scientific analysis. He dismisses the positivists' assumption that the social sciences must formulate universal laws on the grounds that concrete events cannot be "deduced" from laws. It follows that formulation of universal laws in the sociocultural sciences is irrelevant to the goal of those sciences: explanation of the cultural significance of concrete events (1949:135). Subjectivists' assumption that the social sciences must reproduce the immediate experience of social actors in their irrationality and subjectivity is just as easily rejected. Human action, Weber asserts, is no more inherently subjective or irrational than an event in the natural world. Thus no special "subjectifying" method is required for analysis of specifically human events.[2]

But demolishing his opponents' positions on objectivity is not the only purpose of Weber's analysis, for it is not his intent to assert that objectivity in the social sciences is impossible. On the contrary, his aim is to show that what he has revealed as the necessary presuppositions of social-scientific analysis do not rule out objectivity in those sciences. His discussion of this issue is the third theme of his analysis: the logical status of knowledge in the sociocultural sciences. A summary statement of his position can be found in his essay "Science as a Vocation":

> All scientific work presupposes that the rules of logic and method are valid; these are the general foundations of our orientation in the world; and, at least for our special question, these presuppositions are the least problematic aspect of science. Science further presupposes that what is yielded by scientific work is important in the sense of "worth being known." [1946:143]

This statement contains all the key elements of Weber's understanding of the logical status of social-scientific knowledge, but a good deal of "unpacking" is necessary to elucidate what it entails. Weber asserts that two sets of presuppositions are at the basis of all scientific activity: the validity of the rules of logic and method, and belief in the value of scientific knowledge. He identifies the first presupposition as the "least problematic" aspect of science, a status he specifies more clearly in the "Objectivity" article:

> It has been and remains true that a systematically correct scientific proof in the social sciences, if it is to achieve its purpose, must be acknowledged as correct even by a Chinese—or more precisely stated—it must constantly *strive* to attain this goal, which perhaps may not be completely attainable due to faulty data. Furthermore, the successful *logical* analysis of the content of an ideal and its

ultimate axioms and the discovery of the consequences which arise from pursuing it, logically and practically, must also be valid for the Chinese. [1949:58]

Later, Weber reinforces this with the statement that the normative validity of logical and mathematical propositions is the a priori basis of all empirical science (1949:40).

These passages clarify Weber's understanding of this presupposition. When he argues that logic and method are the "general foundations of our orientation in the world," he means they are universal and a priori, not the product of a particular culture. Further, he means this universality to extend to the analysis of values as well as to the rules of logic and method as they are applied to strictly empirical data. His position, then, is that the logical analysis of empirical facts and the empirical implications of value positions can claim universal validity.

Weber's discussion of the second presupposition of scientific activity departs from this theme of universality. His position with regard to this presupposition is somewhat obscure and merits careful attention. He begins by asserting that

for even the knowledge of the most certain propositions of our theoretical science—e.g., the exact natural sciences or mathematics, is, like the cultivation and refinement of the conscience, a product of culture. [1949:55]

At several points in his methodological writings Weber reiterates this theme, making frequent reference to the "value" of scientific truth. He makes it clear that this value cannot be established by scientific activity, but is a culturally bound presupposition of that activity (1975:116). Referring again to the "Chinese," Weber concludes by insisting that

at the same time, our Chinese can lack a "sense" for our ethical imperative and he can and certainly often will deny the ideal itself. [1949:58]

This "ideal" is defined as belief in the value of scientific truth, which Weber identifies as "the product of certain cultures and . . . not a product of man's original nature" (1949:110).

Thus far, Weber's position seems very straightforward: even those from another culture (the "Chinese") must agree with our logic, but they need not agree with our normative commitment to the value of scientific truth. But later Weber adds an important corollary: "Scientific truth is precisely what is *valid* for all who *seek* the truth" (1949:84); and such a search is a product of our "capacity and need for analytically ordering empirical reality in a manner which lays claim to validity as empirical truth" (1949:58). Implicit in these statements is the assumption that belief in the value of seeking empirically valid truth is the basic presupposition of scientific activity and that the methods of scientific analysis are the *only* means by which empirically valid truth can be determined. Thus Weber's position is that although someone from another culture can reject our commitment to the discovery of empirically valid truths about the world, this goal's only means of realization, if it is embraced are the established methods of scientific analysis.

This position has important implications for the contemporary debate over practices of other cultures, such as magic and religion, which, some have claimed, parallel those of Western science. What Weber's theory comes to, quite simply, is that only Western science can supply empirically valid truths about the world. Weber would be the first to insist that magic and religion supply a symbolic ordering of the world, but he claims that "valid empirical knowledge" can only be the product of the Western conception of scientific analysis. This is the case, he asserts, because only science provides "concepts and judgments which are neither empirical reality nor reproductions of it but which facilitate its analytic ordering in a valid manner" (1949:111).

Weber's understanding of the role of these two presuppositions constitutes his conception of the logical status of social-scientific knowledge. Its full implications will be discussed in the examination of contemporary perspectives on objectivity, but before moving to that discussion it is useful to summarize Weber's theory by applying it to the key issue in that debate: relativism. Contemporary discussion of whether social-scientific analysis must be understood as "relative" extends over a wide range of topics, and central to this discussion is the position on relativism commonly attributed to Thomas Kuhn: scientific theories are "incommensurable." Weber's theory speaks to this aspect of the debate over relativism very clearly, if somewhat perfunctorily. Although social scientists with different value systems will choose different topics for analysis, he asserts, it does not follow that their theories are "incommensurable." Because the same rules of logic and method will be employed in those analyses, all social-scientific theories can be assessed with regard to their adherence to these common rules (1949:60). Thus, for

Weber, social science is not to be understood as "relative" in any sense.

Weber's position on another aspect of the debate over relativism, however, is less clear. On the status of scientific knowledge vis-à-vis other cultures, his position is ambiguous. On one hand, he asserts that belief in the value of scientific knowledge is a specifically cultural product. In the context of the modern debate, this position would be labeled "relativism." Although Weber claims that his theory is *not* relativisitic in this regard, it is difficult not to label it as such (1949:18);[3] but Weber's statements about the identification of empirically valid knowledge with science complicates his position. A modern critic would quickly conclude that Weber's comments on this issue smack of ethnocentrism, at the very least. In one sense, this charge is of course true. That acquisition of empirically valid truths about the world is the exclusive product of Western science is clearly an idealization of that activity; and Weber defines this scientific knowledge "among the dynamic forces of our culture" (1949:59). One of Weber's critics interprets this to mean that Weber sees objective knowledge as a historical product; that is, Weber saw attainment of objective understanding as the result of the rational-instrumental method which has developed in modern society (Bauman, 1978:69).

Given this ambiguity in Weber's theory, it is tempting to write off his position as confused or unsophisticated, but such a dismissal would be premature. There is a sense in which Weber's position transcends the dichotomy between "absolute" and "relative" which has dictated the course of the modern debate. Because the principal thrust of Weber's theory is to define objectivity for the community of Western science, he defines it in terms of communication among scientists. For him, it is intimately connected to the ground rules of the scientific community. Although Weber argues that these ground rules are universal, he asserts that the community is not universal. Weber would argue that it makes no sense to talk about "scientific objectivity" with someone who is outside Western culture, because it cannot be assumed that the goal of that community, attainment of "valid knowledge," will be espoused by those outside the Western community. It follows that "objective knowledge" *is* a product of history, but only in the sense that what the Western scientific community defines as objective knowledge was not defined in precisely that way before the community came into existence.

3. The Social Scientist and the Social Actor

The following discussion of the contemporary debate of the logical status of social-scientific knowledge will attempt to develop a concept of objectivity for the social sciences that can be utilized in constructing a postpositivist synthesis. Weber's theory of objectivity will serve as a kind of touchstone for the discussion, but will not dominate the analysis. Although Weber's theory has many virtues, the contemporary debate has raised issues which his position cannot resolve; the most notable weakness in Weber's position is his exclusion of evaluative statements from the sphere of rationality. It will not be the purpose of the discussion, however, to rectify this error in Weber's account; rather, it will focus on the principal question raised by the Weberian theory: the scientific status of the social scientist's concepts. This question will be divided into the three topics mentioned above. Each topic will be assessed with the aim of developing a coherent position with regard to the issues it raises.

The relationship between the concepts of the social actors and those of the social scientists is, in many senses, the most difficult of the three topics, due to the fact that reaction against the positivist position has been the most vehement on this issue. Rejection of the naive positivist position that the "subjective" concepts of the social actors must be replaced with the "objective" concepts of the social scientist has come to be a rallying cry of the antipositivist schools. Certainly it is the clearest point of convergence among these schools.

Against the positivists, adherents of these schools assert that social-scientific analysis must *always* begin with an understanding and assessment of the social actor's "subjective" concepts. With the significant exception of Althusser, all the theorists discussed above strongly advocate this position, and the essential argument in its defense is simple but very persuasive: Social actors' concepts are constitutive of the subject matter of social science, social action; thus, to analyze that subject matter, the social scientist must begin with analysis of those concepts. In the light of this argument, Althusser's rejection of the concepts of the social actors as "ideological" can be identified and, consequently, dismissed as another instance of positivist rejection of the actors' concepts as "subjective."

This designation of the role of social actors' concepts, however, has created a serious problem for the antipositivist schools, which positivists neatly avoided in their understanding of the issue. For positivism, the relationship between the concepts of the social actor and those of the social scientist was settled: actors' "subjective" concepts must be replaced by the social scientists' "objective" concepts; however, antipositivist rejection of this formulation necessitates that the relationship between these two sets of concepts be reformulated. The insistence that social science must begin with social actors' concepts is certainly illuminating, but it fails to answer the further question of the nature of the relationship between the concepts.

Discussions of this issue in contemporary literature have rejected a number of possible answers. First, the position that social scientists' concepts are identical to those of social actors—that is, they only reproduce those concepts—can be dismissed. Weber objected to social scientists' attempt to reproduce actors' concepts on the grounds that complete reproduction is impossible. The argument against this position, advanced in modern discussions, is different but just as effective: Asserting identity between the actors' concepts and those of the social scientist erases the distinction between social science and social action. A second position can also be dismissed: social scientists' concepts are completely divorced from those of the social actors. Social science derives its meaning as an activity from its claim to "explain" social action, and this implies, at minimum, that social scientists' concepts are related to those of social actors and that the relationship is defined by the fact that social scientists' concepts provide a clearer understanding of the social action in which the actors participate.

It was noted above that ordinary-language philosophy has been incorrectly accused of falling prey to the first of these errors: mere reproduction of social actors' concepts. Although much in the work of ordinary-language philosophers would lead to this conclusion, it is not, technically, an accurate representation of their position. The best illustration of the kind of arguments which have led to this erroneous judgment can be found in the work of Winch. Most of his *Idea of a Social Science* is a criticism of social scientists who ignore actors' concepts, replacing them with concepts of their own making. This leads the reader, quite naturally, to conclude that Winch regards social scientists' use of concepts other than those of the actors as illegitimate. This, however, is not the point of Winch's argument. It is perfectly legitimate, he declares, for the social scientist to employ "technical concepts" if these concepts are based on a prior understanding of actors' concepts. But it is easy to overlook this statement because Winch offers only one example of what he means by "technical concepts" based on actors' concepts: the concept of "liquidity preference" as it is used by economists (1958:89). Thus the only argument that his readers are likely to remember is his rejection of concepts that are divorced from those of the social actor.

The ordinary-language position on this question, then, is not much assistance in solving the basic problem. Phenomenologists, like ordinary-language philosophers, have also been accused of the error of only reproducing actors' concepts. It was shown above that this conclusion is similarly unfounded, but it can also be shown that—unlike ordinary-language philosophers—phenomenologists, and specifically Schutz, offer a satisfactory answer to the question.

The preceding discussion of Schutz's elaboration of Weber's ideal-type theory detailed his understanding of how the social scientist, beginning with the ideal types utilized by the social actor, refines and abstracts those conceptions to form concepts which are appropriate to the question posed in the investigation. Schutz's resolution of this process isolates the issue which is central to this transformation: the definition of rationality in the social-scientific community differs from that of everyday life. Although the social scientist begins with the actors' concepts, those concepts must be made to conform to the "postulate of rationality," unique to the scientific community, if they are to be employed in social-scientific analysis.[4]

Schutz's formulation of the relationship between the concepts has two principal advantages. It reveals the nature of the similarity between Schutz's theory and that of ordinary-language analysis. He asserts that the definition of rationality in science is different from that of everyday life and, further, that this difference is definitive of the distinction between these two "provinces of reality." Ordinary-language philosophers cast this difference in terms of the distinction between the two "language games" of social science and everyday life, but it comes to much the same thing. Derek Phillips, whose discussion of this point is particularly useful in highlighting this similarity, makes the point that truth and falsity are part of the language game of science but not of everyday life (1977:98).

The second advantage of Schutz's formulation is in his definition of rationality for the social-scientific community. What is to count as "rational"—that is, what is to count as appropriate to scientific discourse—is determined by the community of scientists. The intersubjective agreement of scientists, not some absolute standard, determines the definition of rationality of the scientific community. Schutz's theory defines the concepts of the social scientist as determined by both the intersubjective understandings of the everyday world and the intersubjective understandings which constitute the community of scientists. Unless they conform to both requirements, they do not qualify as appropriate social-scientific concepts.[5]

Bauman summarized Schutz's position on this issue succinctly: interpretation by sociologists is superior to that of social actors only in that it is done more consciously and methodically (1978:181). This statement may appear to be, on the surface, rather weak, but in contemporary discussions of this issue, Schutz's specification of the difference stands out as significant. Antipositivists' vehement rejection of the positivist position, as noted above, has made the specification of this relationship particularly difficult. Schutz is one of the few antipositivist theorists who has formulated a clear understanding of this problematic relationship.

Critics of Schutz's approach have noted that although he accurately conceptualizes the difference between the concepts, he fails to supply examples of how social-scientific analysis, predicated on this understanding, would proceed. This criticism is undeniably correct. So, to complete the argument for Schutz's understanding of this relationship, an example of this kind of analysis should be supplied, and though Schutz does not offer examples, the empirical analyses of Weber can fill this gap. Weber's famous study of the Protestant Ethic and the spirit of capitalism illustrate the relationship between the concepts of the social actor and the social scientist as Schutz interpreted it.

Weber's examination of capitalism and Protestantism begins with his attempt to understand the social actors' conceptualization of these belief systems. His discussion of capitalism revolves around analysis of how the "everyday capitalist" conceptualizes economic activity. He asks what "subjective meaning" the capitalist brings to that activity and how those meanings evolved. His examination of Protestantism illustrates even more clearly this concern with the social actors' conceptions of their activity. The significant insight is his discovery that the distinctive qualities of the Protestant Ethic are based not on the understandings of theologians but on the subjective understandings of the "everyday Calvinist." His discovery that theologians' orthodoxy was modified by believers' need for psychological security is a clear indication of his paramount concern for the actors' conception of their actions.

But Weber's analysis does not end with the subjective meaning of everyday capitalists and Calvinists. Although he begins with the actors' concepts of these activities, he refines those conceptions according to the logical demands of the problem he posed. Because his purpose is to discover the relationship between these two belief systems, he must refine and abstract the actors' concepts to fulfill that purpose. To create concepts which will facilitate his analysis, he chooses only those aspects of the actors' conceptions which are directly relevant to his attempt to define this relationship. The ideal types of the spirit of capitalism and the Protestant Ethic which emerge from this process of refining and abstracting possess a logical rigor, or, as Schutz puts it, a rationality that is not characteristic of the everyday concepts.

Weber uses these ideal types to advance a particular thesis about the nature of the relationship between these two belief systems, and this thesis embodies an understanding of the relationship between capitalism and Protestantism which is superior to that in the everyday life of the average capitalist or Protestant. It is superior in the sense that it supplies a clearer perspective on the nature of the relationship between the two belief systems by revealing the points at which they converge. These insights into the relationship between capitalism and Protestantism are not part of the everyday understandings of the social actors engaged in these activities. Nor, as Phillips points out, would such insights be appropriate to the language game of everyday life. But they are appropriate to the language game of social science, and, in fact, supply that language game its rationale.

4. The Relationship among Social-Scientific Theories

The common theme of antipositivist understanding of the relationship between the social scientist and the social actor is insistence that social actors' concepts be the starting point of social-scientific analysis. A common theme, the intersubjectivity of the scientific community, can also be identified for antipositivist understanding of this second topic, the relationship among social-scientific theories. Weber's account of the objectivity of social science rests squarely on the assumption of this intersubjectivity, as he asserts that the scientific community is bound together by the "rules of logic and method" and by its belief in the value of scientific knowledge. Weber's treatment of these issues, however, is perfunctory. Almost blithely, he assumes the intersubjectivity of the scientific community, and never bothers to specify what he means by the "rules of logic and method" that bind that community together. But both of these issues, which Weber passes over, have been explored in contemporary discussions. Due largely to the work of Kuhn, the nature of the intersubjectivity of the scientific community has been disputed at length. Also, much has been done to specify the distinctions between the different kinds of logic and method in the scientific community. In the following, it will be argued that certain aspects of these recent antipositivists' discussions have supplied satisfactory answers to the questions raised by both of these issues.

Positivist discussions of the nature of social-scientific theories have traditionally revolved around the elimination of bias. Most simply, it has been the positivist argument that what qualifies analysis as "scientific" is elimination of the personal bias of the investigator. The antipositivist approach, in contrast, has been that posing the objectivity of social-scientific theories in terms of removing personal bias from them is to pose the wrong question. It argues that the positivist question must be replaced with questions of the means by which social scientists communicate with each other, what standards of intelligibility are established by the social-scientific community, and how those standards are enforced. Extensive critiques of positivist definitions of objectivity in terms of eliminating bias and the related conception of a neutral observation language have, by this time, laid both of these conceptions to rest. No participant in the contemporary debate seriously defends either position in anything like its pure form. But these positions, curiously, have not vanished from current discussions. The discredited positivist position performs the function of a strawman in these discussions. Each participant in the debate feels that this position must again be discredited before any discussion of objectivity is attempted. Thus positivism still functions as one extreme pole in modern debate, though only in a rhetorical sense.

The tenacity of the positivist position may be explained by the fact that rejection of the positivist theory of a neutral observation language has raised a very difficult question for the social sciences: If the concept of a neutral observation language is abandoned, do the social sciences have any criteria by which the truth or falsity of social-scientific theories can be assessed? This question set the stage for the contemporary debate on the objectivity of the social sciences. A very persuasive answer forms the second pole of that debate: Kuhn's theory of scientific revolutions. Although in a strictly logical sense Kuhn's position is not the exact opposite of positivism, it serves as the principal foil of positivism in the contemporary debate. In other words, that debate can be characterized as centering around the two poles created by the discredited positivist theory, on one hand, and Kuhn's position on the other. These two positions define the course of the contemporary debate, just as positivism and subjectivism defined the terms of the debate in Weber's time.

Kuhn argues, against the positivists, that there is no neutral observation language; rather, each scientific theory creates its own proof because all observation is theory dependent. Kuhn thus sees the history of science as a succession of what he calls "paradigms," a term which has been widely discussed in the contemporary literature. Broadly, a "paradigm" can be defined as a set of assumptions, ways of doing research, and standards of truth. Central to this concept is what Kuhn has labeled the "incommensurability" of paradigms, by which he means that the terms of one paradigm make no sense in the context of another paradigm. Moving from one paradigm to another is thus like a religious conversion, because, as the consequence of a paradigm shift, the world, in a literal sense, is "seen differently" (Kuhn, 1962).

Kuhn's position on the incommensurability of paradigms has had a profound effect on the discussion of scientific theories. It has shifted the locus of that discussion to examination of the reasons for which one theory is chosen over another, or in other words why paradigms are replaced. Because Kuhn rejects all criteria of the truth of empirical statements except as they pertain to a specific theoretical perspective, the reasons for choosing theories become paramount because they constitute the only means of comparing one theory to another. In *The Structure of Scientific Revolutions*, Kuhn seems to deny the possibility of offering *any* reasons for choosing one theory over another; in subsequent discussions of this issue, however, he has reformulated his position. In an initial reply to critics, he argues that the values of scientists play the key role in this selection process. He insists that "good reasons" may be given for choosing a theory, but that the deciding factor is the values of the scientists, not the rules of choice (1970:260).

In his most recent work, Kuhn modified his position even further. In a discussion of Popper's position, he poses the questions very directly. How do scientists choose between competing theories? How do we understand scientific progress? His first answer is very candid: "There is too much about these questions I do not understand" (1978:288). But he asserts that the answer must be psychological and sociological; that is, it must rest on a description of a value system or ideology and the institutional structure through which that system is transmitted and enforced. Popper's error, he concludes, is to focus on the individual rather than on the psychological makeup of the group (1978:272–91).

But this is not the whole story. Kuhn asserts that theory choice is always a mixture of individual factors and shared canons. He labels the individual factors "subjective" and the shared canons "objective"; then he identifies five of these shared canons: accuracy, consistency, breadth of scope, simplicity, and fruitfulness. The substance of his argument is that since these "objective" criteria of theory choice are imprecise, individual choices are made on the basis of subjective criteria.

> The considerable effectiveness of such criteria does not, I now wish to suggest, depend on their being sufficiently articulated to dictate the choice of each individual who subscribes to them. Indeed, if they were articulated to that extent, a behavior mechanism fundamental to scientific advance would cease to function. What the tradition sees as eliminable imperfection in its rules of choice I take to be in part responses to the essential nature of science. [1978:330]

Finally, he claims that his position is not subjective in the sense that matters of taste are subjective. Even what he labels the "subjective" criteria of choice, employed by individual scientists, are "objective" in the sense that they can be challenged and discussed (1978:337).

Although this formulation of Kuhn's position is more satisfying than its initial form, it is extremely sketchy. His five "objective" criteria of theory choice provide a bridge of sorts from one theory to another. In light of his emphasis on the incommensurability of paradigms, this aspect of Kuhn's theory is easily overlooked—but it is precisely this question, identification of criteria that are independent of particular theoretical perspectives, that is at issue. To explore this issue further, the following argument will turn to what may seem an unlikely source: Wittgenstein's understanding of scientific knowledge.

Although Wittgenstein did not advance an explicit theory of scientific knowledge, or specifically discuss the social sciences, it will be argued that, on the epistemological level, Wittgenstein's position best answers the question which Kuhn's rejection of positivism has posed for the contemporary debate. Wittgenstein's position emphasizes an aspect of scientific analysis and theory choice which tends to be obscured by Kuhn's emphasis on the discontinuity of paradigms: the fact that, underlying the language games employed by scientists, is basic agreement on a mode of argumentation that perpetuates, rather than curtails, scientific discussions.[6] Thus, discussion of Wittgenstein's remarks on this subject must begin with an explication of his concept of a language game.

For Wittgenstein, a language game entails a community of people who share concepts and, hence, standards of intelligibility, rationality, and argumentation; and he provides many examples (1953:56ff.) that show that people who share a language game share an *activity*. He argues that any definable subset of the larger set of social activity constitutes a language game. Activities as diverse as religion, mathematics, chess, and rugby qualify as language games in this sense. But if Wittgenstein's theory is to be applied in this context, the first question which must be addressed is whether social science can be said to constitute a language game.

At the outset, it is not difficult to point to several aspects of social science which would seem to disqualify it as a viable language game in Wittgenstein's sense. To many who are engaged in social-scientific activity, it seems abundantly clear that the discipline does *not* share concepts, standards of intelligibility, or even modes of argument. It seems much more plausible that social science is constituted by a rather diverse set of language games that could be identified as including the four schools discussed above, plus behaviorism, orthodox Marxism, and, perhaps, ethnomethodology. But Wittgenstein's perspective encourages us to examine the broader context in which these disputes take place; that is, to see social science as an activity which has certain rules, standards, and methods which set it apart from other activities in our society. Although he does not discuss the social sciences, what Wittgenstein has to say about scientific activity in general is directly relevant to these disciplines. In *On Certainty* he states:

> All testing, all confirmation and disconfirmation of a hypothesis takes place already within a system. And this system is not a more or less arbitrary and doubtful point of departure for all our arguments: no, it belongs to the essence of what we call an argument. The system is not so much the point of departure, as the element in which arguments have their life. [1972:16]

Later he notes that this activity constitutes the ground of the language game, not our agreement on a set of certain propositions:

> Giving grounds, however, justifying the evidence, comes to an end;—but the end is not certain propositions' striking us immediately as true, i.e., it is not a kind of *seeing* on our part; it is our *acting*, which lies at the bottom of the language-game. [1972:28]

Thus Wittgenstein's perspective entails that, despite the undeniable difference between social scientists, their activity, in the larger context of our society, is clearly distinguishable. Social scientists are, generally speaking, academics and researchers; they teach, write articles, and argue with each other over the fine points of their discipline. Because they share this activity, Wittgenstein argues, they share concepts, modes of thought, and standards of intelligibility. It cannot be denied that the activity of social science is constituted by social scientists' communicating with each other, comparing each other's theories, and trying to persuade each other of their truth or falsity. This is the case, Wittgenstein would point out, because they share something of crucial importance: agreement on what constitutes an argument. Wittgenstein's perspective suggests, then, that although social scientists may engage in different language games, in the larger context of society the social sciences can be identified as a distinctive activity that rests on shared assumptions.

Kuhn's emphasis on the incommensurability of paradigms suggests a different perspective.[7] For Kuhn, no translation is possible between paradigms, and movement from one paradigm to another involves total conversion analogous to religious conversion. Wittgenstein's theory, in contrast, allows us to think of the activity of social scientists as having continuity. The activity of social science presupposes criteria of truth and rationality which transcend various theories propounded by social scientists.

Wittgenstein would not, however, deny that observation is "theory laden." His discussion of "seeing" and "seeing as" reveals that he is well aware of the relationship between theory and observation (1953:193–208). But Wittgenstein sees that the fact that observation is theory dependent does not preclude criteria of judgment for both theories and observations. Rather, observation itself necessarily presupposes the existence of such criteria.

Another aspect of Wittgenstein's approach is useful in explaining the role of these broad criteria in human social life: the theory of forms of life.[8] Wittgenstein defines "form of life" as the network formed by the interrelated language games of a culture (1953:11). In more sociological terms, Wittgenstein's concept can be identified as the set of assumptions and ways of acting that is fundamental to a particular cultural setting. His discussion of forms of life is intimately connected to his understanding of language games. It was noted above that in his examination of language games he asserts that those who share such a language game share criteria as to what is to count as a "good reason," but he also asserts that "at the end of reasons comes persuasion" (1972:81), and in another context:

> If I have exhausted my justifications I have reached bedrock, and my spade is turned. Then I am inclined to say: "This is simply what I do." [1953:85]

On the surface, this statement seems to be an affirmation of Kuhn's position on the incommensurability of paradigms; but what Wittgenstein means is quite different. The "bedrock" he refers to is the form of life in which making arguments and giving reasons takes place. In *On Certainty* he extends this analogy of bedrock to explain the complex relationship between language games, which change over time, and the form of life that encompasses them:

> It might be imagined that some propositions, of the form of empirical propositions, were hardened and functioned as channels for such empirical propositions as were not hardened but fluid; and that this relation altered with time, in that fluid propositions hardened, and hard ones become fluid. The mythology may change back into a state of flux, the river-bed of thought may shift. But I distinguish between the movement of the waters on the river-bed and the

> shift of the bed itself; though there is not a sharp division of
> the one from the other . . . . And the bank of that river con-
> sists partly of hard rock, subject to no alteration or only to
> an imperceptible one, partly of sand, which now in one
> place and now in another gets washed away or deposited.
> [1972:15]

Wittgenstein identifies the elements of this bedrock as
elements of our common life which "stand fast" for us; that is,
those elements which are exempt from doubt. "What has to be
accepted," he argues, "the given, is—so one could say—*forms of
life*" (1953:226). But he also insists that

> what stands fast does so, not because it is intrinsically ob-
> vious or convincing, it is rather held fast by what lies around
> it. [1972:21]

Employing yet another metaphor, he asserts:

> . . . the question that we raise and our *doubts* depend on
> the fact that some propositions are exempt from doubt, are
> as it were like hinges on which those turn . . . it belongs to
> the logic of our scientific investigations that certain things
> are *in deed* not doubted. . . . If I want the door to turn the
> hinges must stay put. [1972:44][9]

For Wittgenstein, then, the elements of our form of life are
not those elements which can be shown to be absolutely certain;
they are the elements that make possible a certain way of living.
Again, he places the emphasis of his argument on *acting*: we can
"turn the door" only if the hinges stay put. That certain things
"stand fast," he asserts, is evidence that "we belong to a community bound together by science and education" (1972:38).

Wittgenstein's theory of forms of life can also be shown to
parallel Weber's understanding of the role played by the rules of
logic and method in scientific investigations. In his discussion of
objectivity, Weber argues that the justification for scientific activity cannot be scientifically established and that the rules of
logic and method are our "general orientation" in the world.
Wittgenstein identifies this general orientation as our form of
life. Fundamental to this form are the traditions of argumentation, demonstration, and testing that structure the language
games of science and also, therefore, those of social science. We do
not offer reasons for these traditions because they form the bedrock of our form of life. They are not established by scientific activity but make that activity possible. They are, in Wittgenstein's

metaphor, the riverbed on which the waters of scientific discourse flow.

Wittgenstein's theory of forms of life can thus be shown to provide an understanding of the continuity of scientific activity and the role this activity plays in the fundamental grounding of our cultural life. I am attempting to argue that although Kuhn's identification of the shared criteria of theory choice points in this direction, Wittgenstein's remarks provide a more complete understanding of the larger nature of scientific activity. Furthermore, it points to the fact that even if the positivist foundation for scientific investigations is discarded, it is not necessary to adopt the position that there is no overarching consensus. Wittgenstein's theory provides a means of establishing the continuity of scientific analysis which does not succumb to the errors of positivist absolutism.

But this is only the first step in explaining the relationship among social-scientific theories. If it can be established that the activity of social science is characterized by standards and rules that provide continuity among the various theories, the next task must be to specify those standards and rules. Such an attempt, however, is not an easy task, principally because it raises the problem of whether the logic that informs the language games of social science differs from that of the natural sciences. Social scientists disputed this issue before the time of Weber and have generated a staggering amount of literature on the subject.

Weber's theory of objectivity was directly concerned with this question, and he replied by arguing that the social sciences are characterized by a logic which is related to, but not identical with, that of the natural sciences; it is a logic adapted to the specific needs of analysis in the sociocultural sciences. But although Weber identifies very precisely the differences between construction of the social scientist's ideal types and the concepts of the natural sciences, he does not address the question of the precise nature of the logic by which those concepts are manipulated, and it is this question which has played a key role in the contemporary debate and is particularly crucial to specification of a postpositivist position. Thus the following assessment will begin with Weber's assumption that the logic of the social sciences is unique and will concentrate on specifying the nature of that uniqueness.

Contemporary attempts to specify the logic of the social sciences have led in several directions. Von Wright has advanced the argument that the appropriate logic is that of the practical syllogism (1971); Scheffler argues that extensional logic, particularly as developed by Quine, is useful in solving some of the problems in comparing social-scientific theories (1976). Both approaches, however, though useful additions to understanding the uniqueness of the logical problems in the social sciences, are in an important sense too narrow. They focus exclusively on showing how the logic employed in social-scientific analysis is as rigorous as that of the analytic syllogism, thus implicitly accepting the latter model as the archetype of logical analysis. However, the logical problems that face the social sciences demand a broader perspective, one which does not reify the analytic syllogism of formal logic, and such a perspective is provided by Stephen Toulmin in *The Uses of Argument* (1958).

Toulmin advances the thesis that "logical argument" extends to many forms of argument other than those that fall under the analytic paradigm of formal logic. Arguments which can be fitted into this analytic paradigm, he points out, are the exception rather than the rule. He traces the dominance of this paradigm to historical developments: because logicians have used the study of the analytic syllogism to develop the categories of formal logic, they have tended to exclude all arguments which do not fit this form from what Toulmin calls the "Court of Reason" (1958:175). Toulmin strongly objects to this identification and counters with the argument that the appropriate paradigm for logical arguments is the lawsuit, where evidence depends on the question at issue.[10] Although logical arguments can be said to have a standard form, the criteria or standards for their validity are "field dependent," which means that the force of a logical argument is always the same. Establishing a valid inference has the same logical force in all logical argument: what varies in the different kinds of logical arguments are the criteria by which a valid inference is established (1958:36).

Toulmin's argument is important in the antipositivist critique for several reasons. Most significantly, it avoids the error that has plagued most attempts to define the logic of the social sciences: mimicking the formal logic in some of the theoretical aspects of the natural sciences. Placing the problem in the appropriate historical perspective, Toulmin shows that the analytic paradigm is not the archetype of all logical argument; it is an exceptional form that can only rarely be applied to concrete problems. This point is missed by Von Wright and Scheffler, who, attempting to derive the logic of the social sciences from the analytic paradigm, too narrowly limit the scope of a "logical argument."

A second reason why Toulmin's approach is significant is that he suggests that *many* kinds of logical arguments are appropriate to different kinds of situations. This implies that the search for *one* logic of the social sciences may be misguided. The social sciences deal with a wide variety of phenomena; they address questions, Toulmin would argue, that must be analyzed by different kinds of logical arguments. He suggests that the model that encompasses all these varieties is the lawsuit, which is open ended; it specifies only that the evidence "suit" the question. Weber attempted to make much the same point in his discussion of the construction of the ideal type: what counts as a relevant fact is determined by the investigator's interest.

From this perspective, Toulmin's theory removes the inferiority complex of the social sciences on the status of their logical arguments. He allows social scientists to assert that they can advance fully valid logical arguments without imitating the analytic paradigm, and further, that it is not incumbent on them to define one logic that is characteristic of all investigations in the social sciences. The intent of Toulmin's book is to open the "Court of Reason" to activities of human beings other than those encompassed by formal logical arguments, but it also achieves the narrower goal of opening that Court to the social sciences.

This section has argued that the perspectives of Wittgenstein and Toulmin are viable alternatives to the positivist position. Together, they supply a more adequate understanding of the activity of social science. The first key element of that understanding is emphasized by Wittgenstein: science (and by extension social science) is an intersubjective activity; the activity of social science is constituted by a set of shared concepts, standards of judgment, and modes of argumentation which provide, at the very least, a basis for communication among the various theories propounded by social scientists, a continuity obscured by Kuhn's theory of the incommensurability of paradigms.

The second key element of that understanding is suggested by Toulmin: arguments in the social sciences can be fully logical and rational without mimicking the analytic syllogism, which, for positivists, is the only valid form of logical argument. Toulmin's argument that the logic by which evidence is presented in a particular case depends on the question posed suggests that many "logics" may be employed by social scientists, not just one. Weber's understanding of the construction of the ideal type was predicated on the same principle. Toulmin's argument extends Weber's principle to manipulation of the concepts, as well as their construction.[11]

5. Social-Scientific Analysis of Other Cultures

The validity of the social scientist's analysis of other cultures is an exceedingly complex problem which has long been of interest to social scientists. Furthermore, it might appear to be only tangentially related to the concerns of this study and, thus, could wisely be avoided. But examination of the issues raised by this question reveals that if the argument is to be successful, it must come to grips with these issues.

The principal argument of this study is that if a postpositivist approach for the social sciences is to emerge, a synthesis of the two major antipositivist critiques is necessary; but it is on the cross-cultural status of the social scientist's method that the two camps appear to diverge most sharply. In the simplest terms, the dispute can be reduced to whether a concept of rationality can be defined that provides a standard which is applicable to all cultures. Those engaged in the subjective critique of positivism seem to suggest that cultures can be characterized by what Gellner has labeled "collective solipsism" (1974:147). By this he means that they take the position that the social scientist can do no more than explore the standards of rationality embodied by a particular culture; thus for the social scientist to apply what can be defined only as "standards of rationality" to another culture is illegitimate. Those in the objective critique, on the other hand, seem to appeal to an absolute, universalistic conception of rationality that transcends all cultural bounds. On this issue, in short, the two camps appear to be at loggerheads.

It will be argued, however, that although important differences exist between these two camps, neither takes as absolute a stand on this issue as first appears. Through close analysis of the theories of Wittgenstein and Habermas, an attempt will be made to show that these representatives of the positions of the two camps are not dogmatically opposed. Rather, each theorist is very cognizant of the arguments offered by the opposing camp and, as a result, the theories converge on significant issues.

To sort out the complex issues in this debate, the discussion will be organized around a distinction among three understandings of the concept "rationality." Because the nature and status of rationality are the central issue in the debate over the cross-cultural status of the investigations of the social scientist and thus must be addressed directly, it will be possible, by explaining the various antipositivist positions with regard to these three definitions of rationality, not only to reveal their points of convergence but also to outline a viable approach to this issue.

The first definition of rationality (Rationality I) which emerges from this debate deals with the underlying logic of social institutions. Those who employ this definition are concerned to explore the logic of a particular society or social institution by uncovering the interrelationships of beliefs and practices that constitute it. Much of Weber's empirical work can be seen as exploration of Rationality I. His examination of the three types of legitimate domination, for example, details how, within a given structure of domination, belief in a particular form of legitimacy determines the other aspects of the social structure: the administrative apparatus, the economic and social order, and the capacity for change. His analysis shows that social systems are "rational" in that the beliefs and practices which constitute those structures fit together in a logical fashion, forming an interrelated and interdependent unit.

The legitimacy of examining social institutions on the level of Rationality I is accepted by all the theorists under consideration here. In fact, such examinations are an integral part of each approach. Schutz's analysis of the "life world," Winch's attempt to discover the rules of "language games," and the concern of Althusser and Habermas with the logic of capitalist society are instances of the examination of Rationality I. The disputes among these theorists with regard to rationality, then, do not concern Rationality I; they arise from claims on the basis of the second and third definitions of rationality which are utilized in the debate.

The second definition (Rationality II) interprets "rationality" to mean the logical system that informs the scientific method and the rules of formal logic; the third definition (Rationality III) interprets "rationality" in terms of a universal standard of judgment, encompassing both the normative and factual spheres.

On the basis of Rationality II, it has been claimed that the logic of the scientific method is different from and superior to that which informs social institutions and practices; and on the basis of Rationality III it has been claimed that societies as a whole can be judged to be "rational" or "irrational" by the universal standards established in this definition. Disputes over the validity of these claims form the core of the debate over rationality in contemporary discussions, and for purposes of clarity, it might be useful to begin with the most extreme position.

David Bloor, arguing for what he labeled the "strong program" for the sociology of knowledge, asserts that the activity of the social scientist must be limited to analysis of the rationality of beliefs that are internal to particular cultures (1976). He insists that social science cannot grant a privileged status to the logic employed in the analysis; it cannot, in other words, regard the logic of the scientific method as in any way superior. He supports this assertion by arguing that the method with which social scientists analyze the logic of institutions of another society is a product of the institutional structure of *our* society. The institutions of each society, as Bloor sees it, produce a logical system unique to that society. *Our* logical system is defined in terms of formal logic and the scientific method; that of a primitive culture may be defined in terms of witchcraft. The point of his argument is that each of these logical systems is a product of that society's institutional structure and has no legitimacy aside from that designation.

Bloor is not arguing simply that each society operates according to Rationality I; he assumes this to be the case without providing an argument to defend it. The point of his argument is that the institutions of each society produce a unique logical system which comes to be defined as the standard of rationality for that culture. Bloor finds unacceptable the elevation of our standard of rationality, Rationality II, to a superior status—and, even worse, employment of Rationality II as a standard of judgment by which the logical systems of another culture are assessed (1976:130). He argues, in short, that Rationality II is applicable only to the culture which produced it, and by implication, Rationality III is a meaningless concept.

Most social scientists find Bloor's attitude toward Rationality II too limited. Even those who reject the positivists' unquestioning acceptance of the objective rationality of the scientific method have a strong tendency to define Rationality II as, in some sense, a more rigorous and thus "superior" form of thought. Again, Weber is a good example of this attitude. Although he devotes much effort to revealing the errors of the positivist understanding of objectivity, he maintains dogmatically that the rules of logic and method are our "general orientation" in the world. They are the "least problematic" aspect of science, an aspect which, he argues, must be accepted even by non-Western cultures. But Weber fails to supply a convincing justification for what he defines as the superior status of the scientific method, and supplying that justification has become a major concern of the contemporary debate.

Justification for the cross-cultural validity of Rationality II revolves around an anthropological question: If it is discovered that another culture's system of thought embodies logical contradictions, violates the rules of inference, or in other words does not conform to the rules of Rationality II, how are these facts to be regarded? The temptation to label such a system "irrational" or "illogical"—that is, to use Rationality II as a universal standard of judgment—is one to which many social scientists have succumbed. Such judgments were common in the past, but in recent years the argument against this position has gained wide acceptance and fewer social scientists accept the universality of Rationality II.

This opposing position has been most clearly articulated by Winch. Beginning in an explicitly anthropological context, Winch attacks Evans-Pritchard's labeling of Azande thought as "irrational" on the grounds that he appeals to a transcultural standard of rationality which is epistemologically unjustifiable (1972:8–49). Winch's argument is very similar to Bloor's "strong program" (discussed above). Like Bloor, Winch argues that each society produces a particular standard of rational thought. Our culture's standard, Rationality II, labels certain sequences of thought "contradictions" because they violate the rules of inference established by the logical system; Azande society, however, appears to have a standard of rationality which permits what we label contradictions. On the basis of this evidence, we *can* label Azande thought "contradictory" and, hence, "irrational," but to do so necessarily involves lifting our standard of rationality from its cultural context and endowing it with universality, which Winch claims is illegitimate.

Winch's statement of the issue set the stage for the ensuing debate over Rationality II, and the question which has dominated this debate is directly related to Winch's thesis: Can a distinction be made between the translation or understanding of the thought of an alien culture and a critical judgment on the logical status of that thought? Several participants have argued that translation of another culture's thought into our own must necessarily invoke our criteria of logic and rationality, and thus entails a judgment of inferiority of systems of thought that violate those standards (Gellner, 1974:24; MacIntyre, 1974:71; Hollis, 1974:23). The argument of these theorists can best be illustrated by Winch's example of the Azande. If we attempt to translate the Azande understanding of witchcraft into the language game of social-scientific analysis, this involves the effort to understand the tradition and context of that activity. It also involves invoking the criteria of rationality that are characteristic of the language game of social science because those criteria are inseparable from social-scientific analysis. And because translating Azande witchcraft into the language game of social science involves discovering the different standards of rationality exhibited by the two systems of thought, it also involves judging the Azande system inferior.

That the distinction between translation and judgment should become the focal point of the debate is not surprising. Once unquestioning belief in the universality of the standards of Rationality II is rejected, the point at which judgments can be made on the logical status of an alien system of thought—if at all—becomes paramount. However, the implications of the argument that translation and judgment are inseparable are disturbing, for it amounts to admission that we cannot avoid universalizing our standards of rationality if we engage in cross-cultural comparison. Thus if we want to avoid such universalization, as Winch claims we must, no comparisons are possible.

An alternative approach, however, avoids both of these alternatives. It can be shown that cross-cultural comparisons are possible because the discovery that the criteria of rationality (embodied in the thought of another culture) violate the standards established in Rationality II need *not* entail the judgment that another culture's standards are inferior. This position, however, is difficult to maintain. It sounds very much like the discredited theory of a clear distinction between the epistemology of factual and evaluative statements, but there are significant differences. It cannot be denied that translation of one language game into the terms of another necessarily invokes the criteria of the translator's language game, but it *can* be denied that this translation necessarily involves a critical judgment on the logical standard of the translated language game.

A few examples are necessary to establish the validity of this argument. Consider a translation from English to German. Knowledge of the rules and definitions of both languages is of course necessary to effect the translation. In the process of translation, further, it would be impossible not to discover that the rules of English and German grammar differ in certain respects, but discovering that the standards of German grammar are different from those of English need not lead the translator to conclude that the German rules are inferior. Rather, it would lead to the conclusion that each set of rules is appropriate to its respective language. An even more relevant example is comparison between the language games of orthodox Christianity and biology. Translated into the language game of biology, the "theory" of the virgin birth of Christ reveals a logical contradiction, but this discovery should not lead the biologists to conclude that the logical system of Christianity is inferior to that of biology. The difference can be recognized and noted without attaching an automatic judgment of inferiority.

The insights of several contemporary theorists can also be used to defend this argument, and Schutz's discussion of the ideal types of the social scientist is particularly relevant. He reveals that the logic or, as he puts it, the "standard of rationality" that is operative in everyday life is distinct from that of the social sciences. Thus when the social scientist translates everyday concepts into social-scientific language, the logic of everyday concepts will be shown to be "deficient," according to the standards of rationality in social-scientific analysis. But Schutz also points out that social-scientific standards of rationality are not appropriate to the concerns of everyday life. In his terminology, social-scientific analysis and everyday life are different "provinces" of reality. Thus social scientists must necessarily utilize different standards of rationality to accomplish their purposes, but this in no way entails that the standards employed in everyday life are "irrational" or in any sense inadequate.

Much the same argument has been advanced by an ordinary-language philosopher. Derek Phillips, drawing on Wittgenstein's work, asserts that the language game of science, which he labels "extra-ordinary," differs from the language game of everyday life in that questions of truth and falsity are paramount in the former, not in the latter. Thus asking whether the practices of everyday life are true or false makes no sense; those practices are, as Wittgenstein points out, simply *what we do*. But in the scientific language game, questions of truth and falsity are highly appropriate; such questions are the whole point of the game and must be carefully examined (1977:89). Phillips' conclusion is thus the same as Schutz's: social science and everyday life are separate language games, based on different standards, but neither standard can be judged to be inferior to the other.

The arguments of Schutz and Phillips for the "separate but equal" status of Rationality II does not, however, satisfy those who maintain the superiority of the standard. Such advocates might offer a final argument in defense of their position: The standards of rationality that inform the scientific method (Rationality II) are more effective than Azande standards of rationality when it comes to practical questions such as making crops grow. Gellner puts this point very forcefully in his discussion of the scientific-industrial form of life:

> The cognitive and technical superiority of one form of life is so manifest and so loaded with implications for the satisfaction of human wants and needs—and, for better or worse, for power—that it simply cannot be questioned. [1973: 71–72]

Gellner is correct in saying that the effectiveness of Western science in the manipulation of physical nature is unassailable, but it must be noted that manipulation of physical nature is only one aspect of social life. To claim that the Azande would be "better off" if they applied the standards of Rationality II to this aspect of their common life could plausibly be argued, but it does not follow that this standard is equally applicable to efficient regulation of the Azande kinship system. Thus Rationality II is superior for the accomplishment of certain purposes, but the standards it embodies are, as Toulmin would put it, "field dependent."

This conclusion on the status of Rationality II falls somewhere between the two extreme positions in this debate: the relativist position, that no comparisons can be made among differing standards of rationality because all comparisons involve critical judgments, and the absolutist position, that Rationality II embodies a universal standard.

The purpose of the foregoing has been to establish that different standards of rationality can be compared, but that such a comparison does not necessarily entail the judgment that our standards are superior to all others. Rather, it should entail recognition that different standards are appropriate to different purposes. This position may not be as intellectually satisfying as either extreme, because it appears more ambiguous, but it has a virtue which both extreme positions lack: it explains what we *do* as social scientists.

The third and final definition of rationality in the contemporary discussion is, like Rationality II, concerned with universal validity, but Rationality III deals with a significantly different aspect. Those who discuss Rationality III propose the identification of universal aspects of human life on both the individual and the social level, and identification of these universal aspects is used to formulate requirements which are applicable to all human societies. These requirements form the basis of the claim that a society cannot be deemed rational unless it satisfactorily meets these requirements.

However, Rationality III must be carefully distinguished from Rationality I. Rationality III is not concerned with how the institutions of society fit together into a cohesive unit, but with whether a societal unit fulfills the universal requirements of human life. It is predicated on four assumptions: (1) the basic requirements of human life can be identified; (2) these requirements have universal validity; (3) any society which does not meet them cannot be deemed rational; and (4) the concept of rationality encompasses both the normative and factual spheres.

Weber had very little to say about the subject matter encompassed by Rationality III, a neglect for which he has been widely criticized. Although he was interested in exploring the rationality of institutions on the level of Rationality I, he refrained from rendering judgment on the rationality of an entire social unit. His reference to the "iron cage," created by the modern world, is the closest he came to labeling a society "irrational" in the sense of Rationality III. It should be noted, however, that Weber's rejection of Rationality III stems from his strongly held convictions that because facts and values belong to different spheres of inquiry, values cannot be scientifically established, and because of the irresolvable conflict among normative positions, no normative position can be declared correct. It follows that, for Weber, declaring a particular normative position to be universally valid is illegitimate.

Rationality III, however, has become a prominent aspect of the contemporary debate, due primarily to the influence of neo-Marxist schools of social theory. For the purposes of this study, the most interesting aspect of this debate is between ordinary-language philosophers and critical theorists, for several reasons. First, these two schools have generally been understood to represent the two extreme positions on Rationality III: ordinary language the relativistic pole, critical theory the absolutist pole. Second, and more importantly, the dialogue between these schools has revealed the complexity of these issues. But I will attempt to show that, on close examination, the positions of ordinary-language philosophers and critical theorists are in agreement on a number of key issues rather than dogmatically opposed. The examination will thus attempt to reveal the complexity of these issues and the points of convergence between these two opposing camps.

The position taken by ordinary-language philosophers, and particularly by Winch, is commonly assumed to be relativistic. He is interpreted as rejecting the possibility of formulating universal standards of human rationality or specifying common aspects of human life. Gellner states this position with his usual wit: for most philosophers, relativism is a problem, but for Winch and Wittgenstein it is a solution. Gellner asserts that the "collective solipsism" entailed by Winch's position results in a situation in which no judgments can be made about the relative merits of one society over another. He interprets Winch as asserting that every aspect of human life, from scientific analysis to moral beliefs, is entirely relative and conventional (1974).

Writing off Winch's position as relativistic, however, is premature. Close examination reveals that his position on this issue is more complex than Gellner's account allows, for Winch denies that his theory is relativistic and this is substantiated in his later work, *Ethics and Action*. In this work he mentions a number of attributes of human existence which he identifies as common to all human life: the moral qualities of truthfulness, integrity, and justice, as well as the biological facts of birth, death, and sexuality (1972:42, 250, 252). Winch does not, however, devote much attention to these universals: he claims that they place constraints on human life but he does not describe how this occurs. The fact that he mentions these universals, however, is significant.

One commentator claims that these universals supply Winch

with the tools for external criticism of societal forms (Derksen, 1978:220), but this interpretation misses the point of Winch's position. Although Winch identifies these elements as common to all human societies, he does not interpret them as a basis for criticism of societal forms. Criticism of this nature goes against the whole tenor of Winch's approach. He deliberately defines these universals so broadly that they can offer very little basis for criticisms. He interprets them as the common forms around which societal conventions develop, rather than rigidly defined principles which create standards by which human social life can be judged.

Gellner's critique of the ordinary-language position places Wittgenstein, as well as Winch, in the relativist's camp; but in this, Gellner's account is even more inaccurate. Wittgenstein can be interpreted to provide a more coherent argument against relativism than is found in Winch's brief account. It can be argued that Wittgenstein takes a stance between the extremes of relativism and absolutism by advancing the thesis that nonarbitrary aspects of language games are rooted in the prelinguistic behavior of the human species. In his words, our *acting* lies at the root of our language games (1972:28). Very few social scientists have seriously explored this aspect of Wittgenstein's work, but it can be shown that his approach to the issues raised by Rationality III offers social scientists a viable alternative to the untenable extremes of this debate.

Wittgenstein develops the position that human social life is not entirely conventional or arbitrary through an indirect and exceedingly subtle argument. He points out that certain elements of our common life "stand fast" for us because they are exempt from doubt. As was noted above, these elements "stand fast" not because of their absolute certainty but because, if they did not "stand fast," basic aspects of our language games, even our form of life, would be altered. Precisely what it means for something to "stand fast," however, is not easily expressed. A conviction which we regard as "unshakable" is "anchored in all my questions and answers, so anchored that I cannot touch it" (1972:16). These unshakable convictions thus have a very ambiguous status: the ground of our belief, they are, at the same time, groundless:

> At the foundation of well-founded belief lies belief that is not well-founded. [1972:33]

Only when Wittgenstein offers examples of the beliefs he places in this category does his theory become clearer. He mentions three of these beliefs in *On Certainty*: the earth is round; water boils at 100°C; the earth has existed a long time (1972:38–39). In *Philosophical Investigations* he labels such beliefs "general facts of nature." These facts, furthermore, form the basis of certain ways of acting that are fundamental to our way of life, and what he means by this comes out most clearly in his discussion of measurement. Our units of measurement are, of course, conventional, but the fact that the activity of measuring makes sense is not conventional; it is dependent on the natural fact that objects have a constant size and shape. To imagine a form of life in which measurement is impossible would be to imagine a very different natural world than the one we inhabit (1953:56).

> I am not saying: if such and such facts of nature were different people would have different concepts (in the sense of a hypothesis). But: if anyone believes that certain concepts are absolutely the correct ones, and that having different ones would mean not realizing something that we realize—then let him imagine certain very general facts of nature to be different from what we are used to, and the formation of concepts different from the usual ones will become intelligible to him. [1953:23]

Thus far Wittgenstein's argument, if not simple, is fairly easy to accept. Most would agree with him that if the earth were *not* round, our form of life would be radically altered. But Wittgenstein applies his argument to another area which is much more controversial. General facts of nature, he asserts, form the ground of certain ways of acting that constitute the "natural history" of the human species. This explains his remark: "If a lion could talk, we could not understand him" (1953:223). But certain ways of acting, for Wittgenstein, entail certain ways of thinking:

> Commanding, questioning, recounting, chatting, are as much a part of our natural history as walking, eating, drinking, playing. [1953:12]

Exploration of what he refers to as the "natural history of man" reveals, then, not only common ways of acting, but common ways of thinking. It even reveals agreement on the "essence of thinking":

> The propositions of logic are "laws of thought" because they bring out the essence of human thinking—to put it more correctly: because they bring out, or shew, the essence, the technique, of thinking. They shew what thinking is and also shew kinds of thinking. [1967:41]

It follows, from this statement and from his remark in *On Certainty*, that if we agree on what belongs to the essence of an argument (1972:10), we must agree on "judgments" as well. This aspect of Wittgenstein's argument would probably not meet with general agreement; however, the only aim of this examination is to point out that this statement of Wittgenstein's theory is not relativistic. It also falls far short of advocacy of universal standards by which all human social life must be judged.

In sum, Wittgenstein's position is this: Certain general facts of nature can be identified which, though not endowed with absolute certainty, are nevertheless the ground of our common form of life; and these general facts of nature have produced ways of acting which constitute the natural history of the human species, a history which reveals not only patterns of acting but patterns of thinking and, consequently, patterns of judgments, the conclusion of thinking. It should also be noted that in all these discussions Wittgenstein makes no distinction between normative and factual statements; his remarks apply equally to both "spheres." The natural history of the human species cannot, in his view, be neatly divided along these lines.

Wittgenstein's approach to this issue, then, appears to defy categorization; however, Phillips' attempt to describe Wittgenstein's position suggests a term which captures the essence of the approach: "dialectical." Phillips interprets Wittgenstein's theory as rejection of both the relativist position that no constants of human social life can be determined and the absolutist position that the basic requirements of human life establish standards by which all social arrangements must be judged (1977:83). He sees Wittgenstein as opting for a dialectical understanding of the relationship between the constants of human social life, revealed in the "natural history of man," and the conventions of human societies. Wittgenstein describes this relationship as one of complex interaction and interdependence rather than strict determination.

The supposedly relativist side of this issue, therefore, can be shown to be less relativistic than its critics have claimed.

However, analysis of the "absolutist" side will reveal that it is less dogmatic than it appears. In contemporary discussion, the theorist who is most noted for a positive theory of Rationality III is Jürgen Habermas.[12] From the perspective of many of his critics, Habermas attempts to establish a universal set of requirements for human social life which are to be understood as absolute standards by which societies are judged; those which do not meet these requirements are "irrational," those which do are "rational." The clearest substantiation of this interpretation of Habermas is in *Legitimation Crisis*, where Habermas attacks Weber's concept of rationality, arguing that it is in error because it excludes all evaluative elements. In opposition to Weber, Habermas sees his task as replacing this definition with a conception of rationality which specifies criteria for a rational end as well as the rational organization of means.

In the above discussion of Habermas' elaboration of this project, it was noted that instead of proposing substantive moral principles and declaring them universally valid, Habermas argues that only the formal criteria of truth claims can be defined as universally valid. In terms of his definition, then, although Habermas is proposing a conception of rationality that is both normative and universally valid, he does not attempt to ground that conception in substantive moral principles but in formal criteria. Thus the interpretation of Habermas as a strict "foundationalist" who seeks to ground knowledge in absolute truth is mistaken.

Although this misinterpretation is less obvious in his critique of Weber, Habermas makes this position quite clear in his recent work. Through his studies of social evolution, moral development, and universal pragmatics, he defines a position that combines sensitivity to the historical conditions of human subjects with an assertion of the formal characteristics of human social life. The conviction that informs all this later work is succinctly stated in the following passage from his earlier work:

> Since empirical speech is only *possible* by virtue of the fundamental norms of rational speech, the cleavage between a real and an inevitably idealized (if only hypothetically ideal) community of language is built not only into the process of argumentative reasoning but into the very life-praxis of social systems. [1973b:185]

This cleavage between, on one hand, empirical speech and,

on the other hand, the fundamental norms of rational speech provides the theme for Habermas' studies in *Communication and the Evolution of Society* (1979). He begins by stating the universalistic aspect of his analysis: "I shall develop the thesis that anyone acting communicatively must, in performing any speech action, raise universal validity claims and suppose that they can be vindicated" (1979:2). The theory that he develops in his subsequent arguments begins with the assumption that communicative competence, like linguistic competence, has a "universal core" that describes a "fundamental system of rules that adult subjects master" (1979:26). Specifically, communicative competence entails the satisfaction of three validity claims: the claim of truth for a particular propositional statement, the truthfulness of the intention of the speaker, and the rightness of the norms invoked (1979:28, 65–66). Furthermore, Habermas asserts, we can examine the truthfulness of statements because they are embedded in "relations to reality" (1979:68).

These aspects of Habermas' approach, as he admits, define the "transcendental presuppositions" of his approach (1979:177), but the other side of the cleavage (mentioned above) is by no means ignored. Habermas is well aware that although ideal speech is anticipated in ordinary speech, truth claims are discursively redeemed in the context of particular cultural settings and the cultural norms constitutive of those settings. His examination of "the structure of intersubjectivity," mentioned in *Legitimation Crisis*, is expanded in *Communication and the Evolution of Society* through discussions of Hampshire, Winch, Austin, and Taylor. The point of these discussions is that although all speech anticipates ideal speech, the realization of universal validity claims is necessarily accomplished in ordinary language and through the operation of culturally defined norms. For example, Habermas, citing Wittgenstein's "use theory of meaning," remarks that "the meaning of a linguistic expression can be identified only with reference to situations of possible employment" (1979:30).

Habermas, in his theory of communicative competence, erects a distinctively new form of the "absolutist" or "foundationalist" position. Instead of espousing substantive moral principles with universal validity, he proposes formal criteria of ideal speech which inform ordinary speech. At the same time, he is concerned to specify the cultural norms through which universal validity claims are realized. Whether this new kind of foundationalism is successful is an open question and will not be addressed here;[13] what *will* be argued is that the universal aspects of human social life that Habermas explores in his recent work have limited usefulness for the practice of social science. The structures of ideal speech, as well as the stages of moral development and social evolution that Habermas develops in *Communication and the Evolution of Society*, provide a general structure in which social-scientific analysis can be conducted. But the abstract formality of these structures raises the question of exactly how they facilitate the analysis of particular societies, which is, as critical theorists admit, the primary goal of social-scientific analysis.

Habermas defends his appeal to universal criteria by claiming that they offer practical guidance for analysis of particular societies. For example, in his discussion of legitimation problems in the modern capitalist state he invokes his evolutionary theory by referring to different "levels of justification"; but the conclusion he derives does not depend on this evolutionary perspective. Rather, he concludes that the central problem of capitalist society is *internal* contradictions within the capitalist system. In other words, Habermas' most damning indictment of capitalist society depends not on his evolutionary theory but on his analysis of the internal logic of capitalism (1979:178–205).

At least at this point, it can be argued that Habermas has not conclusively demonstrated the practical usefulness of his universal criteria,[14] but another conclusion can also be drawn from this aspect of his work. His attempt to integrate the insights of ordinary-language analysis and hermeneutics with his espousal of the universal validity of truth claims produces certain affinities with the positions of Winch and Wittgenstein (as presented above). Habermas admits this: "The use-theory of meaning introduced by Wittgenstein has universal pragmatic aspects" (1979:7). It was noted above that Phillips refers to Wittgenstein's understanding of the relationship between the "natural history of man" and societal conventions as "dialectical," and it is not implausible to apply the same term to Habermas' theory. For Habermas, the linguistic constitution of meaning is a "moment" in the objective system of social reality, also constituted by the "real" factors of labor and domination.

It cannot, of course, be argued that Wittgenstein and Habermas are in complete agreement on this point, but it can be argued that a number of significant similarities between the two theories can be identified: both reject the epistemological distinction between factual and evaluative spheres; both define certain universal criteria of human social and linguistic activity; both emphasize the intersubjective constitution of values in societal contexts; and both define the relationship between universal criteria and intersubjective constitution as one of complex interaction and interdependence. The difference between them is which of these two themes receives primary emphasis. Habermas, centrally concerned with analysis of universal criteria, argues that social scientists must employ these criteria to criticize and assess existing social arrangements. Wittgenstein and Winch, on the other hand, emphasize the intersubjective constitution of meaning; both define the universal constraints on human life so broadly as to render them virtually useless as analytic tools.

The identification of these similarities, however, has great significance for the present study. The gulf between the "relativism" of ordinary language and the "absolutism" of critical theory on Rationality III turns out to be not as wide as it seemed.

It is not the purpose of this study, however, to identify differences and similarities, but to draw conclusions which have implications for the future course of social theory. The conclusion can be simply stated: although certain universal constraints on human social life can be identified, attempts to define their nature result in generalities which are, of necessity, broad and unspecific. As such, they may serve as useful points of departure for the social scientist's examination, but the primary focus will be on how each society decides to define those parameters within its social context. In other words, the direction of social-scientific analysis has been more properly defined by Wittgenstein and Winch than by Habermas.

6. Conclusion

This discussion of contemporary antipositivist understandings of the logical status of social-scientific analysis serves as a fitting conclusion to the concerns of this study. The examination has not, of course, definitively resolved the questions at issue, but a number of themes have emerged which can serve as a base for a postpositivist understanding of the logical status of social-scientific activity. The first theme concerns the raison d'etre of social science: an "explanatory" activity which necessarily involves a "stepping back" from the actors' concepts, a clarification and assessment of those understandings. What antipositivists mean by "explanatory" is, of course, quite different from the positivist position that the social scientist must replace actors' "subjective" concepts with "objective," scientific concepts completely divorced from the actors' understanding. Rather, it was argued that although the social scientist must begin with the social actors' concepts, the understandings supplied by social-scientific analysis must be clearly distinguished from social actors' everyday understanding. Further, it was argued that the best explanation of this relationship is Schutz's theory of the different levels of rationality in these two spheres.

The second theme concerns the intersubjective context of theorizing in the social sciences. It was argued that although positivists' neutral observation language and their rigid adherence to the analytic syllogism must be discarded, this rejection need not entail that the social-scientific community establish no standards by which social-scientific theories can be assessed. Rather, it was argued, on the basis of Wittgenstein's theory, that underlying the various theoretical perspectives that are assumed by social scientists is agreement on the fundamental mode of argumentation. Further, relying on Toulmin, it was asserted that the arguments utilized in such theories can be shown to be fully logical, even though they do not conform to the analytic paradigm employed in some of the physical sciences. Toulmin's understanding of the nature of logical arguments brings both the subject matter and the tools of the social sciences into the "Court of Reason."

The third theme concerns the cross-cultural status of social scientists' activity. It was argued that although certain limiting conditions of human life can be identified, these conditions are so broad as to be of little use to the practicing social scientist. Criticism of social arrangements on the basis of these universal constraints, though not entirely ruled out of consideration, will not be the principal focus of social-scientific analysis. That analysis will be concerned primarily with the structure of inter-subjectivity within those parameters.

These themes are central to the concern that has informed the various topics analyzed: the possibility of providing a comprehensive postpositivist approach to the social sciences that supplies a means of synthesizing the interpretive analysis of social action with the structural analysis of social forms. That such a synthesis is necessary seems obvious from contemporary discussions in the philosophy of the social sciences. In a philosophical sense, the social sciences are floundering. They have discarded the positivist foundations of their discipline; nevertheless, they fail to agree upon a viable replacement. However, the necessary elements of that replacement are becoming clear: a successful postpositivist synthesis must supply a conceptual apparatus which can bridge the gap between interpretive and structural analysis. Although the foregoing has not definitely established this synthesis, it has outlined the parameters and suggested that the elements of the synthesis are emerging from antipositivist critiques. Specifically, interpretive analysis can be wedded to structural analysis without succumbing to positivism or a form of dogmatic absolutism.

This conviction, that such a conceptual apparatus is the most pressing need of contemporary social science, led to reexamination of Weber's perspective. It has been my intention to show that if such a synthesis is the principal problem of contemporary social theory, Weber's concept of the ideal type points to a solution to this problem. His methodology was formulated as an answer to a set of problems similar to those that confront present-day social theory. His ideal-typical methodology supplies a link in his work between interpretive and structural analysis. As such, it is at least suggestive of the kind of synthesis required by contemporary social theory.

In pursuit of this goal, the analysis has effected a kind of reinterpretation of Weber's work from the perspective of contemporary problems.[15] The central endeavor has been to put these contemporary accounts in perspective; that is, to provide a framework in which the strengths and weaknesses of each can be assessed. But the converse has also been accomplished: the analysis has identified the weaknesses and strengths of Weber's theory. At several points in the analysis, weaknesses in Weber's approach were rectified by appeals to one of the contemporary approaches. Yet the contemporary relevance of Weber's work is the principal focus of this analysis.

My intent has been to sketch an outline of the elements of a possible postpositivist synthesis and to show that Weber's ideal type provides a valuable guide for its definition. Therefore this reconsideration of Weber is justified if his work can help social theory find a way out of its present dilemma.

Notes

1. Introduction

1. I am referring here primarily to "realists" and specifically to the discussion by Hesse (1974).

2. Discussions of the implications of realism for the social sciences can be found in Keat (1971), Keat and Urry (1975), and Bhaskar (1978).

3. Outhwaite is the only contemporary social theorist I have discovered who attributes such a synthesis to Weber (1975:84). But even he claims that although Weber's synthesis is "brilliant" it is also "unstable." He notes, however, that because Weber is one of a very few theorists to attempt such a synthesis, his work is the point of reference for contemporary attempts to do so.

4. It will be argued below that Weber's ideal type allows him to move beyond the actors' concepts to an assessment of structural forms. It will also be argued that although some theorists of the subjective critique, most notably Schutz, appear to follow Weber in this respect, they are not as successful as he in wedding the analysis of actors' concepts and structural forms.

5. Because the focus of the following analysis is the relationship between Weber's position and contemporary discussions in social theory, no mention will be made of Parsons' extensive commentaries on Weber. This exclusion can be justified on the grounds, first, that Parsons' position does not figure prominently in contemporary discussions, and second, that the recent revival of interest in Weber involves explicit repudiation of Parsons' interpretation.

194

2. Weber's Theory of the Ideal Type

1. Rickert conceptualized this distinction in terms of the individual versus the general, Windelband in terms of the idiographic versus the nomothetic (Gorman, 1977:8). Weber employs both sets of terms in his analysis.

2. In his recent book (1976), Thomas Burger argues that Weber derived his methodology of the social sciences exclusively from Rickert.

3. Burger also argues that Weber departs from Rickert's formulation by creating a concept distinct from individual and general concepts, but that Weber does so by changing the reality to which his new concept, the ideal type, refers. Ideal types, he argues, refer not to empirical reality but to ideas in the investigator's mind (1976:123).

This is a serious misunderstanding of Weber's reasoning. I have tried to show that both the general concepts of the natural scientist and the ideal types of the social scientist are the result of a synthesis determined by the theoretic interest of the investigator. Burger's position thus makes sense only if it is assumed that the subject matter of the social sciences, the actors' subjective meanings, are less "real" than the subject matter of the natural sciences. This position is not only erroneous but untrue to Weber's account. It leads Burger to an unsatisfactory assessment of ideal-typical analysis that overemphasizes its abstraction from reality (1976:178).

4. Nagel misinterprets this aspect of Weber's theory in his discussion of the ideal type (1963:197).

5. Oakes captures the import of this statement very accurately in his introduction to the essay (Weber, 1977:1–56).

6. It might be objected that in this passage Weber appears to reject the notion that a shared language is essential to meaningful social action because he posits a case in which the two actors do *not* share a language. The statements at the end of the passage make it clear, however, that unless both actors conceptualize the action as an "exchange," the action itself is not "empirically possible." In other words, the *shared* concepts of the two actors constitute the exchange.

7. Weber admits that economics and psychology are concerned to formulate universal laws and that meteorology is concerned with explaining concrete reality.

8. Weber alludes to this distinction between the two branches of science in his discussion of Meyer (1949:134) but does not elaborate on it in this context. A fuller discussion of the distinction between the

sciences of reality and the sciences which formulate laws can be found throughout *Roscher and Knies* (1975).

9. This discussion raises the difficult issue of the possibility of comparative analysis when the units are understood to be the subjective meanings of social actors in different societies. As noted above, Weber gives a very unsatisfactory answer to this question, if he answers it at all. He assumes that sociological investigators, by immersing themselves in analysis of a foreign culture, can apprehend the subjective meanings of the social actors without great difficulty. That this apprehension of meaning is much more problematic than Weber supposes is evident in the vehemence of contemporary debates on this topic, which will be discussed in subsequent chapters.

10. Watkins makes this error in his criticism of Weber's theory (1952:42).

11. Schutz makes much of this deficiency in Weber's account in his analysis of Weber's methodology (1967).

12. Sewart does not provide a source in Weber for this passage but refers to Iggers (1968:164), who also distorts Weber's meaning by taking the passage out of context.

13. This discussion raises questions concerning the reality of structural entities, which will be taken up in chapter 4.

14. Wolfgang Schluchter, in *The Rise of Western Rationalism* (1981), offers what he calls a "re-interpretation" of Weber that is similar to the perspective on Weber's work in this chapter.

3. The Subjective Critique

1. The most prominent of these discussions can be found in Bernstein (1976), Roche (1973), Giddens (1976), Harré and Secord (1972), Sellars (1963), Durfee (1976), and Pitkin (1972).

2. Schutz's critique of Weber provides an interesting parallel between Weber's theory and ordinary-language analysis. Both approaches begin with the social actors' concepts and accept them as, in Schutz's terms, the "irreducible primitive" of social analysis.

3. Whether Husserl succeeded in establishing intersubjectivity on this level has been widely disputed. The application of this dispute to the methodology of the social sciences has been elaborated by N. Patrick Peritore in "Some Problems in Schutz's Phenomenological Methodology" (1974:132–40). He asserts that Schutz's analysis of the constituting process in internal time consciousness begs the question of intersubjectivity, a problem which, Schutz admits, Husserl failed to

solve. This failure, Peritore argues, causes contradictions in Schutz's entire sociological program. Specifically, it causes Schutz to give up the presuppositionless stance which he seeks to establish for social analysis.

4. Peritore makes this point very clearly in his discussion of Schutz's methodology (1974:132–40).

5. Gorman argues that Schutz never proves this hypothesis (1977:49). Schutz's discussion of the intersubjective context of the constitution of meaning, however, can be taken as "proof" of this point. Schutz's point in this regard is, I think, convincing: Common-sense knowledge is typified in the sense that it is constituted through reference to a shared set of meanings.

6. One aspect of Schutz's discussion of the ideal type is his argument that most social scientists make the error of assuming that ideal types "discover" subjective meanings. He counters this with the assertion that ideal types posit meanings rather than discover them (1967:190). It is unclear from the context whether Schutz meant this criticism to apply to Weber. It is not difficult to show, however, that Weber did not make this mistake; he is acutely aware of the distinction between individual subjective meanings and the meaning context of the social scientist's ideal types.

7. In his commentary on Schutz's work, Gorman denies that Schutz effected this synthesis on the grounds that the subjectively meaningful cannot be "objective" in the sense that Schutz declares (1977:140). What he overlooks in this account is the intersubjective element that Schutz's theory stresses (above).

8. Winch claims that in one section of *Critique of Stammler* (1977) Weber "forgets" subjective meaning and focuses instead on the bodily movements of social actors. But a close reading of this passage reveals that Weber is describing a particular set of social actions as bodily movements for the express purpose of emphasizing the oddity of such a description and its lack of utility for social-scientific analysis (1977:101ff.). It is interesting, furthermore, to note that in this article Weber attacks an understanding of the constitutive nature of social rules that is not very different from that espoused by Winch.

4. The Objective Critique

1. Miriam Glucksmann explains this point very succinctly in her work on structuralism in contemporary social theory (1974:45–46).

2. Hindess (1973) provides a useful example of how this process works in his critique of the method of ethnomethodology.

3. MacIntyre makes this point very clearly in his statement that any social theory which criticizes another's lack of objectivity must do so on the basis of its own claim to have found an objective basis (1973:337).

4. A third criticism of Althusser's epistemology is concerned with another aspect of the relationship between thought and reality: the relationship between theory and practice. Although this is of central importance to Marxist theory, it is of little relevance here (Glucksmann, 1974; Callinicos, 1976; Veltmeyer, 1974–75; Geras, 1972).

5. Several of Weber's defenders have attempted to rescue him from structuralists' charges by asserting that Weber's empiricism (in Althusser's definition) does not prevent him from engaging in structural analysis (Roth, 1977:645; Turner, 1977:9). This approach, however, does not solve the question; it sidesteps it. For Althusser, structural analysis is impossible on the basis of an empiricist problematic, and it is this issue which must be dealt with if the problem is to be discussed.

6. The English translation is in Dallmayr and McCarthy (Habermas, 1977b:361).

7. It should be noted, however, that Habermas is reminding Weber of his departure from Kant, which, given Weber's explicit neo-Kantianism, is a significant criticism.

8. Giddens offers two additional objections to the psychoanalytic model: psychoanalysis is dialogue between individuals, critical theory a dialogue between groups; therapeutic dialogue is voluntary, critical dialogue is not (1977:159). Gadamer, in his critique of Habermas' discussion of Freud, objects that use of the therapeutic model raises the possibility of manipulative politics (1971b:283–317).

5. Logical Status of Social-Scientific Analysis

1. Windelband makes this same distinction between the sciences in his discussion of these issues (Iggers, 1968:148).

2. In fact, Weber argues that human action is even more "calculable" than events in the natural world, a point which emerges in his discussion of causality. Although Weber's concept of causality is an important aspect of this theory of objectivity, a thorough discussion of this topic would take the essay too far afield (see Hekman, 1979). It

must be noted, however, that Weber maintained that causal analysis was appropriate to the social sciences. He distinguishes his advocacy of causal analysis from that of the positivists by asserting that although the principle of causality is applicable to all scientific disciplines, its form varies in the different sciences. The form appropriate to the social sciences is borrowed from the legal theorists (1949:167–68).

3. Maurice Natanson claims that because Weber's theory is based on a value choice, it is existential rather than relative (1974:316). In the same vein Schluchter notes: "Weber has been called a nihilist, a relativist, and a decisionist. He is all of these things if you believe in the existence or discernibility of an objective meaning of the world" (Roth and Schluchter, 1979:58–59).

4. The correspondence of Schutz and Parsons identifies this issue of rationality as the principal source of disagreement between the two theorists (Schutz, 1978).

5. An argument which is directly counter to this is advanced by Garfinkel (1974). His conclusion that scientific rationalities can only be employed as ineffective ideals in the analysis of everyday life, however, leads to the position which is rejected in the above argument, that is, that social science can do no more than reproduce social actors' concepts (1974:71). Bauman's comment that the question of truth has no place in ethnomethodological discourse is certainly appropriate in this context (1978:189).

6. In the following argument I am heavily indebted to Derek Phillips' excellent account of Wittgenstein's theory of scientific knowledge in *Wittgenstein and Scientific Knowledge: A Sociological Perspective* (1977).

7. I assume that Kuhn's theory of paradigms can be applied to the social sciences, although this has been a subject of controversy among social scientists.

8. Toulmin and Janik note that the concept of *Lebensformen* was a popular term in intellectual circles in Wittgenstein's Vienna (1973:230).

9. In the literature on Wittgenstein's forms of life it has been disputed whether his concept refers to organic or cultural aspects (Hunter, 1968; Gier, 1980; Rubinstein, 1979).

10. Weber also appeals to the law to establish a logical form appropriate to the social sciences, yet distinct from that of the natural sciences (1949:167–68).

11. Another approach to the logic of the social sciences is suggested by realists' work in the philosophy of natural science. Realists argue that the positivist view of the natural sciences is radically flawed

and that this misconception is at the root of the problem of defining the logic of both the natural and the social sciences. They suggest an alternative model, realism, which replaces positivism's rigid correspondence theory of truth with an understanding of the coherence of a network of theoretical facts (Hesse, 1974). A number of social theorists have begun to explore the implications of this "revolution" in the natural sciences for social science (Bhaskar, 1978; Keat, 1971; Giddens, 1977; Benton, 1977). They argue that equating "scientific method" with the positivist conception of science has cast the issue of the "scientificity" of the social sciences in the wrong terms. If the positivist understanding of science is replaced with that of realism, however, then social science can be truly "scientific" even though it does not meet positivism's criteria of a science. A realist understanding of the sciences would also allow rejection of the gulf between the natural and social sciences that is accepted by some antipositivists (e.g., Winch), as well as by positivists. In this context, Keat remarks, in passing, that Weber was one of a few theorists to try to reject positivism without rejecting the scientific nature of social science (1971:15).

12. The contrast between Habermas and Wittgenstein, which is the point of departure of this argument, is a reflection of Rorty's characterization in *Philosophy and the Mirror of Nature* (1979). His list of philosophers who attempt to "ground" knowledge includes Habermas, and his list of exceptions to this tendency includes Wittgenstein.

13. Beatty (1979) persuasively argues that Habermas is successful in overcoming the objections to a transcultural standard of understanding and judgment.

14. This analysis of Habermas could not make use of his arguments in the recently published two-volume work, *Theorie des Kommunikativen Handeln.*

15. Schluchter uses this word to describe his reconstruction of Weber's "developmental history" (1981).

Bibliography

Abel, Theodore. 1948. "The Operation Called Verstehen." *The American Journal of Sociology* 54:2:211–18.

Althusser, Louis. 1969. *For Marx*, trans. Ben Brewster. London: Allen Lane Penguin Press.

———. 1971. *Lenin and Philosophy*, trans. Ben Brewster. New York: Monthly Review Press.

———. 1976. *Essays in Self-Criticism*, trans. Grahame Lock. Atlantic Highlands, N.J.: Humanities Press.

——— and E. Balibar. 1970. *Reading Capital*, trans. Ben Brewster. New York: Pantheon Books.

Apel, Karl-Otto. 1967. *Analytic Philosophy of Language and the Geisteswissenschaften*. Dordrecht, Holland: D. Reidel.

Aron, Raymond. 1969. *La Philosophie Critique de l'Historia*. Paris: NRF.

Bauman, Zygmunt. 1978. *Hermeneutics and Social Science*. New York: Columbia University Press.

Beatty, Joseph. 1979. " 'Communicative Competence' and the Skeptic." *Philosophy and Social Criticism* 6:3:267–87.

Beck, Lewis White. 1975. *The Actor and the Spectator*. New Haven: Yale University Press.

Benton, Ted. 1977. *Philosophical Foundations of the Three Sociologies*. Boston: Routledge and Kegan Paul.

Berger, Peter, and Thomas Luckmann. 1966. *The Social Construction of Reality*. New York: Anchor Books.

Berger, Peter, and S. Pullberg. 1966. "Reification and the Sociological Critique of Consciousness." *New Left Review* 35:56–71.

Bernstein, Richard. 1976. *The Restructuring of Social and Political Theory.* New York: Harcourt Brace Jovanovich.

Bhaskar, Roy. 1978. "On the Possibility of Social Scientific Knowledge and the Limits of Naturalism." *Journal for the Theory of Social Behavior* 8:1:1–28.

Bloor, David. 1976. *Knowledge and Social Imagery.* London: Routledge and Kegan Paul.

Blum, Alan, and Peter McHugh. 1971. "The Social Ascription of Motives." *American Sociological Review* 36:98–109.

Briskman, Larry. 1978. "Skinnerism and Pseudo-Science." *Philosophy of Social Science* 9:81–103.

Brittan, Arthur. 1973. *Meanings and Situations.* London: Routledge and Kegan Paul.

Burger, Thomas. 1976. *Max Weber's Theory of Concept Formation.* Durham, N.C.: Duke University Press.

Callinicos, Alex. 1976. *Althusser's Marxism.* London: Pluto Press.

Collins, Randal. 1975. *Conflict Sociology: Toward an Explanatory Science.* New York: Academic Press.

Dahrendorf, Ralf. 1976. "Remarks." In *The Positivist Dispute in German Sociology,* ed. Theodore Adorno, trans. Glyn Adey and David Frisby, pp. 123–30. New York: Harper Torchbooks.

Dallmayr, Fred. 1981. *Beyond Dogma and Despair.* Notre Dame, Ind.: University of Notre Dame Press.

———— and Thomas McCarthy, ed. 1977. *Understanding and Social Inquiry.* Notre Dame, Ind.: University of Notre Dame Press.

Derksen, A. A. 1978. "On an Unnoticed Key to Reality." *Philosophy of the Social Sciences* 8:209–25.

Di Quattro, Arthur. 1972. "*Verstehen* as an Empirical Concept." *Sociology and Social Research* 57:32–42.

Durfee, Harold. 1976. "Introduction." In *Analytic Philosophy and Phenomenology,* ed. Harold Durfee, pp. 1–13. The Hague: Martinus Nijhoff.

Fay, Brian, and J. Donald Moon. 1977. "What Would an Adequate Philosophy of Social Science Look Like?" *Philosophy of Social Science* 7:3:209–227.

Fitzgerald, P. J. 1968. "Voluntary and Involuntary Acts." In *Readings in the Theory of Action,* ed. Norman Care and Charles Landsman, pp. 373–402. Bloomington: Indiana University Press.

Gadamer, Hans-Georg. 1970. "On the Scope and Function of Hermeneutical Reflection." *Continuum* (Chicago) 8:77–95.

————. 1971a. "Rhetorik, Hermeneutik und Ideologiekritik." In *Hermeneutik und Ideologiekritik,* ed. Karl-Otto Apel, pp. 57–82.

Frankfurt: Suhrkamp.

_____. 1971b. "Replik." In *Hermeneutik und Ideologiekritik*, ed. Karl-Otto Apel, pp. 283–317. Frankfurt: Suhrkamp.

_____. 1976. *Philosophical Hermeneutics*, trans. and ed. by David E. Linge. Berkeley: University of California Press.

Garfinkel, Harold. 1974. "The Rational Properties of Scientific and Common Sense Activities." In *Positivism and Sociology*, ed. Anthony Giddens, pp. 53–73. London: Heineman.

Gellner, Ernst. 1973. *Cause and Meaning in the Social Sciences*. London: Routledge and Kegan Paul.

_____. 1974. "Concepts and Society." In *Rationality*, ed. Bryan Wilson, pp. 18–49. Oxford: Basil Blackwell.

Geras, Norman. 1972. "Althusser's Marxism: An Account and Assessment." *New Left Reveiw* 71 (Jan.-Feb.):57–86.

Giddens, Anthony. 1971. *Capitalism and Modern Social Theory*. Cambridge: University Press.

_____. 1976. *New Rules of Sociological Method*. New York: Basic Books.

_____. 1977. *Studies in Social and Political Theory*. New York: Basic Books.

Gier, Nicholas, 1980. "Wittgenstein and Forms of Life." *Philosophy of the Social Sciences* 10:3:241–58.

Glucksman, Andre. 1972. "A Ventriloquist Structuralism." *New Left Review* 72 (Mar.-Apr.):68–92.

Glucksmann, Miriam. 1974. *Structuralist Analysis in Contemporary Social Thought: A Comparison of the Theories of Claude Levi-Strauss and Louis Althusser*. London: Routledge and Kegan Paul.

Gorman, Robert. 1977. *The Dual Vision: Alfred Schutz and the Myth of Phenomenological Social Science*. London: Routledge and Kegan Paul.

Gouldner, Alvin. 1970. *The Coming Crisis of Western Sociology*. New York: Basic Books.

Habermas, Jürgen. 1970a. "Towards a Theory of Communicative Competence." *Inquiry* 13:360–75.

_____. 1970b. *Toward a Rational Society*, trans. Jeremy J. Shapiro. Boston: Beacon Press.

_____. 1970c. *Zur Logik der Sozialwissenschaften*. Frankfurt: Suhrkamp.

_____. 1971. *Knowledge and Human Interests*, trans. Jeremy J. Shapiro. Boston: Beacon Press.

_____. 1973a. *Theory and Practice*, trans. John Viertel. Boston: Beacon Press.

———. 1973b. "A Postscript to *Knowledge and Human Interests.*" *Philosophy of the Social Sciences* 3:157–89.

———. 1973c. "Wahrheitstheorien." In *Wirklichkeit und Reflexion*, pp. 211–65. *Festschrift fur Walter Schulz.* Pfullingen: Neske.

———. 1975. *Legitimation Crisis*, trans. Thomas McCarthy. Boston: Beacon Press.

———. 1977a. "Discussion." In *Understanding and Social Inquiry*, ed. Fred Dallmayr and Thomas McCarthy, pp. 66–71. Notre Dame, Ind.: University of Notre Dame Press.

———. 1977b. "A Review of Gadamer's *Truth and Method.*" In *Understanding and Social Inquiry*, ed. Fred Dallmayr and Thomas McCarthy, pp. 335–63. Notre Dame, Ind.: University of Notre Dame Press.

———. 1979. *Communication and the Evolution of Society*, trans. Thomas McCarthy. Boston: Beacon Press.

Hamlyn, D. W. 1968. "Causality and Human Behavior." In *Readings in the Theory of Action*, ed. Norman Care and Charles Landsman, pp. 48–67. Bloomington: Indiana University Press.

Harré, R., and P. F. Secord. 1972. *The Explanation of Social Behavior.* Oxford: Basil Blackwell.

Hart, H. L. A. 1948–49. "The Ascription of Responsibility." *Proceedings of the Aristotelian Society* 69:171–94.

———. 1961. *The Concept of Law.* Oxford: Clarendon Press.

———. 1968. *Punishment and Responsibility.* New York: Oxford University Press.

Hekman, Susan. 1979. "Weber's Concept of Causality." *Sociological Inquiry* 39 (Fall):4.

Hems, John. 1976. "Husserl and/or Wittgenstein." In *Analytic Philosophy and Phenomenology*, ed. Harold Durfee, pp. 55–86. The Hague: Martinus Nijhoff.

Hesse, Mary. 1974. *The Structure of Scientific Inference.* Berkeley: University of California Press.

Hindess, Barry. 1973. *The Use of Official Statistics in Sociology: A Critique of Positivism and Ethnomethodology.* London: Macmillan.

———. 1977. *Philosophy and Methodology in the Social Sciences.* Sussex: Harvester Press.

———. 1978. "Humanism and Teleology in Sociological Theory." In *Sociological Theories of the Economy*, ed. Barry Hindess, pp. 157–89. New York: Holmes and Meier.

Hirst, Paul Q. 1976. *Social Evolution and Sociological Categories.* New York: Holmes and Meier Publishers.

Hollis, Martin. 1974. "Reason and Ritual." In *Rationality*, ed. Bryan Wilson, pp. 221–39. Oxford: Basil Blackwell.

Horton, Robin. 1973. "Levy-Bruhl, Durkheim, and the Scientific Revolution." In *Modes of Thought*, ed. R. Horton and R. Finnegan, pp. 249–305. London: Farber and Farber.

Howe, Richard H. 1978. "Max Weber's Elective Affinities: Sociology within the Bounds of Pure Reason." *American Journal of Sociology* 84:2:366–85.

Hughes, Henry Stuart. 1958. *Consciousness and Society*. New York: Alfred A. Knopf.

Hunter, J. F. M. 1968. "Forms of Life in Wittgenstein's *Philosophical Investigations.*" *American Philosophical Quarterly* 5:233–43.

Iggers, George. 1968. *The German Conception of History*. Middletown, Conn.: Wesleyan University Press.

Janoska-Bendl, Judith. 1965. *Methologische Aspekte des Idealtypus*. Berlin: Dunker and Humblot.

Keat, R. 1971. "Positivism, Naturalism and Anti-Naturalism in the Social Sciences." *Journal for the Theory of Social Behavior* 1:3–17.

_____ and J. Urry. 1975. *Social Theory as Science*. London: Routledge and Kegan Paul.

Kuhn, Thomas. 1962. *The Structure of Scientific Revolutions*. Chicago: University of Chicago Press.

_____. 1970. "Reflections on My Critics." In *Criticism and the Growth of Knowledge*, ed. I. Lakatos and A. Musgrave, pp. 231–78. Cambridge, Mass.: Cambridge University Press.

_____. 1978. *The Essential Tension*. Chicago: University of Chicago Press.

Lecourt, D. 1975. *Marxism and Epistemology*, trans. Ben Brewster. London: New Left Books.

Louch, A. R. 1966. *Explanation and Human Action*. Berkeley: University of California Press.

MacIntyre, Alasdair. 1971. "The Idea of a Social Science." In *Against the Self-Images of the Age*. New York: Schocken Books. Reprint. Notre Dame, Ind.: University of Notre Dame Press.

_____. 1973. "Ideology, Science and Revolution." *Comparative Politics* 5:3:321–42.

_____. 1974 "Is Understanding Religion Compatible with Believing?" In *Rationality*, ed Bryan Wilson, pp. 62–77. Oxford: Basil Blackwell.

Martins, Herminio. 1974. "Time and Theory in Sociology." In *Approaches to Sociology: An Introduction to Major Trends in British*

Sociology, ed. John Rex, pp. 246–294. London: Routledge and Kegan Paul.

McCarthy, Thomas. 1978. *The Critical Theory of Jürgen Habermas.* Cambridge, Mass.: M.I.T. Press.

Melden, Abraham. 1967. *Free Action.* London: Routledge and Kegan Paul.

Munch, Peter. 1975. " 'Sense' and 'Intention' in Max Weber's Theory of Social Action." *Sociological Inquiry* 45:4:59–65.

Nagel, Ernst. 1963. "Problems of Concept and Theory Formation in the Social Sciences." In *Philosophy of the Social Sciences*, ed. Maurice Natanson, pp. 189–209. New York: Random House.

Natanson, Maurice. 1974. *Phenomenology, Role and Reason.* Springfield, Ill.: C. C. Thomas.

Outhwaite, W. 1975. *Understanding Social Life: The Method Called Verstehen.* London: Allen and Unwin.

Peritore, N. Patrick. 1974. "Some Problems in Schutz's Phenomenological Methodology." *American Political Science Review* 69:1:132–40.

Peters, R. S. 1958. *The Concept of Motivation.* London: Routledge and Kegan Paul.

―――. 1969. "Motivation, Emotion, and the Conceptual Schemes of Common Sense." In *Human Action*, ed. Theodore Mischel, pp. 135–65. New York: Academic Press.

Pettit, Philip. 1972. "On Phenomenology as a Methodology of Philosophy." In *Linguistic Analysis and Phenomenology*, ed. W. Mays and I. C. Brown, pp. 241–55. London: Macmillan.

Phillips, Derek. 1977. *Wittgenstein and Scientific Knowledge: A Sociological Perspective.* Totowa, N.J.: Rowman and Littlefield.

Pitkin, Hanna. 1972. *Wittgenstein and Justice.* Berkeley: University of California Press.

Radnitzky, Gerhard. 1970. *Contemporary Schools of Metascience.* New York: Humanities Press.

Rex, John. 1971. "Typology and Objectivity." In *Max Weber and Modern Sociology*, ed. Arun Sahay, pp. 17–36. London: Routledge and Kegan Paul.

―――. 1974. *Sociology and the Demystification of the Modern World.* London: Routledge and Kegan Paul.

Rickert, Heinrich. 1962. *Science and History: A Critique of Positivist Epistemology*, trans. George Reisman. Princeton, N.J.: Van Nostrand.

Ricoeur, Paul. 1975. "Phenomenology of Freedom." In *Phenomenology and Philosophical Understanding*, ed. E. Pivcevic, pp. 173–94. Cambridge: Cambridge University Press.

_____. 1977. "The Model of the Text." In *Understanding and Social Inquiry*, ed. Fred Dallmayr and Thomas McCarthy, pp. 316–34. Notre Dame, Ind.: University of Notre Dame Press.

Roche, Maurice. 1973. *Phenomenology, Language and the Social Sciences*. London: Routledge and Kegan Paul.

Rorty, Richard. 1979. *Philosophy and the Mirror of Nature*, Princeton, N.J.: Princeton University Press.

Rose, Gillian. 1978. *The Melancholy Science*. New York: Columbia University Press.

Roth, Guenther. 1977. "Review of Hirst, *Social Evolution and Sociological Categories*." *Contemporary Sociology* 6:6:644–45.

_____ and Wolfgang Schluchter. 1979. *Max Weber's Vision of History: Ethics and Methods*. Berkeley: University of California Press.

Rubinstein, David. 1979. "Wittgenstein and Science." *Philosophy of the Social Sciences* 9:341–46.

Runciman, W. G. 1972. *A Critique of Max Weber's Philosophy of Social Science*. Cambridge: Cambridge University Press.

Scheffler, I. 1976. *Science and Subjectivity*. Indianapolis: Bobbs-Merrill.

Schluchter, Wolfgang. 1981. *The Rise of Western Rationalism*, trans. and with introduction by Guenther Roth. Berkeley: University of California Press.

Schutz, Alfred. 1962. *Collected Papers*, vol. 1, ed. Maurice Natanson. The Hague: Martinus Nijhoff.

_____. 1964. *Collected Papers*. vol. 2, ed. Avrid Brodersen. The Hague: Martinus Nijhoff.

_____. 1967. *The Phenomenology of the Social World*, trans. George Walsch and Frederick Lehnert. Evanston, Ill.: Northwestern University Press.

_____. 1978. *The Theory of Social Action: The Correspondence of Alfred Schutz and Talcott Parsons*, ed. Richard Grathoff. Bloomington: Indiana University Press.

_____ and Thomas Luckmann. 1973. *The Structures of the Life-World*. Evanston, Ill.: Northwestern University Press.

Sellars, Wilfred. 1963. *Science, Perception and Reality*. London: Routledge and Kegan Paul.

Sewart, John. 1978. "Verstehen and Dialectic: Epistemology and Methodology in Weber and Lukacs." *Philosophy and Social Criticism* 5:3–4:319–66.

Taylor, Charles. 1969. "Neutrality in Political Science." In *Philosophy, Politics and Society*, 3d ser. ed. Peter Laslett and W. G. Runciman. Oxford: Basil Blackwell.

Toulmin, Stephen. 1958. *The Uses of Argument.* Cambridge: Cambridge University Press.

———— and Allan Janik. 1973. *Wittgenstein's Vienna.* New York: Simon and Schuster.

Touraine, Alain. 1974. "Towards a Sociology of Action." In *Positivism and Sociology,* ed. Anthony Giddens, pp. 75–100. London: Heineman.

Tucker, William. 1965. "Max Weber's *Verstehen.*" *Sociological Quarterly* 6:157–65.

Tugendhat, Ernst. 1972. "Description as the Method of Philosophy: A Reply to Mr. Pettit." In *Linguistic Analysis and Phenomenology,* ed W. Mays and I. C. Brown, pp. 256–66. London: Macmillan.

Turner, Bryan. 1974. *Weber and Islam.* London: Routledge and Kegan Paul.

————. 1977. "The Structuralist Critique of Weber's Sociology." *British Journal of Sociology* 28:1:1–16.

Veltmeyer, Henry. 1974–75. "Towards an Assessment of the Structuralist Interrogation of Marx: Claude Levi-Strauss and Louis Althusser." *Science and Society* 38:4:385–421.

Wakins, J. W. N. 1952. "Ideal Types and Historical Explanation." *British Journal for the Philosophy of Science* 3 (May):22–43.

Weber, Max. 1946. "Science as a Vocation." In *From Max Weber,* ed. H. H. Gerth and C. Wright Mills. New York: Oxford University Press.

————. 1949. *The Methodology of the Social Sciences,* trans. and ed. Edward Shils and Henry Finch. New York: The Free Press.

————. 1968. *Economy and Society,* ed. Guenther Roth and Claus Wittich. New York: Bedminster Press. 3 vols.

————. 1970. "Essay on Some Categories of Interpretive Sociology," trans. Edith Graber. Unpublished master's thesis, University of Oklahoma.

————. 1975. *Roscher and Knies,* trans. Guy Oakes. New York: The Free Press.

————. 1977. *Critique of Stammler,* trans. Guy Oakes. New York: The Free Press.

————. 1978. "Anti-Critical Last Word on *The Spirit of Capitalism.*" trans. Wallace Davis. *American Journal of Sociology* 83 (5).

Wellmer, Albrecht. 1971. *Critical Theory of Society.* New York: Seabury.

Wild, John. 1976. "Is There a World of Ordinary Language?" In *Analytic Philosophy and Phenomenology,* ed. Harold Durfee, pp. 190–207. The Hague: Martinus Nijhoff.

Wilson, H. T. 1976. "Reading Max Weber: The Limits of Sociology." *Sociology* 10:2:297–315.

Winch, Peter. 1958. *The Idea of a Social Science and Its Relation to Philosophy*. London: Routledge and Kegan Paul.

_____. 1972. *Ethics and Action*. London: Routledge and Kegan Paul.

Wittgenstein, Ludwig. 1953. *Philosophical Investigations*. New York: Macmillan.

_____. 1967. *Remarks on the Foundation of Mathematics*. Oxford: Basil Blackwell.

_____. 1972. *On Certainty*, ed. G. E. M. Anscombe and G. H. von Wright. New York: Harper and Row.

Wright, G. H. von. 1971. *Explanation and Understanding*. Ithaca, N.Y.: Cornell University Press.

Index

Abel, Theodore, 45, 91
action theorists, 92, 94
Althusser, Louis, 17, 103, 105–123, 130, 146, 150, 161, 177
antipositivist approaches, 5, 9, 14–16, 61–64, 75, 161, 177
Apel, Karl-Otto, 6, 140
Aristotle, 124, 125, 141
Aron, Raymond, 58
Austin, J.L., 189

Bachelard, Gaston, 106
Bauman, Zygmunt, 164
Berger, Peter, 10, 12
Bernstein, Richard, 4, 6
Bloor, David, 178, 179
Blum, Alan, 93
Brittan, Arthur, 15
Burger, Thomas, 14

critical theory, 7, 17, 63, 64, 101–104, 123–148, 184, 191

Dahrendorf, Ralf, 13
Dilthey, Wilhelm, 18, 126

empiricism, 105, 106, 108, 110, 112, 114, 117, 121, 123
ethnomethodology, 6, 169
Evans-Pritchard, E.E., 179

Fay, Brian, 8, 9, 14, 151
Fichte, J., 126
Freud, Sigmund, 127

Gadamer, Hans-Georg, 129, 140, 144, 151
Gellner, Ernst, 176, 182, 184, 185
Giddens, Anthony, 2, 4, 6, 11, 14
Gouldner, Alvin, 4

Habermas, Jürgen, 10, 15, 17, 97, 103, 104, 123–149, 151, 154, 176, 177, 188–191
Hampshire, Stuart, 189
Harré, Rom, 4
Hart, H.L.A., 93
Hegel, G.W.F., 126
hermeneutics, 6, 10, 128, 129, 130, 140, 190
Hindess, Barry, 113, 115, 119
Hirst, Paul, 113–115
Husserl, Edmund, 68, 81, 82, 89

ideal type: Weber's theory, 1, 15–16, 18, 61, 85, 87, 90, 94, 112, 114, 115, 120, 153, 154, 155, 163, 165, 175, 176, 193; Schutz's theory, 70–76, 98, 181
intersubjective meaning, 46, 65–70, 76, 77, 82, 83, 95–98, 100, 101, 111, 112, 142, 165, 166, 191

James, William, 73

Kant, Immanuel, 126, 140
Keat, Russell, 9, 10, 14
Kuhn, Thomas, 159, 166–171, 173, 175
Lask, Emil, 19
legitimacy, 136–138, 140
legitimate domination, 51, 52, 54, 114, 177
Louch, A.R., 77, 80, 84, 86–88, 99
Luckmann, Thomas, 10–12, 98
McHugh, Peter, 93
Martins, Herminio, 8
Marx, Karl, 102, 105–107, 111, 112, 118, 119, 126
Marxism, 37, 169
mental events, 80–84, 95–97
Methodenstreit, 18–20, 26, 62, 90
methodology of the social sciences: current issues, 1, 8, 9, 12, 13, 15, 16, 146; Habermas' approach, 123–145; ordinary language approach, 77–100; Schutz's approach, 66–77, 94–100; Weber's approach, 18–64
Moon, J. Donald, 8, 9, 14, 151
Munch, Peter, 91

natural sciences, 2–4, 19–27, 34–36, 38, 60, 86, 90, 121, 125, 127, 141, 155, 156, 173, 174
neo-Kantians, 20

objectivity, 17, 27, 29, 34, 64, 69, 75, 101–104, 116–119, 120, 122, 136, 141, 142, 145–148, 161, 166, 167; Weber's concept, 152–160, 165, 173, 178, 179
ordinary language analysis, 6, 7, 10, 17, 33, 45, 63–65, 75, 77, 101, 103, 110, 122, 130, 150, 162, 163, 184, 185, 190, 191

Peirce, Charles, 126
Peters, R.S., 92, 95
phenomenology, 5–7, 10, 17, 45, 63–77, 81–84, 95–101, 103, 110, 122, 130, 150, 163
Phillips, Derek, 163, 165, 181, 182, 187, 190
philosophy of the social sciences, 120, 122; contemporary debate, 2–15, 48, 149
Pitkin, Hanna, 89
Popper, Karl, 168
positivism, 2–9, 13, 14, 16, 18, 26–28, 30, 45, 49, 53, 61–63, 65, 75, 84, 85, 100–102, 104, 105, 113, 116, 122, 123–128, 130, 131, 134, 137, 138, 145, 146, 148, 152–156, 161, 162, 164, 166, 167, 169, 173, 175, 176, 178, 192, 193
postpositivist synthesis, 9, 16–17, 62–64, 103, 104, 145, 149, 161, 176, 192–193
Protestant ethic, 55, 164, 165
probability, 44, 49, 51–53
Pullberg, S., 10, 12

Quine, W., 174

Radnitzky, Gerhard, 5, 9
rationality, 134, 136, 138, 140, 163, 164, 169, 176–184, 188
relativism, 102, 113, 114, 129, 139, 140, 159, 160, 184, 187, 191
Rex, John, 43, 49, 55, 58, 59
Rickert, Heinrich, 18, 19, 21, 22, 24, 25, 35, 39, 40, 41, 43
Ricoeur, Paul, 94, 95, 97
Roche, Maurice, 6
Runciman, W., 31

Scheffler, I., 174
Schutz, Alfred, 15, 66–77, 79, 80, 82–84, 87, 89, 95–99, 132, 142, 163–165, 177, 181, 182, 192

Secord, P.F., 4
Sewart, John, 55–58
Simmel, Georg, 18
sociology of knowledge, 178
Stammler, 29, 30, 64
Strauss, L., 15
structuralism, 7, 17, 63, 64, 101–122, 123, 145, 147
subjective meaning, 3, 7, 14, 15, 21, 29, 33, 34, 40, 44–55, 57, 58, 61, 63–66, 70, 73, 77, 84, 90–95, 101, 112–116, 130, 132, 146, 149, 150, 153, 164, 165
subjectivists, 19, 26–28, 30, 153–157

Taylor, Charles, 189
Toulmin, Stephen, 153, 154, 174–176, 182, 192
Touraine, Alain, 8
Tugendhat, Ernst, 83

Urry, J., 9, 10, 14

values, 20, 21, 28, 31, 72, 113, 114, 116, 117, 125, 134, 137, 138, 153–155, 157–159, 183, 191
Verstehen, 45, 46, 49, 90, 91

Weber, Max: concept of objectivity, 152–162, 165, 167, 172, 173, 177, 178, 179, 183, 188; contemporary relevance, 61–64, 151, 164, 165, 193; critiques of, 66–67, 70, 71, 76–80, 84, 85, 87, 90, 91, 95, 98, 99, 101, 112–117, 120, 121, 125, 136–141; ideal type theory, 18–60, 66, 94, 163, 175, 176; methodology of the social sciences, 1, 4, 12–17
Winch, Peter, 15, 49, 77, 78–80, 84–89, 91, 92, 95, 129, 132, 142, 151, 152, 162, 177, 179, 180, 184, 185, 189–191
Windelband, Wilhelm, 18, 19, 21
Wittgenstein, Ludwig, 33, 78–83, 88, 89, 96, 129, 140, 151, 153, 169–173, 175, 176, 181, 184–187, 189, 190–192
Wright, G.H. von, 173, 174